A Dark and Bloody Ground

TEXAS A&M UNIVERSITY
42
MILITARY HISTORY SERIES

A Dark and Bloody Ground

The Hürtgen Forest and the Roer River Dams, 1944–1945

EDWARD G. MILLER

Texas A&M University Press

College Station

Maps © 1994 by Donald S. Frazier and Anne-Leslie Dean

The paper used in this book meets the minimum requirements
of the American National Standard for Permanence
of Paper for Printed Library Materials, z39.48–1984.
Binding materials have been chosen for durability.

∞

Library of Congress Cataloging-in-Publication Data

Miller, Edward G., 1958–
    A dark and bloody ground : the Hurtgen Forest and the Roer River
dams, 1944–1945 / Edward G. Miller.
        p.   cm. — (Texas A&M University military history series ; 42)
    Includes bibliographical references and index.
    ISBN 0-89096-626-5
    I. Hürtgen, Battle of, 1944.   I. Title.   II. Series
D756.5H8M55   1995
940.54'213551—dc20   94-45333
                                                             CIP

To E. H. Miller

Man is the fundamental instrument in war;
other instruments may change,
but he remains relatively constant.

U.S. Army Field Manual 100-5 (Operations), 1944

Contents

Illustrations   ix

Foreword   xi

Preface   xiii

Abbreviations   xvii

1. The VII Corps Enters the Forest   1

2. Early Operations of the 9th Division   20

3. October Deadlock   36

4. Origins of the Second Battle of Schmidt   47

5. The 28th Division Attack Begins   56

6. Disaster at Vossenack   78

7. The November Offensive   93

8. The Battles in the North   99

9. Stalemate in the Center   124

10. The Capture of Hürtgen   141

11. The Capture of Grosshau, Kleinhau, and Bergstein   154

12. Operations to 16 December   168

13. Final Battles and Capture of the Dams   190

14. Analysis   203

Appendix   213

Notes   217

Index   243

Illustrations

Lt. Gen. Courtney H. Hodges   3

Generalfeldmarschall Walter Model   7

Bradley, Eisenhower, Gerow, and Collins   10

Generalleutnant Hans Schmidt   34

Brandenberger   43

Bruns with his aide and driver   54

Soldiers of Company E, 110th Infantry, south of Germeter   63

Platoon leader Ray Fleig   68

M-10 Tank Destroyers of the 893d Tank Destroyer Battalion   76

Company E, 47th Infantry, and tanks of TF Richardson near
   Nothberg   111

Warren B. Eames   116

Capt. Don Warner   122

Soldiers of 8th Infantry Regiment northeast of Schevenhütte   126

M4 Tanks near Hürtgen District office   151

S.Sgt. Marcario Garcia   155

Hürtgen, 30 November 1944   159

Jeeps of 22d Infantry in Grosshau   160

Pfc. Joseph Sorobowski and Pvt. Roy E. James   166

Company C, 2d Ranger Battalion, near Bergstein   170

Pfc. Thomas W. Gilmore   173

Schwammenauel Dam   199

Hürtgen Forest in 1946   205

MAPS

1. The Hürtgen Forest and Roer River Dams   4
2. 9th Infantry Division Operations, 6–16 October 1944   22
3. 28th Infantry Division: Schmidt/Vossenack, 2–11 November 1944   57
4. The Capture of Hürtgen, Kleinhau, and the Brandenberg-Bergstein Ridge, 21 November–7 December 1944   94
5. 1st Infantry Division, November–December 1944   101
6. 4th Infantry Division, November–December 1944   174
7. 78th Division and the Capture of the Schwammenauel Dam, December 1944–February 1945   194

Foreword

Infantry combat is a brutal, personal thing, and the battle of the Hürtgen Forest saw some of the most intense close combat of World War II. The Hürtgen Forest was a beautiful place in peacetime, but in war it became the infantry soldier's worst nightmare.

The American leadership grew overly optimistic for success during the pursuit of the German Army across France and Belgium. When the Americans approached Germany, commanders expected the pursuit to continue as it had so far. Confident of success, the First Army commander, Lt. Gen. Courtney H. Hodges, permitted operations in the forest at a time when most thought that the war would be over in a matter of weeks or months. This was hardly the case, and by entering the difficult forest terrain, the Americans gave up the advantages in mobility and firepower that had helped get them to Germany in the first place.

The First Army's VII Corps set out to clear the Hürtgen Forest of German troops who might use it as a base from which to counterattack a flank. The German Army was not a significant threat at the time, and American commanders failed for weeks to notice that the forest shielded objectives of great importance. Tragically, thousands of soldiers became casualties before senior commanders recognized that the objectives were a series of dams constructed before the war to control the level of the Roer River. By the time the Americans realized this, the outcome of the Allied offensive aimed at the heart of Germany depended on whether they controlled the dams.

This is the first complete, single-volume account of the battle. It is well documented and will stimulate the reader's mind and help the reader better understand the causes of this tragic series of actions in 1944–45. The book covers high-level decisions; more important, it covers the impact of these decisions on the infantry soldier.

Wesley Hogan
Major General, U.S. Army (Ret.)
Commander, 3d Battalion, 121st Infantry, 1944–45

Preface

The literature on the experience of the U.S. Army in World War II is extensive, and the 50th anniversary of the battle for Germany has brought still more. With the exception of the official histories, or "Green Books," most authors have concentrated on the better-known battles and campaigns such as Normandy and the Battle of the Bulge. Many of the books, no doubt in an effort to be readable, lack analysis, adequate documentation, and objectivity.

I have tried to avoid some of these problems in this history of the little-known, bloody battles in the Hürtgen Forest, 1944–45. The more famous campaigns and battles noted above have overshadowed this important struggle in the forest south of Aachen, Germany. Perhaps this is because the American approach to the Hürtgen Forest resulted in a bloody battle of attrition aimed at the wrong objectives. Readers who have grown up with the typical books, motion pictures, and veteran's "war stories," which lead one to believe that the U.S. Army effortlessly swept away enemy resistance, might be surprised at the following account.

The events in the Hürtgen Forest are important to today's reader because they show what can happen when commanders and their staffs are slow to see an objective in the proper context. They also demonstrate the need for the operational commander to state in clear, unmistakable terms the intent, or vision, for conduct of an operation. It took the Americans weeks after they entered the forest to recognize that the significant operational objectives there were not road junctions and towns but rather the Roer River dams. These dams controlled the level of the major water obstacle standing between the First U.S. Army and the Rhine. The Americans could not safely cross the Roer unless they controlled the dams, but at first they sought only to sweep the forest of enemy soldiers and take several road junctions, key terrain, and towns. Some attacks along such lines were necessary, but the Americans operated in the forest for over two months before they launched an attack directly on the dams.

The terrain was some of the most difficult along the German frontier. It was certainly not the place for the Americans to put their tactical doctrine of combined arms into practice. Yet the repeated attacks in the forest did little more than cancel the effects of the air, armor, and artillery support that had been critical to success in Normandy, northern France, and Belgium. Had the First Army set out early on for the Roer dams, one might suppose that fighting in an area that prevented it from making good use of its superiority in air, armor, and artillery was worth the risk. Unfortunately, this was not the case. What began as a continuation of the pursuit across France ended as a battle of attrition deep in a forest filled with mud and mines.

My interest in this subject stems from a lifelong study of the military history of the Second World War. While stationed in Germany with the U.S. Army between 1984 and 1988, I decided to learn more about the events in the Hürtgen Forest. I found out firsthand that it is one thing to sit in the comfort of one's office or home and study a terrain map; it is another to walk through the hilly forest in a chilling autumn rain.

This book is the result of my desire to produce as complete an account as possible of the activities at the company, battalion, and regimental levels. It was here that soldiers had to carry out the "command decisions" and implement doctrine. I describe high-echelon decision making to the extent necessary to set the stage for the reader.

My sources include correspondence and interviews with both German and American veterans, government records, and secondary sources. Several persons in the United States and Germany assisted me with this project. Any errors in the text are, of course, my responsibility. At the risk of omitting an individual or group, I would like to thank the following for their assistance. **United States:** Dempsey Allphin, Billy F. Allsbrook, John B. Beach, Dr. William S. Boice, Richard Boylan (National Archives), Marlin L. Brockett, William M. Cowan, Warren B. Eames, Lt. Col. (Ret.) Raymond E. Fleig, Dr. Christopher Gabel, Col. (Ret.) William A. Hamberg, Roy M. Hanf, Col. (Ret.) Chester B. Hansen, Michael Harkinish, Lt. Col. (Army National Guard Ret.) William O. Hickok, Bruce M. Hostrup, Col. (Ret.) John R. Jeter, Chester H. Jordan, Col. (Ret.) Harry M. Kemp, K. Wayne Kugler, Robert N. Laurent, Earl L. Lutz, Lt. Col. (Ret.) William L. McWaters, Brig. Gen. (Ret.) Lewis E. Maness, Sidney C. Miller, Robert H. Moore, Randall Patterson, William M. Pena, Robert Pettee, Bill Petty, Edward B. Phillips, Col. (Ret.) Richard W. Ripple, Maj. Gen. (Ret.) Robert H. Schellman, Paul Stevenson, John. F. Votaw (1st Infantry Division Museum), Donald A. Warner, Karl Wolf. **Germany:** Hubert Gees, Oberstleutnant (a.D.) Gevert Haslob, Oberst (a.D.) Wilhelm Osterhold, Klaus R. Schulz, Albert Trostorf, Günter von der Weiden, Eugen Welti, and Generalmajor (a.D.) Heinz-Günther Guderian.

Finally, this project would have been impossible to complete without the understanding and support of my wife and daughter.

Abbreviations

AP	Armor piercing
AT	Antitank
BAR	Browning Automatic Rifle
CCA	Combat Command "A"
CCB	Combat Command "B"
CCR	Combat Command Reserve
CP	Command Post
COMMZ	Communications Zone
ETO	European Theater of Operations
FO	Field Order
G-1	Personnel Officer (division and higher staff)
G-2	Intelligence Officer (division and higher staff)
G-3	Operations Officer (division and higher staff)
G-4	Logistics Officer (division and higher staff)
HE	High Explosive
HQ	Headquarters
LD	Line of Departure
M4	"Sherman" medium tank
M5	"Stuart" light tank
M10	Tank destroyer armed with a 76mm gun
M29	"Weasel" tracked cargo carrier
MG	Machine gun
MSR	Main Supply Route
OP	Observation Post
RJ	Road Junction
S-2	Battalion or regimental intelligence officer

S-3	Battalion or regimental operations officer
TAC	Tactical Air Command
TD	Tank Destroyer
TF	Task Force
TOT	Time on Target

A Dark and Bloody Ground

1
The VII Corps
Enters the Forest

The forest up there was a helluva eerie place to fight . . . Show me a man who went through the battle . . . and who says he never had a feeling of fear, and I'll show you a liar. You can't get all of the dead because you can't find them, and they stay there to remind the guys advancing as to what might hit them. You can't get protection. You can't see. You can't get fields of fire. Artillery slashes the trees like a scythe. Everything is tangled. You can scarcely walk. Everybody is cold and wet, and the mixture of cold rain and sleet keeps falling. Then they jump off again, and soon there is only a handful of the old men left.

T.SGT. GEORGE MORGAN,
1ST BATTALION, 22D INFANTRY

The Hürtgen Forest was the scene of the worst experience in the lives of most of the thousands of German and American soldiers who fought there. The veterans remember the constant cold rain, fog, and mist, which left no chance of getting dry. They recall the mud, the mined firebreaks, the tree bursts, and the showers of wood splinters. They survived the hunger, thirst, and filth that was part of fighting in the seventy square miles of forest south of Aachen.[1]

Many people familiar with the U.S. Army's successful engagements are not aware of its failure in the Hürtgen Forest. The Americans failed to understand that the objectives worth fighting for were not always road junctions, forested hills, and farming villages. The important targets in this case were the dams that the forest shielded, but these were not the objectives of nearly three months of hard fighting.

The decision to fight in the forest originated in the heady days of Allied optimism in the late summer of 1944. The unexpected success of the Normandy breakout led the GIs of the First Army's VII Corps (and the rest of the Allies for that matter) to believe they were fighting a defeated enemy. The Americans were eager to smash through the German border defenses and cross the Rhine. Barring the way to the Rhine, however, was the Roer River. And between the VII Corps and the Roer were a densely populated, but narrow, terrain corridor and a large forested area south of Aachen. The terrain corridor was too narrow to accommodate more than one or two regiments and therefore was not well suited for large-scale pursuit operations. The forest, of course, was not a good place to conduct maneuver warfare either, but both the corps commander, Maj. Gen. J. Lawton Collins, and the army commander, Lt. Gen. Courtney H. Hodges, looked at the forest and saw a harbor for a counterattack force. They decided to sweep the forest.

It appeared to be a reasonable task. When the VII Corps entered the forest, however, it forfeited its superiority in air power, artillery, and armor support. That might have been an acceptable risk had the Americans in September, or even October, aimed for an important objective— one that would contribute to the crossing of the Roer. Unfortunately, in their haste to enter Germany, the Americans overlooked the single most important objective barring the approaches to the river.

Neither Collins nor Hodges made plans to capture the flood-control and hydroelectric dams located on or near the Roer, just inside the forest. It would be dangerous to put troops across the river without control of the dams because the Germans might open the floodgates, which would trap the troops on the opposite bank. Though the dams were the key to the Roer, one division after another fought in the forest to capture towns and control roads before Hodges directed an attack against them.

In September, 1944, the 3d Armored Division fought the first engagements in the forest. It was followed by the 9th Infantry Division in September and October. In early November the 28th Division failed to take the road center of Schmidt. Beginning in mid-November, several more divisions and a host of supporting units battered without success at the German defenses deep in the gloomy woods (the 1st, 4th, 8th, 9th (-), 78th, and 83d Infantry Divisions and the 5th Armored Division and 2d Ranger Battalion). Only in late November did Hodges press for air attacks on the dams. These failed, and it was mid-December, three months after the first GI set foot in the forest, before the Americans launched a ground attack on the dams. Three days into this operation, the Germans launched their Ardennes offensive. It was February, 1945, before the Americans had control of the dams and could with confidence put troops on the east bank of the river.

Lt. Gen. Courtney H. Hodges, Commanding General, First U.S. Army (Courtesy U.S. Army)

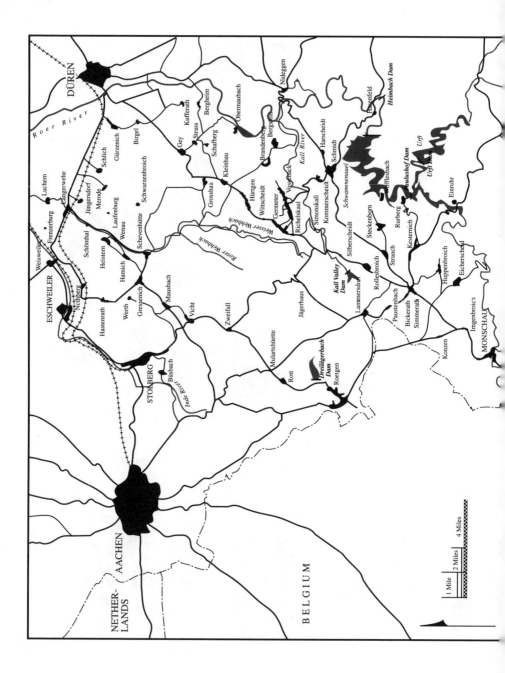

This battle brought out the best and the worst in the American soldier. There were several awards of the Medal of Honor and Distinguished Service Cross. No doubt there were many other acts of heroism that will never be told. Other stories, however, show the iron grip of fear on men who had seen too much fighting. In some cases, men ran when there were no enemy soldiers nearby, and others would not move without the support of tanks. Tank crews sometimes refused to move without the protection of infantry, and GIs of all ranks broke down under the strain of continuous combat.

Defense of the forest served two purposes for the Germans. It was a convenient place to delay and wear down the Americans while the Germans reconstituted forces and put them back into the line. This was the kind of fight they were well suited to engage in, for even weak units could do well behind strong defenses in very rugged terrain. The other reason involves preparations for the Ardennes counteroffensive. Security for the attack depended on a firm northern shoulder anchored in the vicinity of the Roer dams. If the Americans held the dams, they could safely counterattack across the Roer and thus hit the main effort, the 6th Panzer Army, from behind. Simply put, the Germans had to get the attack underway before the Americans crossed the Roer.

To understand how the First Army lost the race for the Roer River and became embroiled in a battle of attrition in some of the worst ground along the western front, it is necessary to review the events leading to the American entry into Germany.

THE GERMAN SITUATION

The late July breakout by the Americans from the hedgerow country of Normandy hit the Germans like a sledgehammer. Rather than withdraw behind the Seine River, as urged by Field Marshal Gunter von Kluge (who was both Commander in Chief–West and commander of Army Group B), the Germans—at Hitler's explicit orders—stood and fought for every foot of French ground.[2] This policy caused nearly irreparable damage to Kluge's forces. The Americans and the 21 Army Group, were, unfortunately, unprepared to take advantage of the tactical situation. Historian Martin Blumenson believes one reason for this was the unexpected success of the Allies. Eisenhower and his senior generals thought the Germans were, in fact, finished as a threat. The Allied generals believed the Germans would be unable to recover from the disaster that resulted from their ill-fated counterattack into the Allied flank near Falaise. The success here, as well as with operations in general after July, helped cause a surge in Allied optimism after the terribly slow battle of attrition behind the beaches in Normandy. This mind-set was prevalent throughout the First U.S. Army well after the slowdown of operations outside of Aachen along the Westwall.

The result of this optimism, according to Blumenson, led Eisenhower, Montgomery, Bradley, and others to look at future operations even before the end of the battles near Falaise. Rather than concentrate their energies and attention toward a battle of annihilation, they stopped short and began to look east, toward Germany. Thus the Allies failed to gain a complete victory—the destruction of the German armies in Normandy. This was because the Allied leadership evidently deemed the capture of terrain rather than the destruction of the German armed forces the key to victory.[3] The Germans were able to withdraw several thousand soldiers— and even more important, headquarters staffs—from France and move them behind the relative security of the German border. This would prove a very critical factor during the coming weeks as the First Army reached Germany.

Still, the Germans had lost 50,000 POWs, 10,000 men killed, and nearly 400 tanks and assault guns.[4] The skies belonged to Allied fighter-bombers, and the rolling fields belonged to their tanks. Though "apathy, despair, terror strained at the fabric of German discipline,"[5] the German army was not defeated. One American battalion commander likened it to "a wounded tiger" that would turn "now and again to slash its tormentors, each slash drawing blood."[6]

During the third week in August, Field Marshal Walter Model replaced Kluge, who had been implicated in the July bomb plot against Hitler. Before he departed his headquarters, Kluge prepared a letter that implored Hitler, "Make up your mind to end the war . . . [and] put an end to this frightfulness." The despondent field marshal committed suicide on his way back to Germany.[7]

Hitler ordered the ruthless, 53-year-old Model to restore the situation. Since 1940, Model had commanded a panzer division, a panzer corps, a field army, and two army groups. When he took command of Army Group Center in Russia, he threatened his commanders with court-martial if they failed to hold their positions. He "slept little, restlessly roamed the front . . . bullying his commanders in coarse language . . . overruling his intermediate commanders."[8] In the process, he gained a reputation as a master of defensive fighting. His performance against the First Army during the coming months proved such assessment correct.

Model was an aggressive commander, with ties to the Nazi regime, but he was also a realist. When he took over as both Commander in Chief–West and commander of Army Group B, he told Hitler that "the unequal struggle cannot long continue." Hitler, of course, would hear none of this, and he relieved Model from his dual command (he let him keep command of Army Group B). In early September, Hitler returned

Generalfeldmarschall Walter Model during a visit to the 89th Infantry Division CP, east of Schmidt, late November 1944. (Courtesy G. Haslob)

the elderly Field Marshal Gerd von Rundstedt to his former position as Commander in Chief–West. Model probably decided that, in view of the situation, he could not effectively handle the dual responsibilities.[9] The return of Rundstedt perhaps contributed in an indirect way to the German success in the Hürtgen Forest. It allowed Model to concentrate on what he did very well—fight a defensive battle. He could devote time and attention to halting the American attack into Germany. Had he retained two important command roles, he would not have had time to do this.

Rundstedt, a paragon of Prussian military elitism, and Model had to buy enough time to reconstitute the shattered combat units around the staffs that had survived the battle of France. They also had to assemble enough men and equipment to fortify the western border defenses, which included the outmoded Westwall, or, as it was known to the Americans, the Siegfried Line. Four years of neglect (1940–44) had taken its toll on the Westwall. The first German troops to occupy the defenses found no mines, wire, weapons, communications equipment, or, in most cases, even garrison soldiers. Farmers had used many of the bunkers for storage of beets and potatoes, and stragglers sometimes caused more damage than engineers could repair.[10] The Americans had no way to know this, and concerns about the strength of the Westwall weighed heavily on the minds of commanders.

The Westwall stretched from the Dutch-German border near Kleve to just north of Basel, Switzerland. It consisted of thousands of mutually supporting concrete bunkers and other positions emplaced in depth. Some bunkers were built into the sides of hills overlooking important roads. Others were designed to resemble buildings and power stations. The original purpose of the Westwall was to delay an enemy until the Germans could bring up mobile reserves. By 1944, however, such reserves no longer existed.

Construction began in 1936, and by 1938, nearly 500,000 men worked on the project day and night. The typical machine-gun bunker had a reinforced concrete roof nearly seven feet thick, a front wall about four feet thick, and a rear wall about eight feet thick. The average size was about 30 by 36 feet. The Americans later found that it required at least 400 pounds of TNT to destroy one bunker. The Westwall in the Hürtgen Forest consisted of two bands of defenses—the original Schill Line, and an outer band, called the Scharnhorst Line, built just before the war to augment the Aachen defenses.

A row of antitank obstacles the Americans called dragon's teeth blocked the approaches to the Westwall where the terrain might support a tank attack. These obstacles consisted of multiple rows of reinforced concrete pyramids nearly 5 feet high, at a depth of about 30 feet, set into a gridlike concrete base. Each kilometer of dragon's teeth required more than 100 tons of steel and 2,000 cubic meters of concrete for construction.[11]

The other problem involved regeneration of the units that had been destroyed in France and Belgium. Rundstedt and Model sent urgent requests to Berlin for men and equipment. In response, Hitler sent two newly formed divisions to Army Group B and also earmarked several fortress infantry battalions for service in the West. Hitler ordered the formation of another 25 divisions, and he told Rundstedt to hold Holland, the border defenses, the Moselle River, and the Vosges Mountains until the new units could stabilize the situation.[12]

The most pressing task in the central sector of the German front was delaying the advance of the First U.S. Army.[13] This mission went to what remained of the 7th Army, commanded by 52-year-old General der Panzertruppen Erich Brandenberger.[14] The 7th Army's LXXXI Corps (Generalleutnant Friederich-August Schack) defended Aachen and the terrain corridor to the south. General der Infanterie Erich Straube's LXXIV Corps covered the important Stolberg-Monschau-Hollerath sector. On the army's south wing, the I SS Panzer Corps defended 50 miles of front south of Ormont.[15]

The Germans would call this resurgence of combat power the Miracle of the West. It began to take shape in early September, and it would surprise those Americans who thought the end of the war was near.

THE ALLIED SITUATION

Midsummer 1944 was time of unbridled Allied optimism. Given the results of the campaign in France, it is easy to see why. One intelligence report stated that "the end of the war in Europe is within sight, almost within reach."[16] The observations of a 3d Armored Division reconnaissance sergeant also make it easy to understand why many soldiers of all ranks thought victory was so close. In Belgium, he saw "a sea of bedraggled enemy troops . . . traveling from west to east in a desperate run to reach their beloved fatherland."[17]

The successful campaign in France enabled the Allies to drive east well ahead of the schedule that planners had prepared before D-Day. The targets within Germany included the industrial regions of the Ruhr and Saar—areas critical to Germany's ability to prosecute the war. The supreme commander, Gen. Dwight D. Eisenhower, ordered the 21 British Army Group (Field Marshal Sir Bernard L. Montgomery) to make the main effort north of the Ardennes. The ports necessary to sustain the armies were concentrated in the northern half of the Allied zone of attack, as were the best routes to the Ruhr and V-weapon launching sites. Most of the withdrawing German formations were moving in the

Left to right: Lt. Gen. O. N. Bradley (12th Army Group), Gen. Dwight D. Eisenhower, Maj. Gen. L. T. Gerow (V Corps) and Maj. Gen. J. L. Collins (VII Corps), 1944 (Courtesy U.S. Army)

same direction, and the Allies naturally wanted to inflict as much damage as possible on them before they reached the border defenses. But Eisenhower was reluctant to expose the northern wing of the armies to the chance of a concentrated German counterattack. He directed the 12th U.S. Army Group to make a secondary advance south of the Ardennes to draw German strength from the north.

Montgomery then asked for an American field army to guard the right flank of his army group, and over Bradley's objections, Eisenhower gave this task to the First Army.[18] Bradley argued that the British would need at most a single corps. The rest of the 12th Army Group, he said, should move on the Rhine between Mainz and Karlsruhe. Eisenhower, however, believed that it would do little good to reach the Rhine without the means to properly exploit a crossing. An attack north of the Ardennes, through Belgium, would at least offer the chance to capture the port of Antwerp. Montgomery ordered Hodges to attack east as far as the Maastricht-Liège area.[19] This put the Hürtgen Forest, Aachen, and the Roer River opposite the First Army (and VII Corps) zone of advance.

The VII Corps drew the task of protecting the 21 Army Group flank. The Corps spent the first days of September clearing the shattered remains of five enemy divisions from the "Mons Pocket" in southeast Belgium.[20] With "sun and dust and victory in the air,"[21] the Corps then crossed the Meuse River and took Liège, Malmedy, Spa, and Eupen in quick succession.[22] The situation continued to look promising as the Corps neared Germany, and General Hodges remained "quite optimistic about his ability to push through the Siegfried Line and on to the Rhine."[23]

A RECONNAISSANCE IN FORCE

During the second week of September the First Army was in position to carry the battle into Germany, but it was too short on supplies to do so. The problem involved supply dumps that for the most part were still in Normandy, several hundred miles from the front-line units, and the lack of transportation to carry the supplies forward. Both men and machines were worn out from the almost nonstop pace of operations in France and needed time for recovery and maintenance.

The First Army needed to receive 5,000 tons of supplies per day just to sustain current operations, and it also had to accumulate reserves of gasoline and artillery ammunition. Given the logistic problems, however, this level of support would have to be at the expense of the Third Army. To provide the Third Army with a minimum amount of supplies, Bradley reduced the First Army's allocation to 3,500 tons per day. Then, on 10 September, Bradley and Hodges learned that it would be 15 September before enough artillery ammunition would be available to support just five more days of intense fighting. Hodges ordered the First Army to hold in place for two days to allow time to bring up the artillery ammunition needed for the initial attack against the Westwall. He would permit only limited reconnaissance while waiting to renew large-scale operations about 14 September.[24] This was a prudent order, but it was unfortunate that Hodges did not know just how weak the defenses were.

The temporary halt concerned the impatient and aggressive General Collins. He believed that his VII Corps had the momentum it needed to get past the Westwall south of Aachen before the supply situation would force the corps to stop and wait for supplies.[25] On the afternoon of 11 September, Collins approached Hodges with a plan to conduct a reconnaissance in force aimed at breaching the Westwall before the Germans had a chance to defend it in force. The operation would involve more resources than the missions envisioned by Hodges, but it would not be a full-scale attack that would deplete the supplies then being stockpiled for later use. Hodges told Collins to go ahead, on the condition that if the VII Corps failed to achieve a quick breakthrough, it would stop and await resupply. Hodges told Maj. Gen. Leonard T. Gerow, commander of V Corps, to plan a similar operation.[26] According to the army's basic manual concerning combat doctrine, FM 100-5, a reconnaissance in force was considered the "best means of clearing up an uncertain situation." It involved making local attacks to locate the enemy's main defensive line and drive the covering forces from their outposts.[27] The situation along the border at the time was uncertain indeed.

At this time, the VII Corps had three divisions—the 1st and 9th Infantry and the 3d Armored—plus the 4th Cavalry Group. The corps was spread on a wide front stretching from the Dutch-German border on the north to Elsenborn, Belgium, on the south. To the front lay the urban sprawl of Aachen and the adjacent, relatively narrow, terrain corridor. To the south of Aachen was the 70-square-mile area of the Roetgen, Wenau, and Hürtgen state forests. The Americans called the area Hürtgen, after one of the small farming villages in the area.

The Hürtgen Forest is an extension of a larger wooded region stretching into eastern Belgium and lies in the square formed by Aachen, Düren, Heimbach, and Monschau. A ridge system runs through the area from southwest to northeast. The highest parts (over 2,100 feet in elevation) are west of Monschau and fall to an elevation of about 600 feet within a few miles of Düren. The ridge splits into three segments near Monschau. One ridge line runs northwest of Simmerath to the Roer near Nideggen. Another runs east from the vicinity of Germeter, and the third runs north from the head of the Weisser Weh Creek and flattens out near Gressenich. Each ridge dominates the surrounding ground through which any attacker must pass. The cold, rushing streams and narrow rivers running through the forest have steep, sometimes nearly vertical, approaches: the Vicht Creek along the western edge of the forest, the Weisser Weh Creek in the center, and the narrow Kall River, which empties into the Roer River east of Bergstein.

The east-west road network was limited, and the major north-south routes ran along the fringes of the most heavily forested area. None of the roads was able to support a large volume of traffic. The logistic implications are obvious. As long as VII Corps operated in the Aachen area, the roads, bad as they were, were critically important as supply routes for support of the attack to the Roer. Even the narrow forest trails took on great importance. But one road took on special significance. The road is in the eastern part of the forest and passes through Simmerath, Germeter, Hürtgen, Grosshau, and Gey before reaching the Roer at Düren. Because the road was for so many weeks an objective of V and VII Corps, and to ease the reader's task, I will call it the Simmerath-Düren road.

The forest was well suited for the defense. Many districts had trees that grew to 100 feet or more in height. The trees grew so closely together and blocked out so much light that it was difficult for one to see more than a few feet in any direction. An attacker traveling from west to east faced, quite literally, an uphill fight. Except for the areas around the farming villages, there were no large clearings.

Collins issued orders to his division commanders late on 11 September. He chose the terrain corridor south of Aachen, later known to the Americans as the Stolberg Corridor, as the route for the 3d Armored Division. Should the division penetrate the two bands of the Westwall that bisected the Stolberg Corridor, the 1st Infantry Division would move on Aachen. The 9th Infantry Division would protect the south flank of the corps by securing key high ground near Monschau and sweeping through the Hürtgen Forest to secure Roer River crossing sites south of Düren.[28]

Hodges might never have considered such an operation as that planned by the youthful, aggressive, energetic Collins. At 48 years of age, Collins was younger than many division commanders. He also carried much more weight with Hodges than did the other corps commanders in the First Army. Collins did not see combat during World War I, and between the wars he spent several years as either a student or an instructor in the army's professional school system. This was especially important for Collins because at Fort Benning he caught the critical eye of the future army chief of staff, George C. Marshall. This probably helped Collins to rise quickly in later years to higher levels of responsibility. He became VII Corps chief of staff in January, 1941. Following the Pearl Harbor debacle, he was chief of staff of the Hawaiian Department, and in December, 1942, he took the 25th Infantry Division to Guadalcanal. Marshall was instrumental in Collins's reassignment to the European Theater of Operations (ETO), where he took command of VII Corps in February, 1944.[29] His intellect, reputation, and past links to Marshall and Hodges gave Collins substantial credibility among peers and superiors alike. Bradley later said that Collins "was not a deep thinker or a strategist. He was a 'doer,' an action man."[30] His personal leadership style frequently took him out of his headquarters. "Every day I was out in the field visiting as far [forward] as I could the critical point of action. Where the crux of the fighting was likely to be was the place I headed for."[31]

Courtney Hodges, in contrast, was not a West Point graduate. He failed the course of instruction there and instead received his commission from the ranks. Little has been written about Hodges, and this is unfortunate in view of his role in the war. In 1944 Hodges was 57 years old, of medium height and build, the "model of a rumpled, unassertive small-town banker."[32]

The young Hodges commanded a battalion during World War I and received the Distinguished Service Cross for leading a reconnaissance into enemy lines. He came to know Marshall between the wars, and in 1941 Marshall brought Hodges to Washington as chief of infantry. He was later deputy commander of First Army under Bradley and then took command of the army after Bradley went to 12th Army Group. Bradley "had always liked and admired" the "reclusive" Hodges,[33] but when Hodges took over First Army, Bradley "began to fret privately. Courtney seemed indecisive and overly conservative. I hoped that my veteran First Army staff . . . would keep a fire under him."[34] Bradley thought Hodges lacked color and a forceful personality. Some historians maintain that Hodges had a quick temper and that he was prone to relieve senior officers first, and ask questions later. However, a member of his personal staff cannot remember any incidents of the kind.[35]

THE VII CORPS ENTERS GERMANY

The 3d Armored Division (one of three divisions in the VII Corps) penetrated the Westwall first. This division was built around two combat commands, A and B. (These commands were brigade-sized headquarters that could control several tank, infantry, and artillery battalions task-organized for particular missions.) Combat Command B (CCB) comprised Task Force 1 (TF1), commanded by Georgia Tech Graduate Lt. Col. William B. Lovelady, and Task Force 2 (TF2), commanded by Lt. Col. Roswell H. King. Brig. Gen. Maurice Rose, the division commander, told the commander of CCB, Brig. Gen. Truman E. Boudinot, to begin "vigorous patrolling" not later than 8:00 A.M. on 12 September, to "determine the strength and dispositions of the enemy defenses."[36]

Lovelady's own 2d Battalion, 33rd Armored Regiment, then located near Kettenis, Belgium, formed the core of TF1. The remainder was the 2nd Battalion, 36th Armored Infantry (less one company), Reconnaissance Company, 33rd Armored Regiment (less one platoon), a platoon of armored engineers, a platoon of M10 tank destroyers, a battery of M7 self-propelled howitzers, and a maintenance detachment.[37]

The first day of the battle for the Hürtgen Forest and Roer dams, Tuesday, 12 September, 1944, began as had so many others for the tankers and armored infantrymen. The men rose early and went quietly about the business of making precombat checks of their equipment and vehicles. Gunners checked their sights and firing controls, drivers performed last minute maintenance, and vehicle commanders checked their radios. Engines turned over, and the stench of gasoline exhaust hung in the morning mist.

There were problems from the start. Several vehicles in the first element to move—1st Platoon, 33d Reconnaissance Company, supported by tanks and armored infantry—became mired along a muddy trail, and shortly before noon Lovelady ordered Reconnaissance Company's 2d Platoon, a company of armored infantry, and a combat engineer platoon to take the road leading from Eupen, Belgium, to the northeast. At 2:51 P.M., this element reached open ground near an undefended customs station marking the Belgian-German border near Roetgen, Germany. Lovelady informed CCB headquarters by radio that the task force was in Germany. Boudinot told a radio operator, "Tell Lovelady he's famous! Congratulate him and tell him to keep on going!"[38] Roetgen was a collection of buildings scattered in a large clearing in the western end of the Hürtgen Forest. It was the first German town to fall to the U.S. Army in World War II.

There was little resistance. Most of the residents remained inside their homes. The young GIs who saw the residents looking out from behind drawn curtains thought their enemies looked "half-frightened [and] dazed."[39] Sgt. Robert Laurent said, "I rolled my armored car down the center of main street like a victory parade in a cemetery—and prayed."[40]

The tanks and half-tracks passed the drab buildings, some of which displayed white sheets hung from the windows, and proceeded to the northern outskirts of town, where the GIs first encountered the Westwall. Multiple rows of gray-brown, concrete dragon's teeth blocked a patch of open ground to the left of the road. Behind this and to the right were steep, wooded hills. A crater blown by German combat engineers blocked the road to the front.

There was no resistance until elements of Company E, 36th Armored Infantry Regiment, dismounted and moved toward the crater. A sniper's bullet then killed the company commander. Other Germans opened fire from positions in the high ground. The Americans returned the fire with their vehicle-mounted machine guns. The riflemen ran for cover between the dragon's teeth. The artillery was not very effective, and the Germans stood firm. Lovelady told Budinot that his men would have to remain in place for the night. Boudinot told Lovelady to keep the task force moving. Lovelady complied, but German fire later stopped the infantry, and he had no choice but to order his men to dig in for the night.[41]

Wednesday, 13 September, dawned cool with a light haze and more promise. The Company E infantry, covered by the tanks, was able to move along the road toward the neighboring town of Rott. Company D, meanwhile, cleared two concrete bunkers built into the side of the hill adjacent to the Dreilägerbachtal Dam, located in the same area. A platoon of infantry moved directly through the streambed, and combat engineers blew a path through the dragon's teeth.

German tank and antitank fire later accounted for five tanks and two half-tracks at Rott, but American artillery and tank fire eventually silenced the resistance. The task force moved on to Mulartshütte, where it spent the night.[42]

13–14 SEPTEMBER

The reports that reached VII Corps headquarters during the night of 12 September indicated that the reconnaissance in force would not produce a decisive breakthrough in the Stolberg Corridor. Collins looked at his options and decided to limit the advance of the corps for the time being to the west bank of the Roer. He directed the 3d Armored Division to seize the roadnet near Eschweiler. The 1st Infantry Division (16th, 18th, and 26th Infantry Regiments) would skirt Aachen on the south and take the high ground and road centers northeast of the city and protect the corps left flank until the arrival north of Aachen of the main body of the XIX Corps. Aachen was a significant target, but not an immediate objective as long as other options remained available. The 9th Infantry Division (39th, 47th, and 60th Infantry Regiments) would outflank enemy positions on the southern fringe of the Stolberg Corridor near Zweifall and Vicht by moving through the Hürtgen Forest. The 4th Cavalry Group would maintain contact with the V Corps on the south (right) flank.[43] Collins knew that the forest might be difficult to take "on the run," but he also had to assume that Aachen was heavily defended and would be much more difficult to secure. Collins did not have enough troops to take Aachen as well. He probably chose the most promising, though more limited objectives, based on his estimate of the tactical situation. But events proved even this set of goals was too ambitious. It is impossible to determine if persistent optimism played a role in the decision to push simultaneously through both the Stolberg Corridor and the Hürtgen Forest, but the scope of VII Corps operations at the time leads one to think this is the case.

Ironically, the city of Charlemagne was not defended at all. The commander of the LXXXI Corps, Generalleutnant Schack, late on 12 September had ordered the commander of the 116th Panzer Division, Generalleutnant Graf Gerhard von Schwerin, to take command of the Aachen sector. Schwerin hoped his troops would get a chance to recover from the withdrawal through Belgium, but the tactical situation prevented this. Schwerin departed for Aachen after his meeting with Schack. Aachen had hardly any defenses at all, and Schwerin assumed the Americans would attack the city within hours.[44]

He arrived in Aachen late the same night and found that "women, with small children and babies, had loaded their last possessions on small hand carts and prams and walked into the night without having any idea where to go; they were driven only by fear and the threats of the

[Nazi] Party that every person who did not leave the town would be shot as a traitor. This was our own country! . . . Had we not silently but deeply sympathized with the misery of millions of refugees . . . and thought, 'Thank God things like that don't happen at home'?"

Schwerin had to stop the panic. He did not want his soldiers to see the terror in the streets—his men were exhausted and demoralized as it was. Members of his staff reported that there were no police, fire, or emergency services. The civilians were on their own. He sent his officers back into the city to tell the civilians that the army was now in charge. This calmed many of them, but Schwerin knew that a fight for the city would bring nothing but more innocent casualties. He found an official of the telephone service and convinced him to deliver a note to the Americans as soon as they occupied Aachen. He did not intend to force them to fight for the city. The note asked the Americans to "take care of the unfortunate population in a humane way." Unfortunately, Schwerin's letter ended up in the hands of the Nazi Party, not those of Joe Collins.

American difficulties in the woods south of Aachen nearly spelled the end of Schwerin. Rather than taking Aachen within hours, as Schwerin had assumed, the Americans delayed the attack. This helped stabilize the front and make things easier for the German troops, but it also convinced party leaders that perhaps Schwerin was not a man to trust because he had countermanded a Führer order to evacuate Aachen. An SS officer visited Schwerin a few days later. The general understood the signal. He spent the night at the CP of the 60th Panzergrenadier Regiment. His troops would protect him.

He went to Schack's headquarters about the 17th, where he was informed that Model wanted him arrested. Schwerin decided to return once again to the front, where he knew the police would dare not go. Nevertheless, he later presented himself to military authorities and ultimately survived the war. Generalmajor Siegfried von Waldenberg took command of the "Windhund Division;" Model relieved Schack, the corps commander, on 21 September. The "unfortunate" population of Aachen soon received new orders to leave the city.[45]

What could the 7th Army do to stop the Americans? Senior commanders were surprised that the American attack came much slower than they had expected. But this was fine, for Army Group B had no reserves to speak of, and if the Americans spilled into the Stolberg Corridor, they might envelop the forest and outflank German positions between Aachen and Monschau.[46] There was a chance, however, that a fresh unit en route from the east, Oberst Gerhard Engel's 12th Infantry Division, would arrive in time to shift the balance of power in the Stolberg Corridor in favor of the Germans. On 12 September, Berlin had ordered the division to move by train to the Aachen sector, where it would attack to restore the front. Though General Brandenberger told Engel his intention was to commit the division as a whole, the situation was so serious that Engel realized this would be impossible.[47]

The first elements (1st and 3d Battalions, 27th Grenadier Regiment) of the division arrived at Jülich and Düren on 16 September and during the next few days engaged elements of the 1st Infantry Division and 3d Armored Division.[48] Until this time, the Germans had been powerless to stop a strong American attack in the Stolberg Corridor—or the Hürtgen Forest—had they been able to mount one.

The division's 48th Grenadier Regiment, commanded by Oberst Wilhelm Osterhold, a young, decorated veteran of the eastern front, arrived in Cologne just before midnight on 16 September. The sight of the division "made a deep impression on both the military and civilian population. Here was the first full-strength, rested and fresh division, composed of young, healthy and well-trained men that the Germans in the West had seen in a long time. The appearance of this division greatly boosted the morale of the troops and the civilians in the area."[49]

TF Lovelady, meanwhile, had continued its drive against light resistance as far as the eastern outskirts of Mausbach, where a half dozen assault guns and two Panther tanks firing from surrounding high ground caught the column in the open. The Germans first opened fire from the flanks. Their antitank rounds slammed into several tanks before the Americans could return the fire. When they did, the other vehicles opened fire from the high ground to the front. Tanks caught fire and ammunition exploded, as the crews tried to escape. Seven tanks, a tank destroyer, and an ambulance were hit. The survivors withdrew to reorganize.[50]

TF Lovelady tried unsuccessfully during the next four days to break out of Mausbach. By 20 September, one tank company was down to 5 of its authorized 17 tanks, and it had no officers; another company had 6 tanks and one officer. The men were "physically exhausted to near the breaking point. They were tired and dirty. . . . Eyes were bloodshot, cheeks hollowed, shoulders bent forward."[51] TF Lovelady had earned the dubious distinction of being the first unit to fight in the Hürtgen Forest.

Collins later said that a combination of logistic problems, bad weather, and shortages of ammunition combined to stop the VII Corps at the Westwall.[52] Every mile of advance took the Americans farther away from their supply bases and brought the Germans closer to their own. The VII Corps was well established inside Germany by the last week of September. But that was all the Corps could achieve. Collins was justified in conducting the reconnaissance in force—the Americans had to get past the Westwall and the potential gains were well worth the risk.

But the VII Corps was tired, and the Germans managed to throw together enough resistance at critical times and places to stop the Americans.

Had Collins sent even a reconnaissance element to Aachen before 15 September, he would have found that the city was his for the taking. If the Americans had taken Aachen at this time, it is possible that the Germans would have pulled out of at least the western half of the Stolberg Corridor and saved the Americans the trouble of fighting for nearly every yard of it. But there were other tasks such as securing a good supply route and protecting the Stolberg Corridor penetration against counterattack. The Roer dams were not on Joe Collins's mind as September drew to a close. The river was. And the dams remained dangerous and inviolate.

Later parts of this book may give the reader the impression that the army had no systematic approach to small-unit combat. This is not true. Army doctrine in 1944 envisioned the rifleman as the terrain-holding spearhead of a combined arms team using firepower and shock effect delivered in overwhelming mass at the decisive time and place. The mission of the infantry in the attack was to close with and destroy the enemy; in the defense it was to hold ground and wear down the opponent. But no single arm could succeed on the battlefield of the early 1940s. Armor, effective artillery fire, and close air support were integral parts of the equation for success.

Doctrine and training emphasized the coordinated application of infantry, armor, artillery, and air power. "No one arm wins battles," stated FM 100-5; "the combined action of all arms and services is essential to success."[53] The manual correctly stressed that such precepts were simple in concept but hard to carry out. As the following chapters show, this statement was particularly true in the case of the Hürtgen Forest, where combat often resembled nothing more than the gathering of a few riflemen and tanks and then hoping for the best.

2
Early Operations of the 9th Division

"**W**e were just ordered to defend [the Westwall] in a 'fight and die' manner," said the chief of staff of the German 7th Army.[1] This order by the Nazi leadership, coupled with the VII Corps operations at Aachen and in the Monschau Corridor, led to the first large-scale operations in the forest. General Collins, the VII Corps commander, now wanted the 9th Infantry Division to help widen the narrow penetration of the Westwall (in preparation for exploitation at a later date) and protect the south flank of the corps by taking key high ground south and east of Monschau. This forced the division to operate on a 19-mile-wide front, one that doctrine deemed too wide for a division in the attack. (FM 100-5 recommended a frontage for a supporting attack with two regiments on line of about four miles.)[2] The scope of the 9th Division's mission might have stemmed from overly optimistic estimates of American capabilities and German weakness. It also grew out of necessity. There were no extra troops for use in the area. The attack, therefore, developed into several fragmented actions, none of which supported the other.

THE BATTLE FOR SCHEVENHÜTTE

The 47th Infantry Regiment, operating in the northern fringe of the forest alongside the 3rd Armored Division, made the 9th Division's main effort. (The 39th and 60th Infantry are discussed below.) Though units of rearguard German infantry had counterattacked elements of the regiment's 3d Battalion on 15 September, the Americans remained unconvinced that they faced a resurgent enemy because there were so many reports of success. For example, riflemen entered one Westwall bunker and found only a pot of potatoes cooking over a wood fire. In another incident, a mess sergeant driving a jeep took six German soldiers prisoners; when his jeep became stuck in the mud, he had the Germans push it free. A GI awaiting evacuation for acute appendicitis even took a prisoner. An officer later saw the soldier, bent over in extreme pain, walking down the road with the German ahead of him. Another prisoner was a middle-aged veteran of only two weeks' service.[3]

Another story that made the rounds throughout the 9th Division featured the exploits of a cook. During an attack on the 2d Battalion, 47th Infantry, a cook "discarded his meat cleaver for a bazooka" and managed to knock out a German tank that had entered the battalion trains area. "What a man!" sighed members of the company. "If he could only cook!"[4]

Col. George W. Smythe, the commander of the 47th Infantry, was unaware of the presence of the 12th Division. Like so many others, he thought the counterattacks were only local efforts to shore up the line, not coordinated attacks aimed at stopping the Americans altogether. This led him to order his battalion commanders to continue their attacks on 16 September. The 3d Battalion shot ahead of the rest of the regiment, and Company K reached the wooded hills southwest of Schevenhütte, a nondescript crossroads town located in the valley of the Wehe Creek, on the edge of the forest along the Stolberg Corridor.[5] The GIs moved so quickly that they captured a German colonel on reconnaissance. He had no idea the Americans were in the area until he looked up from his map and saw their M1 rifles pointed in his direction.

"None of us had ever heard of a Kraut officer going anywhere alone. . . . We grabbed guns and ran or fell down the steep slope [to Schevenhütte]," recalled 1st Lt. Chester H. Jordan, a platoon leader in Company K. Jordan further reported, "As we raced through the back yards, I looked for the handiest back door. . . . The door I opened led into a small commercial kitchen and then directly into the tap room of a small hotel. The only inhabitant was a dignified old man with a large mustache who was wearing a frock coat and a shirt with winged collars."[6]

The Americans were now four miles east of Stolberg (ten miles inside Germany) and only seven miles from the division's objective—Roer River crossing sites at Düren. The capture of Schevenhütte was not decisive, however, because the Americans lacked the strength to push any farther up the Stolberg Corridor. This was unfortunate because the Germans had no improved defenses in the area. General Schack, the commander of LXXXI Corps, for example, had to place the bulk of his troops in the Aachen-Stolberg Corridor area. He had to risk putting only roadblocks in the forest. The neighboring LXXIV Corps, located to the south, in the

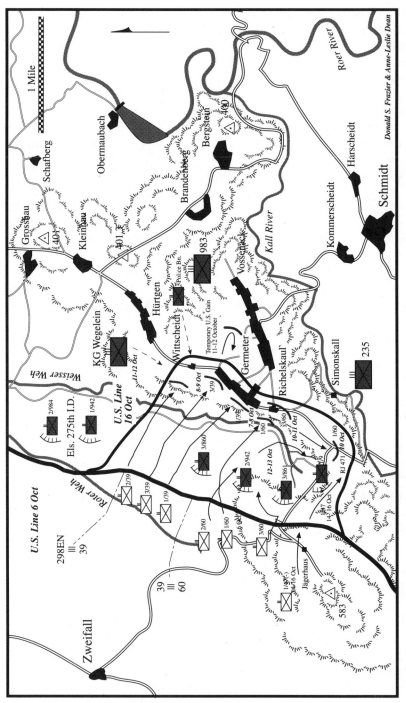

Map 2. 9th Infantry Division Operations, 6–16 October 1944

Donald S. Frazier & Anne-Leslie Dean

Monschau Corridor, was in no better condition. On 10 September, its 347th Infantry Division had 170 combat soldiers, including 40 men assigned to a bicycle-mounted rifle company. Two 150mm cannon represented the entire division artillery. About 1,700 more men reached the division late in the month.[7]

As darkness fell on 16 September, the Americans in the Schevenhütte-Stolberg area heard a great deal of vehicle traffic to their front. Observers reported the findings up the chain, and to be safe, Colonel Smythe ordered his forward elements to remain in their present locations.[8] He did not realize that retreating, rather than reinforcing, German troops were creating most of the noise, and he canceled a planned two battalion attack on Gressenich. Had Smythe been able to determine correctly the reason for the activity behind German lines and permit his men to continue the attack, the 47th Infantry Regiment might have prevented the 12th Infantry Division from influencing the battle in the Stolberg Corridor. Smythe, of course, had no way of knowing that the German soldiers crossing into sanctuary opposite the 9th Infantry Division were only "a conglomeration of clerks, personnel of base installations, . . . some personnel of the German administration in France as well as [remnants] of combat troops, many of them barely cared-for casualties."[9]

The American occupation of Schevenhütte was a threat to the south (left) flank of the newly arrived 12th Division, and Engel ordered a series of counterattacks to retake Schevenhütte. On 17 September, elements of the 2d Battalion, 47th Infantry, decimated a battalion of Oberst Osterhold's 48th Infantry Regiment. American sources also reported a pre-dawn attack on 18 September by about 90 infantry from another battalion of the regiment. This force reportedly broke though a 3d Battalion, 47th Infantry, roadblock northeast of Schevenhütte. The Americans claimed that they had restored the position before daylight, but Osterhold recalls that his battalion commander made no mention of an attack. Engel ordered Osterhold to try again on 22 September.

This attack failed also. The commander of the lead company was killed on reconnaissance. His men then attacked Schevenhütte directly rather than bypassing the center of the town as Osterhold had ordered.[10] The Americans were caught unprepared, but they reacted swiftly. Every officer in the German battalion was killed or wounded, and only one returned to friendly lines.

"Our troops bled themselves to death," said Engel after the war. The 3d Battalion, 47th Infantry, lost about 34 men wounded and another 13 killed. The Germans lost an estimated 150 killed, over 30 wounded, and 45 prisoners. The Americans held Schevenhütte, though their front-line positions were located in the buildings on the eastern edge of town.[11]

Osterhold's soldiers did not know it, but their attack also disrupted the 9th Division's other operations then underway to the south.

THE MONSCHAU CORRIDOR

At the same time as the 47th Infantry was fighting for Schevenhütte, Col. Jesse L. Gibney's 60th Infantry Regiment fought to secure the open high ground in the western reaches of the Monschau Corridor near Höfen. This would flank the Westwall in the southern fringe of the forest and establish the right wing of the VII Corps on good ground prior to crossing the Roer.

The defending German 89th Infantry Division had nearly been destroyed earlier in the summer, but in mid-September it was reorganizing behind the concrete and steel of the Westwall. It had occupied positions held at first by the poorly equipped 416th Grenadier Training Regiment (later attached to the division and renamed the 1055th Infantry Regiment). Some troops were between 50 and 60 years old, and their small arms dated from World War I. One battalion had no trained infantrymen at all, and most of those soldiers present had just returned from the hospital. The division had a few pieces of artillery, and for a time in mid-September, only three 75mm antitank guns and a few panzerfaust (a shoulder-fired, single-shot weapon firing a hollow-charge projectile) constituted its antitank defenses. The 416th Regiment at first had a single 150mm Italian howitzer that soon ran out of ammunition. Rather than relegate the howitzer to the rear, Oberst Eberhard Rösler, the division commander, had his men tow it around in full view of the approaching Americans to give the impression of strength. The division also had no medical, supply, or service troops, and officers assembled "commando detachments" to scavenge supplies from nearby units.[12]

The Americans had their own problems in the five-day fight for the Höfen-Alzen Ridge (14–18 September). On 14 September, Lt. Col. Lee W. Chatfield's 1st Battalion, 60th Infantry, left its assembly area near Camp Elsenborn, Belgium, and entered Germany that afternoon at Kalterherberg. When enemy fire finally halted the battalion near Alzen, General Craig committed the regiment's 3d Battalion through Monschau to approach the ridge from the northwest. This battalion took Höfen, but the Germans turned back a two-company probing attack on Alzen.

There was little additional progress until 17 September, when Colonel Gibney permitted Chatfield to attack the ridge from the northwest. Chatfield sent his attached tanks, tank destroyers, and other vehicles back to Kalterherberg while the infantry marched cross-country in a steady rain. The radios became damp and quit working, and commanders lost control of their dispersed units. The convoy reached the site of a destroyed bridge at dawn on the 18th, but a tank slid off the road and blocked the rest of the column. It was daylight before the battalion renewed its attack, but the ridge was in American hands by evening.[13]

The idea was sound—to seize a good position for the southern wing of the VII Corps. Yet the increasing German resistance on the periphery of the forest, coupled with the lack of American strength to commit to the attack, assured there would be no decisive outcome such as capture of any part of the Simmerath-Düren road. The hard fighting in the Monschau Corridor made it apparent here, as it had in the Stolberg Corridor, that it would take several more days to gain a good foothold in Germany.

The 39th Infantry Regiment (Lt. Col. Van Hugo Bond), meanwhile, on 14 September had also entered the forest. Its mission was to push through the Monschau Corrider from the west and cut the Simmerath-Düren road well into the forest.

The regiment's 1st Battalion (Lt. Col. Oscar H. Thompson) passed through the northern reaches of Monschau Corridor. One company moved without difficulty through Lammersdorf, a village sprawled near a line of dragon's teeth, but later came under automatic weapons and mortar fire from enemy bunkers located in the fringe of the forest. A second company tried unsuccessfully to encircle the enemy position. At dusk, Thompson sent his reserve company into the forest to the northwest to bypass the enemy, but it became engaged in a firefight and could not continue.[14]

The 3d Battalion (Lt. Col. Robert H. Stumpf) tried, but failed, to secure Rollesbroich and cut the Simmerath-Düren road.[15] The battalion also failed for several days to take the highest ground in the area, Hill 554, at Paustenbach, near Lammersdorf. From this hill, the Germans controlled all movement from Lammersdorf into the forest and the Monschau Corridor. The battalion made several unsuccessful attacks to take the hill, which today is topped by a large religious cross. Oberst Hasso Neitzel, the operations officer of the 89th Division, later said that "the enemy attacked five to six times. The regularity was amazing, the more so since each attack was repulsed mostly with great losses. For the latter reason, the enemy requested a short, one-day armistice to recover wounded and bury the dead. That was granted. Nevertheless, the attack was repeated the following day at the usual time." The Americans did not occupy the hill until 29 September.[16]

Colonel Bond, meanwhile, had sent the 2d Battalion (Lt. Col. Frank Gunn) on 15 September through the forest against the rear of the Lammersdorf defenses.[17] A rifleman in Company G, Billy F. Allsbrook, recalled, "I clearly remember entering Germany with no opposition. I thought, boy, this is not bad at all! I recall seeing fortifications that were deserted. We were in two columns, one on each side of the road, with no problems at all. That all changed when we set up in the forest."[18]

A roadblock held up supporting tanks and forced Companies E and F to dig in for the night. Company G, meanwhile, set up two roadblocks on trails to the north, and the next day captured a set of maps and overlays that revealed the location of several Westwall bunkers.[19] But this served little immediate purpose, given the unexpected strength of the defenses and the lack of reinforcing troops.

The Germans were unable to eject the Americans from the Monschau Corridor, but they prevented them from outflanking the Hürtgen Forest and from pushing up the Simmerath-Düren road. Thus they continued to threaten the 9th Infantry Division's flank and rear and, for all practical purposes, eliminated the threat to the Monschau Corridor posed by the 60th Infantry near Höfen. The combat strength of the division was spread from Monschau to the Stolberg Corridor.[20] Concentration was impossible. It was clear to General Craig that the attempt to pay a cheap price for entry into the forest had failed. The American approach to combat was sound in terms of doctrine. The 9th Division in the Monschau Corridor used armor and infantry reserves and tried when possible to flank strongpoints. But commanders at all levels faced problems in maintaining control of their dispersed units the minute they entered the forest and confronted well-defended positions without the benefit of close fire support.

These early engagements along the Westwall brought with them the problem of reducing the huge steel-reinforced concrete bunkers. The 9th Division eventually developed tactics using a rifle platoon to make the initial approach to a bunker. A tank, TD, or riflemen with bazookas would support the attack. The unit would first smother the bunker with mortar and artillery fire to kill the infantry defending the site from nearby foxholes or trenches. The supporting armor then fired at the weapons apertures. An infantry platoon would close on the bunker while firing rifles, BARs, and machine guns.[21]

During one two-day "bunker busting" operation near Lammersdorf, riflemen of Company K, 39th Infantry, exploded a charge against the outer door of a bunker. This failed to get the enemy to surrender. So did the gasoline the Americans poured around the door and ignited with a thermite grenade. The next morning, they set off a German mine that only blew off the cover of a ventilation pipe. The GIs then exploded three dozen more mines on the roof of the bunker. They followed this by exploding a mine placed to blow away the earth covering part of a wall. The riflemen then exploded a half dozen more mines against the exposed concrete. The total penetration was less than three feet. Flamethrowers and bazookas also failed to convince the Germans to give up. It took 300 pounds of TNT exploded on the surface of the bunker to get the Germans to surrender.

An officer taken prisoner reported that while some smoke entered the crew area through the firing apertures, none came in through the vents or the door. The air became bad and the Germans smelled the vapor of the burning gasoline, but enough fresh air entered through the firing apertures to keep them alive. The officer ordered his men to evacuate the bunker because he feared the Americans might block an exit door.

It might also take up to a dozen direct hits by 155mm shells to force the Germans to surrender a bunker. That many rounds created enough dust to make breathing difficult.[22]

Attacks employing fire and movement were the safest way to reduce a Westwall bunker without sustaining undue casualties. Unfortunately, the Americans reached the defenses without the proper equipment for such attacks and with little training in the tactics required to assault the bunkers.

THE FIRST ATTACK ON HÜRTGEN

The failure in the Monschau Corridor led to the first of several attacks through the center of the forest. The VII Corps front during the third week of September was wide, thinly held, and overall unsatisfactory as a point of departure for an attack toward the Roer. On 18 September, General Collins ordered the 3d Armored Division, 47th Infantry Regiment, and the 1st Infantry Division to pause and consolidate before continuing the attack. The rest of the 9th Division would continue working to clear the forest. Collins saw this as a way for the division to join its widely separated regiments, then located at Schevenhütte (the 47th) and in the Monschau Corridor (the 39th and 60th), position the south wing of the corps well through the forest, and give it control of much of the Simmerath-Düren road.[23] Collins probably expected this to force the Germans to evacuate the forest and make it easier for the Americans to reach the Roer.

The initial objectives of the 9th Division were the towns of Hürtgen and Kleinhau. Lack of troop strength forced General Craig to pin hopes for success on a force composed of battalions from both the 60th and 39th Infantry Regiments. The 1st Battalion, 60th Infantry, would attack from Zweifall and seize a wooded ridge north of a marsh known to the Germans as Todtenbruch, or "Dead Man's Moor," located deep within the forest about three miles southeast of Zweifall. The battalion would continue to Germeter, where it would cut the Simmerath-Düren road. The 1st Battalion, 39th Infantry, would capture a trail network in the Weisser Weh Valley and then move on Hürtgen and Kleinhau.[24]

The attack began on 19 September. The 39th Infantry soon found that control of formations larger than platoons was nearly impossible. Troops over a few feet apart could hardly see each other. There were no clearings except for narrow firebreaks and trails. Maps were of little value for terrain association; navigation was primarily by compass.[25] The only thing working in the Americans' favor was the lack of resistance. But that would soon change.

The Americans reached the gorgelike valley of the Weisser Weh on the first day and dug in for the night on its steep, wooded western slope, unaware that the battle was already moving in favor of the Germans. By the next morning, parts of the 1st Battalion, 942d Infantry Regiment, and the XX Luftwaffe Fortress Battalion, controlled by the 353d Infantry Division, were in the area.[26] Two more days of hard fighting brought no results. Then, on 22 September, Craig told Colonel Gibney to move the battalion as fast as possible to reinforce the battalion in Schevenhütte, then under attack by General Engel's 12th Infantry Division.

The march through the same terrain they had already attacked through was exhausting, and the reinforcements arrived at Schevenhütte only to find that they were not needed. When the Americans returned to the Weisser Weh Valley, they learned that the Germans had moved into their old foxholes. They had to enter new positions about a mile west of the creek.[27] This was as close to Kleinhau and Hürtgen as the Americans came during September.

Things were equally difficult for the Germans. The commander of the opposing 353d Infantry Division, Generalleutnant Paul Mahlmann, later said that his troops "were fighting in deplorable conditions, exposed to incessant enemy fire, fighting daily without relief, receiving little support from their own weak artillery; hampered by insufficient supplies of ammunition, out on a ration barely sufficient to ward off hunger, drenched by frequent rain, and without the possibility of changing clothes."[28]

There was a shortage of men with combat experience, and morale suffered because of the poor state of the military postal service. Frequent changes in parent unit assignment, disruption of transport, and families forced to evacuate their homes all combined to cause delays in mail delivery. Some soldiers went for weeks without mail.[29]

Mahlmann also believed that the front-line soldiers felt hemmed between the Americans on one side and their own National Socialist leadership on the other. "Hence, forsaken as they were," he thought, "the troops had no choice but to hold out. In their hopeless resignation, some became fatalities, others sought consolation in religion. After collapse of the confidence in its leadership, the troops, in point of fact, continued fighting only for their personal security."[30]

Mahlmann and his staff departed the Hürtgen area in early October to take charge of another division. Most of the combat troops of the 353d

Division remained in place and came under control of the 275th Infantry Division (discussed below). The division returned to the Hürtgen area in early December. Mahlmann, like so many of his troops, fell ill and gave up his command before the end of the year.

The experiences of the 1st Battalion, 60th Infantry, provide a good example of the thoroughly confused nature of the September battle deep in the forest. On the first day of the attack, Company A took the wrong trail, got lost, and ended up in the area of the 1st Battalion, 39th Infantry. The company did not rejoin its parent battalion until the next day.

Company C, meanwhile, stalled at a trail crossing protected by a roadblock. The company remained in place while Company B attacked a concrete bunker located nearby. This company was armed with only small arms and a few bazookas, not the proper weapons required to eliminate a bunker. The GIs had to shower the position with grenades and fire bazookas at point-blank range at the weapons apertures before the Germans surrendered. The company commander then set up his command post by the bunker. Minutes after the commander had gathered his key personnel to issue new orders, a sudden, unexplained explosion wounded or killed the entire group. Germans in nearby bunkers opened fire on the dazed survivors. This single incident rendered temporarily ineffective a quarter of the combat strength involved in the attack.

The battalion reorganized and continued operations until an enemy counterattack in the late afternoon of 22 September threatened to break through Company C. The battalion commander, Lieutenant Colonel Chatfield, sent first a platoon and then the remainder of Company B to assist Company C, which by that time was in a hand-to-hand fight. He remembered that "the fighting was a small-arms battle, rifle and machine gun, since the enemy was too close in even to use mortars." Both sides drew back exhausted.

The German shelling continued throughout the night. Shells with fuses designed to explode on contact hit the trees and burst above the infantrymen. To dive to the ground for cover, as the men had been trained, meant exposing much of the body to a rain of hot metal and wood splinters. The best way to survive, the Americans learned, was to crouch under, or quite literally hug, a tree. That way, they exposed only the much smaller target of their head (covered by a steel helmet). A new term, "tree burst," entered the vocabulary of the soldiers of the First Army.

Early on 23 September, the Germans overran a platoon of Company A, poured through the resulting gap in the line, and for a time threatened to split the battalion in two. Another counterattack began that afternoon, and this time the Americans did not stop the enemy infantry until they were within small-arms range of the battalion CP. According to Chatfield, "The enemy seemed to be everywhere, and in the darkness of the thick trees the confusion and firing seemed everywhere."

The battalion fought off another counterattack at dusk. The GIs spent another night in the dismal forest with no hope of relief, struggling to stay awake, and listening in the darkness for any sign of the Germans, who roamed at will throughout the area. No one dared venture from the comparative safety of his foxhole, or he might never find his way back. Some men who left were never heard from again. The forest floor, covered with a thick carpet of pine needles, was treacherous with every step. Metallic mine detectors could not locate the wooden-cased antipersonnel mines, which could blow off a foot or part of a leg.

Progress on 24 September was limited, and a few minutes after 1:00 A.M. on the 25th, a white flare shot up into the sky over the German positions. Within minutes, a company of German infantry had surrounded the concrete bunker housing the Company A CP. They took four officers and 45 enlisted men prisoner, virtually annihilating the company. It now had only 30 riflemen—fewer than a full-strength platoon. The Germans launched another attack just as a new commander tried to reorganize the company. The American line held, but at noon the Germans counterattacked once again. The quick response of mortars and artillery broke up the attack and saved the battalion. When Chatfield tried to organize one last attack, the Company B commander told him that his men could not move. Chatfield relieved the officer. A new commander led the attack to a point about two-thirds of the way through the Todtenbruch. By then, the combined strength of the three line companies in the 1st Battalion, 60th Infantry, was less than 200 men, with replacements. The same day, Colonel Gibney ordered a final attempt to clear the Todtenbruch and link the positions there with elements of the 39th Infantry north of Lammersdorf. This attack, by the 1st Battalion, 39th, and 3d Battalion, 60th Infantry, eventually cut the road north of Lammersdorf near a hunter's cabin called Jägerhaus.[31]

The September attack ended with the 39th Infantry about three miles southeast of Zweifall and the 60th Infantry in the Todtenbruch. The 9th Division also held the high ground near Monschau but had failed to clear the Simmerath-Düren road north of Simmerath. Progress by the 1st Infantry Division and the 3d Armored Division to the north was also disappointing. The reconnaissance in force and follow-up attack failed to put the VII Corps along the Roer, but it did firmly establish it in the Westwall.

The Germans in mid-September did not think they would be able to hold the Americans in the Westwall. Many, in fact, thought they would be lucky to hold them at the Rhine. But the tactical situation south of Aachen had turned in their favor by the end of the month. The Americans chose not to concentrate the First Army north of Aachen and in the Stolberg Corridor, as Gersdorff, for one, thought they would. After the war, when an interviewer asked him if he thought a concentrated drive would have left the Americans with exposed flanks, General Gersdorff answered, "If you had known about our weakness in the Line, you would not have worried about your flanks."[32] The Germans won the race for the Westwall and border defenses near Aachen by a narrow margin, but it was clear that as long as the Americans remained interested in the forest, a few thousand of their own men could tie down a significant part of a corps.

The decision that led to the next attack in the forest came in late September. On the 22d, Eisenhower reaffirmed to his chief subordinates that the Allies would first build up their forces along the Rhine before making the final drive into the interior of Germany. The initial phase of the attack, Eisenhower said, would be the double envelopment of the Ruhr by the 21 Army Group and the First U.S. Army. Because Montgomery's ongoing requirements took so much manpower, the First Army would make the main effort. The remainder of the 12th Army Group, principally Patton's Third Army, would continue its offensive into central Germany as far as its resources would allow, but this effort would not divert supplies from the main effort in the north.[33]

"No one is more anxious than I to get to the Ruhr quickly," wrote the supreme commander. Almost as an afterthought, he added that Bradley's 12th Army Group was "fearfully stretched south of Aachen and may get a nasty little 'Kasserine' if the enemy chooses at any place to concentrate a bit of strength."[34] Bradley realized that it was "now quite apparent that we were not going to run through Germany as we had run through France."[35]

Bradley reduced the frontage of the First Army by placing the newly arrived Ninth U.S. Army (with only the VIII Corps) in the Ardennes. He gave the First Army an "on order" mission to protect the right flank of the 21 Army Group, and thrust "vigorously" to Cologne and Bonn. Preliminary operations designed to stabilize the front between Aachen and Monschau included an attack by the VII Corps' 1st Infantry Division and elements of the XIX Corps to clear Aachen. The 3d Armored Division would continue its drive up the Stolberg Corridor. General Gerow's V Corps shifted its sector a few miles to the north to take over ground at Monschau held by VII Corps. This reduced the VII Corps front from about 35 miles to 20 miles and enabled Collins to concentrate the 9th Infantry Division for the push to the Roer.[36]

Collins and Hodges designated the road center of Schmidt as the next target of the 9th Division. Schmidt was located a few miles south of Germeter and Hürtgen on ground overlooking the approaches to the largest of the dams (the Schwammenauel). The two generals evidently viewed the town only as a road center of value in an attack toward the Roer. It is impossible to determine whether or not they had an attack on the dam in mind when they ordered the 9th Division to attack Schmidt, but it is certain that neither general issued a written order to that effect.[37]

THE ROER RIVER DAMS

If the corps and army commanders neglected to consider the importance of the dams, what about their staff officers? The only staff officer as early as the first week of October to discuss in a written report the value of the dams was in no position to impact directly the chain of operational decision making. This officer was the 9th Division G-2, Maj. Jack A. Houston. On 2 October he wrote that the Schwammenauel Dam and powerhouse were "targets of great importance." Houston understood the importance of the dams to future operations, and it was tragic that his final comment was all but ignored for weeks: "Bank overflows and destructive flood waves can be produced by regulating the discharge from the various dams. By demolition of some of them great destructive flood waves can be produced which would destroy everything in the populated industrial valley as far as the Meuse and into Holland."

The two largest and most important of the dams are the Urftalsperre (Urft Valley Dam), and the Rurtalsperre Schwammenauel (Rur Valley Dam, Schwammenauel). In 1944 the Urft Dam regulated the flow of the Urft River and provided hydroelectric power for Aachen, Düren, Schleiden, and Monschau. The 50-meter-high Schwammenauel Dam, built between 1934 and 1938 as a public works project intended to regulate the flow of the Roer River, was made of earth with a concrete core. The reservoir, located southwest of Schmidt, impounded about 81,000 acre-feet of water. The other, less important dams were located near Obermaubach, Heimbach, Lammersdorf, Rurberg, and Roetgen.[38]

The First Army G-2 was quick to dismiss Houston's report with the comment that destruction of the dams "would cause at the most local floodings for about 5 days counted from the moment the dam was blown until all the water had receded." However, on 5 October the army engineer commented that destruction of the two major dams would produce "widespread flooding." The XIX Corps engineer's estimate was the most realistic appraisal. Although this report did not fully analyze the impact of destruction of the dams (they all were in the VII Corps sector), on 8 October the corps chief engineer noted that a flood of the Roer might reach up to 500 yards in width across the entire front of XIX Corps. Such a catastrophe would shut down the northern wing of the First Army for several weeks.[39]

THE DEFENDERS

On 1 October the 275th Infantry Division (Generalleutnant Hans Schmidt) assumed responsibility for defending the Hürtgen Forest. Schmidt called the forest a "weird and wild" place, where "the dark pine trees and the dense tree-tops give the forest even in the daytime a somber appearance which is apt to cast gloom upon sensitive people."[40] The 49-year-old general had not expected to take responsibility for the defense of a gap between the 12th Infantry Division and the 353d Infantry Division, then located south of Schevenhütte.

The organization of the division was far different than that of the opposing 9th Infantry Division. What the German division lacked in combat power, however, it recouped in the advantages the forest gave to the defender. The 1st Battalion, 984th Regiment, was the product of grouping several miscellaneous units under a single headquarters. The 2d Battalion was under the command of a 50-year-old captain and covered the division's north wing (south of Schevenhütte). The 942d Infantry Regiment, originally part of the 353d Division, along with the XX Luftwaffe Fortress Battalion defended the thickly wooded east bank of the Weisser Weh Creek. About 1,100 men of the 253d Grenadier Training Regiment, another composite unit consisting of battalions from a half dozen regiments, were dug in northwest of Germeter. Schmidt also had a partially motorized battalion under the command of a Major Riedel, designated the 275th Fusilier Battalion. This unit had good fighting spirit and would perform well in the days to come.

Prior to the American attack, Schmidt formed a field replacement battalion to conduct special training courses for noncommissioned officers. The division artillery consisted of 105mm howitzers well supplied (by German standards) with ammunition. Six assault guns supplied mobile fire support.

Clouds and morning fog often kept American planes grounded and spared the Germans the daily air attacks they had experienced throughout the summer. The cool, intermittent rains of early autumn made the trails and firebreaks barely passable, even for foot soldiers. The men had inadequate rations, and most were without overcoats or cold-weather clothing. Sickness spread; General Schmidt recalled that some of his soldiers died from exposure and exhaustion.

A defensive position is never considered complete. One can always do something to improve fields of fire, cover, and concealment. The 7th Army permitted use of the dilapidated Westwall bunkers only for protection from artillery. The infantrymen dug their fighting positions near the bunkers. They reinforced the new defenses with logs and placed the firing apertures close to ground level to permit grazing fire. They also

Generalleutnant Hans Schmidt, commander of the 275th Infantry Division. (Courtesy Bundesarchiv-Militararchiv)

built camouflaged perches where snipers using rifles fitted with telescopes could avoid the dense tree growth close to the ground.[41] General Schmidt's 6,500 soldiers were working feverishly on these defenses when the first GI of the 9th Infantry Division left his foxhole to begin the second battle of the Hürtgen Forest.

3
October Deadlock

General Collins did not have enough troops to allow him to devote an entire division to sweeping the center of the forest and simultaneously securing the Stolberg Corridor. The 47th Infantry had to hold the salient at Schevenhütte, and this left Craig only two-thirds of his division with which to make the October attack against Schmidt.

The 9th Division plan called for the 39th Infantry Regiment (Bond) to cross the Weisser Weh Creek, seize Germeter, and cut the Simmerath-Düren road. The regiment would then head east and capture the windswept Vossenack Ridge, which was a logical jumping-off spot for an attack against Schmidt. The farming village of Vossenack, perched on the open high ground, occupied most of the length of the ridge, which was about a mile and a half long. The inherent risk in the 9th Division's plan was that because the 47th Infantry was unavailable for commitment, the 39th Infantry would attack without a secure north flank.

The 60th Infantry (Gibney), on the right of the 39th, would first take the settlement of Richelskaul, located just south of Germeter. The regiment would then turn southwest to capture Road Junction (RJ) 471 and Raffelsbrand, located near the Simmerath-Düren road. This would allow the division to move from the north against the Westwall defenses in the Monschau Corridor. These positions had stopped the 39th Infantry in mid-September.[1]

The Americans banked heavily—perhaps too heavily—on fighter-bombers to isolate the battlefield and compensate for the lack of troop strength. Only two regiments were attacking on a front just two and a half miles wide, through very difficult terrain. But the aircraft could not operate around the clock, and they would be of limited use until the GIs reached the clearings where Germeter, Hürtgen, and Vossenack were located.

Even had aircraft isolated the battlefield from reinforcement, the Germans soldiers already there would be able to hold their own against any infantry attacks that were not accompanied by close air and artillery support.

Fighter-bomber strikes and artillery preparatory fires proceeded the attack, which began at 11:30 A.M., on Friday, 6 October.[2] The 1st and 3d Battalions, 39th Infantry, ran into elements of the 942d Infantry Regiment just minutes after crossing the LD. Even the most experienced American scouts had trouble locating the well-camouflaged bunkers in the forest darkness. The first indication of the enemy was usually the sharp, cracking sound of German bullets hitting the trees.

A few men overcame the initial shock of contact with the enemy and pressed the attack. Company B captured three bunkers, but a fourth was well protected by automatic weapons dug in nearby. Enemy observers also called down deadly accurate mortar fire, and the attack ground to a halt. The 39th Infantry was still about a mile west of Germeter when it dug in late in the day.[3]

The 60th Infantry fared just as badly. The first objective of Maj. Lawrence L. Decker's 2d Battalion at that time was RJ 471, little more than a muddy, narrow intersection of forest-cloaked paths in Dead Man's Moor at the present-day highway B-399. The lead elements of the battalion had moved less than a half mile when fire from a concrete bunker pinned down several riflemen on the wet forest floor and brought the attack to a halt. One of the companies ended the day with 62 men left out of its original strength of about 130.[4] William M. Cowan, then a member of the 2d Battalion, 60th Infantry, remembered, "The machine-gun and small-arms fire, as I recall, was no more than about three feet above the ground."[5]

German mortar crews walked their fire forward and backward and side to side. The fire created tree bursts that caused heavy casualties in Decker's battalion.[6] By evening, some of the Americans had managed to reach positions within a few yards of the Germans, but it would be 11 October before they took the area.

The grind began again on the 7th. By 11:00 A.M., the 1st Battalion, 60th Infantry, was within a few hundred yards of Richelskaul, but Lieutenant Colonel Chatfield, the battalion commander, was reluctant to continue the attack without tank support. This would be slow in coming. Accurate German artillery fire and the muddy, mined trails and firebreaks had combined to slow the supporting tanks. The Germans usually planted their antitank mines two or three deep. When engineers removed a mine, they often did not look for another buried in the same location. The following tanks might hit the remaining mines, block trails, and force operations to halt until engineers could return and sweep the trails.[7] According to the 9th Division Report of Operations for October 1944, "Everywhere, the advance was slowed by numerous mines and obstacles on the roads and firebreaks." It was too late in the day to mount an attack when the tanks finally reached the infantry.[8]

German artillery fire throughout the night of 7–8 October battered the 1st Battalion, 39th Infantry. Things improved when one company maneuvered through a gap in the German defenses, bypassed several concrete bunkers, and reached the edge of the woods west of Germeter. The battalion commander, Lt. Col. Oscar H. Thompson, exploited this welcome gain with the rest of the battalion, but it would be late on 8 October before tanks arrived to support the infantry.[9]

The available German records indicate that the Americans were not alone in neglecting the dams. The Germans were thinking in terms of stopping a quick American push to the Roer at Düren. General der Infanterie Karl Püchler, acting commander of the LXXIV Corps, for example, thought the Americans were after the dominating heights in the area that overlook both the Roer Valley and the critical supply routes nearby, which would sustain such an attack.[10] General Schmidt, commander of the 275th Division, thought the Americans would try either to reinforce their salient at Schevenhütte in an effort to encircle Aachen or to take Germeter, cut the Simmerath-Düren road, and mount a stronger attack against the bunker line south of Raffelsbrand.[11] At first, he did not believe the Americans intended to take Vossenack and Schmidt, because he did not think such objectives justified "the large commitment of troops and expenditure of ammunition."[12]

Postwar interviews with senior German generals indicate that through October at least they were more concerned with preventing the Americans from reaching the Roer near Düren than with protecting the Roer dams and using them to flood the Roer plain behind the Americans. Also, there is no specific mention of the value of the dams in terms of flank security for the Ardennes counterattack, then scheduled for December. Of course, as more generals learned of the highly secret plans for the Ardennes attack, interest in defending the dams grew. Mention of the value of the dams coincides with the interviews which discuss operations after mid-November. Ironically, German interest in the dams picked up not long before the Americans realized their importance.

Though the scope and location of the attack came as a surprise, Schmidt quickly shifted troops to the threatened sector opposite Germeter. He could do this only because the VII Corps was spread too thinly to mass at more than one place. Still, it was a narrow victory. Major Riedel's 275th Fusilier Battalion failed to stop the 39th Infantry on the morning of 7 October, though it did slow them down.

Eighteen-year-old Hubert Gees was a member of Riedel's battalion.

Gees remembers facing "the combined fire of rifles, grenade launchers, and artillery. There was no breakthrough. We had to go back and dig in quickly ourselves. I ducked more every day in the Hürtgen Forest than in my entire basic training."[13]

Gees's company lost 35 men of about 100 assigned. Both the company commander and Major Riedel were wounded. The replacement company commander lasted three days; the third company commander was a 23-year-old lieutenant.[14]

General Schmidt tried again on 8 October, when he sent about 600 men of the 983d Regiment against the 60th Infantry. This attack also failed to stop the Americans, and it cost the 275th Infantry Division many dead and wounded. "During the day, our strength grew weaker and the [division was] pushed back along the entire front. The fighting here was difficult and costly," said Schmidt.[15]

The fighting was also very hard for General Craig's infantry. Entries from the 39th Infantry's operations journal reflect this fact:

7:20 A.M. Heavy artillery barrage has fallen on position for last 30 minutes.

8:00 A.M. (1st Battalion): All companies in small-arms fight.

8:02 A.M. (3d Battalion): "L" Co. somewhat disorganized by artillery fire. Be a little time before Bn can jump off.

8:50 A.M. Many casualties from artillery. . . .

10:58 A.M. "G" Co. knocked out three machine-gun positions.

2:45 P.M. "G" Co. in firefight, small arms and mortars.[16]

Schmidt's division was holding, but it was growing weaker by the minute. His corps commander ordered nearby artillery units, including those of the neighboring 89th Infantry Division, to support the 275th Division. In desperation, Schmidt moved his replacement training battalion—instructors, trainees, and all—into the line. A police battalion composed of men between 45 and 60 years of age armed only with rifles also arrived from Düren. "It hurt me to commit these family men," said Schmidt, "but I had no choice in this critical situation."[17]

The 275th Division suffered nearly 550 battle casualties between 6 and 9 October. It seemed to Schmidt that the Americans were constantly moving up new units because their attack never appeared to lessen in intensity.[18] The Americans were lucky they could create that impression. Their situation was not much better than the Germans', and the rifle platoons had to rely on badly needed riflemen to hand-carry the supplies that reached the foxholes.

Despite the problems, Chatfield's battalion was ready to move on Richelskaul by the morning of 9 October. This attack is an example of successful tank-infantry cooperation. Ten minutes of preparatory artillery fire crashed down on the Germans. Just minutes after the last shell exploded, riflemen supported by tanks pouring machine-gun fire on the German positions burst from the woods and sped toward the settlement. A brave, but rather foolish, German officer stood up at the German foxhole line and fired a panzerfaust that hit a tank but did no damage. The tank then literally cut him in half with a 75mm shell. The remaining Germans either fled or surrendered. The battalion consolidated the positions and remained in place for the rest of the day.[19]

The battalion's next target was the Raffelsbrand road junction. There was a steady rain at midday on 10 October, when Chatfield's battalion moved out. A few men from Company A found a way around the enemy positions and caught the Germans by surprise. They surrendered in large numbers. The battalion was now threatening the rear of the line of concrete bunkers north of the Kall River, but the men were far too tired to continue the attack.

Several men from the 39th Infantry's 1st and 3d Battalions meanwhile managed to reach Germeter on the 9th, but the resistance was so strong that they could not reach Vossenack. A near-disaster struck that night and the next day when the Germans infiltrated between two platoons of Company I and the rest of the 3d Battalion. The Germans killed, wounded, or captured all but a few of the GIs as detailed below. Meanwhile, the 2nd Battalion worked hard to secure the regiment's north flank.[20]

THE BATTLE OF THE WITTSCHEIDT SAWMILL

Like so many other Germans, Oberleutnant Eugen Welti, commander of Headquarters Company, 73d Engineer Battalion, did not expect an American attack in the center of the forest. Elements of his battalion had made little headway against the 39th Infantry. The fighting grew heavier, and on 9 October, a cold, cloudy, rainy day, the battalion, reinforced by the police from Düren, lost the settlement of Wittscheidt, with its sawmill, to the 3d Battalion, 39th Infantry.

At 5:00 the next morning (10 October), Oberleutnant Herbert Seidel led a composite force under the control of the 73d Engineer Battalion to retake the sawmill. The engineers charged across the Germeter-Hürtgen road, burst into the administration building, and surprised two American sentries. Seidel's men overwhelmed a few other Americans, and the police secured the area. Seidel thought any Americans remaining at the sawmill would be in the cellar of the administration building. He waited at the top of the steps leading to the basement and whispered for his messenger to fire an illumination flare through the window. The messenger fired a whistling-type flare by mistake. The flare crashed through the window and by chance ignited in the middle of several Americans who had taken refuge from the attack. The flare's piercing shrill sound and blinding light frightened them into immediate surrender. Seidel was shocked to see 20 Americans standing with their hands raised in surrender.

Late in the afternoon, three M4 tanks accompanied by infantry counterattacked Seidel's men. The tank fire set stored wood on fire. The police broke and ran, and the engineers could not stop them. Seidel had to order his engineers to evacuate the sawmill. He later said, "When we had to give up this important position to the Americans, we had a successful day behind us and [we knew] that for a time we had interrupted the advance of the Americans."[21]

11–12 OCTOBER

This period was the high-water mark of the first attack on Schmidt. The 39th Infantry, despite repeated attempts to do so, could not gain Vossenack. The 60th Infantry was making progress, but it was too weak to be a significant threat to the bunkers in the Monschau Corridor. The Germans strengthened their defenses and prepared to launch what they hoped would be a decisive counterattack.

On 11 October the 2d Battalion, 60th Infantry, now commanded by Maj. Quentin R. Hardage (Major Decker had been wounded), finally took the strongpoint that had delayed it since 6 October. The battalion dug in within a few hundred yards of RJ 471, but it was late on 13 October before the battalion finally took it. Two companies from the 1st Battalion, 47th Infantry, moved south from Schevenhütte, and a tank company from the 3d Armored Division arrived soon afterward from the Stolberg Corridor to reinforce the 60th Infantry.[22]

Despite these successes, the battle for the Germeter area continued to rage, and the 3d Battalion, 39th Infantry, was unable to move through the wooded draw between Germeter and Vossenack. German artillery fire pummeled the battalion whenever it tried to enter the draw, and the companies were strung out in a thin, pencil-like column. Lieutenant Colonel Stumpf, the commander of the 3d Battalion, had to halt the attack to avoid losing contact with the 2d Battalion.[23]

Michael Harkinish, then a rifleman in Company K, recalls moving with his squad through the draw outside Vossenack. The GIs spotted some Germans, and Harkinish and the others dropped to the ground to fire. When the Germans returned the fire, a GI near Harkinish fell mortally wounded. A bullet also hit the company commander in the face. Despite the wound, he remained at his post.

The enemy fire seemed as constant as if every German held an automatic weapon. Harkinish fired his M1 as quickly as he could reload.

About this time, a machine gunner came up, but he was killed before he could set up his weapon. A second later, Harkinish's own luck ran out, as an enemy rifleman shot him in the jaw. "I was spitting out teeth, and the blood was gushing out. I was hysterical. . . . I never became unconscious, but my worst fears were that I would never see my first child, Diane, who was born when I was stationed overseas," he later recalled. A medic arrived, gave Harkinish a shot of morphine, and bandaged the wound. The medic himself was killed a moment later. Harkinish was later evacuated. During the arduous trip to the rear, medics placed him on his stomach so he would not choke on his own blood.[24]

KAMPFGRUPPE WEGELEIN

Generalleutnant Schmidt spent most of 9 October on the phone, trying desperately to pry reinforcements from LXXIV Corps. Finally, about 2:00 A.M. on 10 October, the corps agreed to release to the 275th Division two infantry companies from the 89th Division. These units would not arrive until midday on 11 October. Meanwhile, during the afternoon of 10 October, Generals Brandenberger and Straube traveled to Schmidt's command post to discuss a larger counterattack against the Americans. They told Schmidt he would receive a new unit, Kampfgruppe Wegelein, for use against the enemy north flank.

At the same time that Schmidt worked tirelessly to prevent an American breakthrough, several miles to the south in Luxembourg, Oberst Wolfgang Wegelein loaded his 1,200 young, well-trained officer candidates and other veterans into cargo trucks for the road march to the Hürtgen Forest. Wegelein had orders to attack south from the woods near Wittscheidt and hit the exposed American left (north) flank. If the kampfgruppe could push the Americans from Germeter, Wegelein would continue the attack to the south, where it would hit the 60th Infantry's flank. Success depended upon surprise and the controlled employment of the officer candidates. Wegelein intended to enter attack positions before midnight on 11 October, but his men did not reach the Germeter-Hürtgen area until early the next morning. Wegelein asked General Schmidt to delay the attack, scheduled to begin just after dawn. He told Schmidt he needed more time to prepare his communications network. Schmidt refused the request, telling Wegelein that he would report him for cowardice if he did not attack on the morning of Thursday, 12 October, as planned.[25]

It was a clear and cool morning. Artillery fire hit the 39th Infantry beginning at 6:50 A.M., and Wegelein's young soldiers began their attack about ten minutes later. They caught the Americans by surprise, pushed

General der Panzertruppen Erich Brandenberger (Commander, 7th Army). (Courtesy Bundesarchiv-Militärarchiv)

between Companies F and G, 39th Infantry, and for a time threatened the 2d Battalion's forward CP.[26]

The attack also cut the supply line to Germeter. Lieutenant Colonel Thompson, the commander of the 1st Battalion, 39th Infantry, committed two companies to prevent this, but there was no division reserve, and the regiment's 3d Battalion could assist only by withdrawing Companies K and L from the hard-won positions near Vossenack. General Craig alerted elements of the 47th Infantry for a possible move south.[27]

The Americans managed to keep their communications system in place. In contrast, every step the German infantry took further separated them from Oberst Wegelein, who was now losing control of the battle. Wegelein called off his attack at 11:00 A.M., regrouped his men, and tried again that afternoon. But the renewed attack failed, and by dark the kampfgruppe had suffered over 500 more casualties. Schmidt later remarked that it was "a pity to waste the ammunition" on such a futile effort. A change in corps plans late on 12 October dashed Schmidt's expectations for a renewed attack when he received an order directing the immediate reassignment of the officer candidates. This reduced the kampfgruppe's strength by half. Schmidt had no choice but to end the attack and attach the remaining members of Kampfgruppe Wegelein to the 275th Division.[28]

Shortly before 8:00 A.M. on 14 October, Oberst Wegelein and his adjutant approached the forward positions of one of his rifle companies. Soldiers told Wegelein to be careful because the Americans (in Company E, 39th Infantry) had sharpshooters in the area. Wegelein was nevertheless determined to get as far forward as possible. He and his adjutant had walked no more than 15 yards when the Germans heard the crack of a rifle. Wegelein was dead. They could not leave the protection of their foxholes to recover his body; the Americans who reached him found that he was unarmed.[29]

THE END OF THE OCTOBER ATTACK

The battle was a stalemate by 13 October. Some of the American rifle companies were little more than platoons led by corporals and privates instead of officers and NCOs. The only surviving officers in Company K, 39th Infantry, were two replacement lieutenants with two days' experience. Many of the men were physically and mentally exhausted from fighting in an area where "the sun was blotted out by the density of the trees." Men wondered if they would ever see the outside world again because all they "ever saw was wild deer and Jerries, and trees, firebreaks and more trees."[30]

"Cloudy weather and the natural darkness of the forest made it totally black. . . . men rarely moved about alone in the forest, and when it was necessary, . . . the individual observed to his flanks and rear," a staff officer wrote in the 9th Division's October report of operations.[31]

Navigation was always difficult, because every tree, trail, and fire-break looked identical. "The same trees, the same firebreaks—even if you were in a different area, the 'sameness' seemed to prevail. You would advance and dig out the Jerries, and that place would look like the same area you had just left," recalled Billy Allsbrook.[32] If one was lucky enough to have a map (and few men did, except for officers), cement survey markers on the ground matched corresponding forest district numbers printed on maps. Simply matching the numbers provided one's location; however, German forward observers using similar maps needed only to relay the numbers to their artillery and mortars.[33]

The odds from the start were against the Americans, and they paid a high price. Between 6 and 16 October, the 9th Infantry Division gained 3,000 yards of forest-cloaked ground near Germeter but lost about 4,500 men to all causes—more than one casualty per yard. German losses are much harder to assess, though Schmidt estimated them at 3,300. About 2,000 of them were killed or wounded; the remainder were victims of disease or combat exhaustion.[34]

The manuals written at the Infantry School predicted everything—except the conditions found in the Hürtgen Forest. The staff of the 9th Infantry Division prepared a five-page report dated 31 October, titled, "Notes on Woods Fighting." The lessons learned included the following:

> It is strongly recommended that units . . . be given previous training in this type of fighting. . . . Woods fighting is radically different from ordinary operations, and a knowledge of its basic requirements will save lives and insure success.
> Individual protection against enemy shell fire in dense woods presented a difficult problem. Practically all rounds were tree bursts, and ordinary foxholes or slit trenches proved ineffective. . . . Lying prone exposed a greater portion of the body to shell fragments.
> Night operations were . . . physically impossible.
> Unless a route has definitely been established, do not travel in the woods at night without a compass.
> Never send replacements to a company in the heat of battle. . . . Replacements should not be sent forward during hours when enemy barrages are likely.[35]

Despite the disappointing outcome of the October attack, commanders still had their sights set on the road hub of Schmidt. The Roer still barred the way to the Rhine, and the roads in the eastern reaches of the Hürtgen Forest remained important supply routes as long as the Americans made their main effort against Düren, and the Roer, from the east. General Collins recognized several competing tactical requirements (securing Aachen, crossing the Roer, and securing the flank of the VII Corps), which led him to prioritize the commitment of his divisions against an important array of targets. Unfortunately, he did not recognize the most important of them all.

The end of the first battle for Schmidt coincided with a high-level conference that established Allied priorities for the coming months. The senior commanders who attended this meeting decided to launch a major attack that would begin in November. They hoped the attack would end the war, but they were willing to settle for a large foothold inside Germany. The First Army was the spearhead, and the preliminary attack that started it all resulted in one of the army's most costly division-level battles of the war. It was another attack against Schmidt. The Roer dams did not enter the picture.

4
Origins of the Second Battle of Schmidt

Mid-October 1944 was, according to General Bradley, a "time of utmost frustration in the Allied ground command. . . . Every day that passed gave the Germans more time and opportunity to build defenses."[1] Most accounts of the period reflect a prevailing attitude of dejection among commanders and staff officers alike. There was little if any significant progress on the long western front, and SHAEF planners faced the distressing prospect of a winter campaign. It was now quite apparent the war would not end in 1944.

The Allied leadership had to make a choice. They could redouble their efforts to reach the Rhine by year's end, or they could hold in place to rest and refit during the fall and winter months. The first option was more desirable, though it obviously carried more risk. Yet the second would trade what initiative the Allies still had for an attack in better weather and after the logistic bases were more able to handle the strain of a major operation. Even limited operations to give new units experience at the front without committing them to a major battle would be more desirable than halting altogether. Some worried that the high morale of summer might erode if troops faced the prospects of a winter on the defensive. There were other factors to consider as well. Early war estimates of casualties did not envision the summer's attrition in infantrymen. Planners had overestimated the need for armor, artillery, and support soldiers, and by autumn the Americans faced the unpleasant prospect of the war's outlasting the manpower pool.[2]

Estimates of German losses during the summer also justified continuing offensive operations. The SHAEF G-2 estimated that through attrition alone the Germans sustained a casualty rate of 4,000 men per day in the West between mid-September and mid-October. This was a daily loss equivalent to a division about the size of Hans Schmidt's 275th Infantry. A halt might give the Germans time to improve their defenses further or let them take advantage of Allied inactivity to launch their own attack. It might also allow the Germans time to increase the production of jet aircraft. Also ominous was the prospect of German discovery and use of the secret radio proximity (VT) fuse against Allied bombers.[3]

Eisenhower weighed the alternatives and decided that continued large-scale offensive operations would shorten the war. His plan called for the First Army to attack on or about 5 November to gain a Rhine bridgehead south of Cologne. The Ninth Army would protect the First Army left flank and also move on the Rhine. The 21 Army Group would take the port of Antwerp before joining the attack. If the logistic situation permitted, the Third Army would attack a few days later to protect the First Army right flank. Once the 12th Army Group was across the Rhine, the Ninth Army would drive north of the Ruhr and the First Army would encircle it from the south. An objective look at the tactical and logistic situation, however, would have told Eisenhower that he might realistically expect only to have his armies clear the west bank of the Rhine.[4]

FIRST ARMY PLANS — VII CORPS

Two factors—one operational and one personal—led Hodges to select the VII Corps to make the main effort of the First Army. (The V Corps would enter the battle at a later date and help exploit any success.) The bulk of the corps was located in the relatively open, but narrow, Stolberg Corridor. This would allow Collins to concentrate his available combat power in the best ground to the corps' front. The second reason was that Hodges had the highest confidence in Collins's ability to produce results. Collins made two plans, one for a three-division attack beginning on 5 November, and a second involving a four-division attack to begin between 10 and 15 November. The initial VII Corps objectives were the Eschweiler-Weisweiler industrial area, the Hamich Ridge (important terrain to the corps front that blocked the Stolberg Corridor), and the northern part of the Hürtgen-Kleinhau-Gey roadnet (the objective of the 9th Division in October). It would then drive to the Roer.[5]

Hodges gave the V Corps responsibility for the forest south of Hürtgen. He wanted Gerow's corps to help secure the VII Corps flank and to seize the southern part of the roadnet mentioned above. He directed the 28th Infantry Division to conduct a preliminary attack to provide the VII Corps' 4th Infantry Division with a Line of Departure (LD—a coordinating measure, usually an easily recognizable terrain feature, to ensure that all attacking units strike the enemy at the designated time) for use in the main attack. This would allow the 4th Division to avoid a costly fight to secure its own attack positions.

The 28th had several important missions. It would complete the job started by the 9th Division by seizing the Vossenack Ridge and the adjacent woods as far north as Hürtgen. The division would also send part of one regiment against Schmidt and the high ground overlooking the Roer Valley. The division would also engage German reserves to prevent them from influencing the VII Corps attack (scheduled to begin on 5 November).[6] General Gerow, a VMI graduate and former chief of the Army General Staff's War Plans Division, also directed CCA, 5th Armored Division, to secure Kesternich and Simmerath after the 28th Division had captured Schmidt. The 28th Division would then attack the Monschau Corridor village of Steckenborn and then assume the defense of Kesternich and Simmerath from the 5th Armored Division.[7]

The Schwammenauel Dam was not an objective. None of the V Corps orders for the period (Field Orders 30, 31, and 32, dated 21 October, 8 November, and 14 November) mentioned the dams as a target. The detailed V Corps Report of Operations called the 28th Division's attack a prelude to the VII Corps attack—nothing more.[8] Only in postwar comments by American generals does one find evidence of concern with the dams as early as the last week of October. Bradley stated in the early 1980s that at first commanders did not appreciate the value of the dams, but "by mid to late October we were very much aware of the threat they posed." He added that the dams were a matter of discussion, and this concern "led directly to the decision to order . . . [the] 28th Division . . . to attack the town of Schmidt on November 2."[9]

This reconstruction is difficult to accept. For example, on 29 October Hodges said in a letter to Bradley that "present plans of this Army do not contemplate the immediate capture of these dams." Hodges, in fact, became interested in the dams only after the Germans brought the 28th Division to a halt at Schmidt.[10]

The most significant change to the First Army plan came a few days before the scheduled start of the V Corps attack. Collins had to have another division in order to assemble the force necessary to ensure success of the main effort. When Bradley informed Hodges that another division (the 104th Infantry, then attached to the British) would not be available before 5 November, Hodges told Collins to postpone the attack until no later than 16 November.[11] Hodges was probably more comfortable with the prospects of a delayed four-division effort than he was with a three-division attack launched a few days earlier.

This change made questionable the need to conduct a preliminary attack two weeks before the main attack. Yet there is no written evidence that Gerow asked Hodges for permission to delay it until closer to the expected date of the VII Corps' attack. (In fairness to Gerow, there are few written records of high-level meetings and phone conversations between Hodges and his corps commanders.) To compound the makings of a disaster, bad weather in late October made air support a doubtful prospect. Yet air support was essential to success. Hodges permitted Gerow to postpone the attack because both were aware of the critical need for responsive and accurate air support, but Gerow finally had to order the division commander to begin the attack on 2 November. Had the VII Corps attack began on 5 November, the 28th Division would have had to contend alone with the Germans for only five days. With the change to the four-division plan, however, the 28th Division would have to face the enemy single-handedly for nearly two weeks while it made the only attack on over 150 miles of First Army front.

THE 28TH INFANTRY DIVISION PLAN

The 28th Infantry Division (Pennsylvania National Guard) fought in six campaigns in World War I. The division commander at the time of its February 1941 activation, Maj. Gen. Edward Martin, later left federal service to run successfully for governor. Maj. Gen. G. J. Ord, a Regular Army officer, commanded the division through the first half of 1942, and then Maj. Gen. Omar N. Bradley took command on 26 June. Bradley was careful not to begin a wholesale replacement of the division's National Guard officers. Not only would this cause a furor in Pennsylvania, but such a move would have also endangered promotion prospects for competent Guard officers. Bradley also ended the flood of transfers of the division's best soldiers to assignments such as Officer's Candidate School.

Bradley departed in February 1943, and Maj. Gen. Lloyd D. Brown took the division overseas in October.[12] Lackluster performance by the division in the early stages of the Normandy campaign resulted in his relief in early August. His replacement, Brig. Gen. James E. Wharton, held command for only a few hours before he was mortally wounded on 13 August. Brig. Gen. Norman D. "Dutch" Cota took command the next day. The 51-year-old Cota was a 1917 graduate of West Point who did not see combat in World War I. After the usual assignments between the wars, Cota became executive officer of the 16th Infantry in 1940 and chief of staff of the 1st Infantry Division when it went overseas in 1942. After working with the British Special Operations Headquarters in 1943, he was assigned as assistant division commander of the 29th Infantry Division. He landed with the assault units on D-Day and disregarded enemy bullets to exhort the men to get off the beach and move toward higher ground.[13]

The division's first patrols entered Germany on 11 September. It sustained well over a thousand casualties during its operations along the Luxembourg-German border. The replacements were, for the most part, former antitank, antiaircraft, or Army Air Forces ground personnel with limited training and little combat experience. Prior to the attack on Schmidt, the division was almost at full strength, with 825 officers and 13,107 enlisted men present for duty. Attachments added about 2,200 more men to the total.[14]

Gerow fully understood the difficulties of the mission he had given Cota, and he strongly reinforced the 28th Division. One of the attachments was Lt. Col. Richard Ripple's new 707th Tank Battalion, which would be entering combat for the first time. Bruce M. Hostrup, the commander of Company A, later recalled, "We did know as we entered the Hürtgen Forest that we were to relieve the 9th Infantry [Division] who had been battered. . . . This did disturb Colonel Ripple and myself, for we knew that this was not tank country, and . . . that the Germans held the high ground and that their artillery fire was pin-pointed and fierce. . . . [The 9th Infantry Division] was really torn up and tired."[15]

Many postwar accounts of the battle for Schmidt criticize Gerow for his extensive involvement in preparing the division's plan. His staff indeed did most of the planning, and they left Cota little latitude. Yet a report made shortly after the battle stated that the plans were "generally agreed upon by all concerned."[16] It is difficult to assess the impact of this kind of planning on the outcome of the battle, but Gerow and his staff were not the cause of many of the events described in the next two chapters. In short, the disaster at Schmidt resulted from several causes, both within and without the division. It is unfair to say that all reasons for failure lay in the involvement of the V Corps staff in the preparation of the 28th Division's plan.

At any rate, a review of the plan is essential if one is to understand the battle. The plan called for the division to send its three infantry regiments against separate targets. The route of attack as far as Vossenack was much the same as that used by the 9th Division in October. Terrain between Vossenack and the wooded Kall River Valley would force the 28th Division to move under the observation of Germans dug in on a nearby ridge topped by the villages of Brandenberg and Bergstein (not designated objectives because of lack of troops). The Burgberg, or Castle Hill, located on the east end of the ridge, was higher still. The "B-B Ridge," as the troops called it, would play a significant role in the battle.

One regiment (Lt. Col. Daniel B. Strickler's 109th Infantry) would push north from Germeter to secure the LD for the 4th Division and guard against another attack such as that made by Kampfgruppe Wegelein in October. Lt. Col. Carl L. Peterson's 112th Infantry Regiment would make the division's main effort, beginning with an attack on Vossenack by its 2d Battalion. The 1st Battalion would then attack through Richelskaul to cross the Kall River south of Vossenack and occupy the village of Kommerscheidt. The 3d Battalion would then pass through the positions there and take Schmidt. The third regiment, Col. Theodore A. Seeley's 110th Infantry, would attack south across the Kall River Valley to take the road running from Schmidt to Strauch. This road would become the main supply route for the battalions in Schmidt and Kommerscheidt. One of Seeley's battalions would serve as Cota's only reserve.[17]

THE GERMAN SITUATION

General Brandenberger's chief of staff, Generalmajor Rudolf von Gersdorff, believed that the Ruhr was the ultimate objective of the American attacks in the sector south of Aachen. According to Gersdorff, "The main reason for the tenacious German defense was to prevent the defense of the West Wall from being crumbled . . . a defense in the forest was more favorable, as there the enemy supremacy in tanks and in the air would not be so effective as in open terrain." Gersdorff added that the Germans "took it for granted that it was of primary importance for the American command to capture the commanding heights of Bergstein and Schmidt via Vossenack . . . in order from there to cross the [Roer and capture] the dams. . . ." He continued, "In view of the Ardennes offensive, which was planned already at this time, this enemy intention had to be prevented at all costs."[18]

Gersdorff's comments regarding this American attack show the growing German interest in protecting the Roer dams because of their importance to the security of the north flank of the Ardennes attack. OB West (Oberbefehlshaber West—the highest German ground forces headquarters in the West) had assembled a staggering amount of men and matériel for the upcoming attack and was keeping the preparations a closely guarded secret. Even Rundstedt could not authorize use of the divisions earmarked for the Ardennes offensive. The problem for the Germans, then, was to halt the enemy threat to an important upcoming operation with the forces already in the line and without using the growing pool of men and arms which had to remain in reserve for use in December.

The plan of deception included a transfer on 23 October to the Aachen area of the headquarters of the 5th Panzer Army, now part of Army Group B. It entered the line north of the 7th Army, where it assumed command of the LXXXI Corps and the XII SS Panzer Corps. The 7th Army then became responsible only for the Eifel sector, where its LXXIV Corps faced the VII and V U.S. Corps. General Brandenberger ordered

General Straube, commander of the LXXIV Corps, to continue the defense of the Hürtgen Forest sector.[19]

The battered 275th Infantry Division's 984th Regiment covered the Weisser Weh Creek; the 2d Battalion, 985th Regiment, and the 73rd Engineer Battalion (with remnants of the XX Luftwaffe Fortress Battalion) covered the sector southwest of Hürtgen to Wittscheidt. The 983rd Regiment defended the line from Vossenack south to the division's boundary with the 89th Infantry Division, near Raffelsbrand. The 275th Engineer Battalion, the 253d Grenadier Training Regiment, and other units were also dug in near Germeter with their backs to the Kall River Valley near Simonskall. The division strength amounted to about 5,500 effectives.[20]

Generalmajor Walter ("Papa") Bruns's 89th Infantry Division (formerly commanded by Rösler) would play an important role in stopping the 28th Division. It consisted of the XIV Luftwaffe Fortress Battalion; the 1055th, 1056th, and parts of the 860th Infantry Regiments; the weak 189th Artillery Regiment (15 105mm howitzers); and later the 341st Sturmgeschutz Brigade. Two tank battalions (1st Battalion, 24th Panzer Regiment, and the 2d Battalion, 16th Panzer Regiment) of about 15 tanks each, the 518th Panzerjäger (tank destroyer) Brigade (6–8 Jagdpanthers), and a brigade of 155mm self-propelled assault guns called Hummels were attached to the division after 2 November.[21] The division had been in the Monschau area for several weeks.

THE 28TH DIVISION ENTERS THE FOREST

The soldiers of the 28th Infantry Division saw a ghastly sight when they entered the Hürtgen Forest. The cold October rain and misty gray skies gave the forest a dismal, almost depressing look. Weeks of almost incessant artillery fire had left whole sections of the woods looking as if some giant scythe had shredded the treetops, and tens of thousands of broken, yellow-gray tree trunks littered the steep hills. The men saw the tense, exhausted veterans of the October fighting stagger out of their foxholes. Equipment littered the area. Here and there lay a piece of a wool shirt or cotton field jacket with one or two finger-sized holes in a patch of dried blood. Some items of personal gear even hung from the trees, blown there when the wearer stepped on a mine. No one could remain unaffected by such devastation.

The miserable living conditions in the forest affected morale. Keeping dry was an impossibility in a place where water stood in pools on the saturated ground. Cases of respiratory sickness spread quickly throughout the line units. Some men would begin the attack with severe colds and, in some cases, walking pneumonia. The division was critically

Generalmajor Walter Bruns, Commander of the 89th Infantry Division, with his aide, Leutnant Gevert Haslob *(rear of vehicle)*, and driver on the Schmidt-Nideggen road, about 7 November 1944. (Courtesy G. Haslob)

short of overshoes, and cases of immersion foot were all too common. The upcoming attack would be strenuous even for men rested from the rigors of combat. For men afflicted with sickness and exhaustion caused by the weather and lack of shelter, negotiating the terrain would require almost superhuman effort.[22]

The problems that contributed to the outcome of the November fight for Schmidt did not end there. The 28th Division and the new 707th Tank Battalion, for example, had just a few days during late October during which to train together. The leader of the 1st Platoon, Company A, 1st. Lt. Raymond E. Fleig, recalled that the training served little purpose.

> You'd never know we were in the same Army. We married up with the infantry on the run. There was little or no coordination of communication, routes of attack, etc. Even though each tank had an external telephone for ground forces to [use], the infantry didn't know that, and the usual method of communication was to bang on the side of the tank until you got the tank commander's attention and then point to the target. Often the infantry would not approach the tank because they feared that it would draw artillery and mortar fire. . . . Neither the

tankers nor the infantry nor the engineers knew the capabilities or limitations of the other.

"Either the 28th Division or the 707th Tank Battalion was plagued by misfortune, for all our encounters were at the crisis level and ended in disaster," added Fleig.[23]

On 1 November, General Hodges visited the 28th Division command post at Rott, where he approved Gerow's plan. He left with the impression that the division was ready and optimistic for success. The problem was that the American attack required overwhelming tank, aircraft, and artillery support. This did not materialize, and the Germans responded with unexpected ferocity. The results are described in the following chapters. The Germans would call the division's red keystone-shaped patch *Der blutige Eimer*, or "Bloody Bucket."

5
The 28th Division
Attack Begins

T he next phase in the fight for control of the Hürtgen Forest began on the cold and foggy morning of 2 November 1944. Preparatory fires began at 8:00 A.M. An hour later, thousands of soldiers from the 28th Infantry Division left their foxholes and moved into the misty woods.[1] The worst enemy at first was the forest itself. A few days before his death at Vossenack, the commander of the 109th Infantry Regiment's 1st Battalion, Maj. James C. Ford, Jr., said, "If anyone from a private on up to myself said he knew where he was at any one time, he was a damned liar!"[2]

The men found that the thick tree growth prevented aimed rifle fire—grenades became the weapon of choice. The losses were heavy. Company A, 109th, for example, lost about half of its riflemen before it was even half way to its first objective. The commander combined the 1st and 2d Platoons into one. The company's 3d Platoon was not directly engaged, yet two squad leaders and the platoon leader were killed soon after the start of the attack. Several men in the battalion's reserve company were injured by tree bursts.[3] The headquarters suffered also: the battalion operations officer (S-3), two company commanders, and several enlisted men were wounded or killed.[4]

Despite the losses, the battalion overran the enemy outpost line and was on the initial objective, a wooded area a few hundred yards north of Germeter, less than six hours after the attack began. But this was no indication of future progress. Instead, it represented nearly all the ground the regiment would take before it ultimately withdrew from the battle.

The 109th Infantry's other attacking battalion, the 3d, made far less

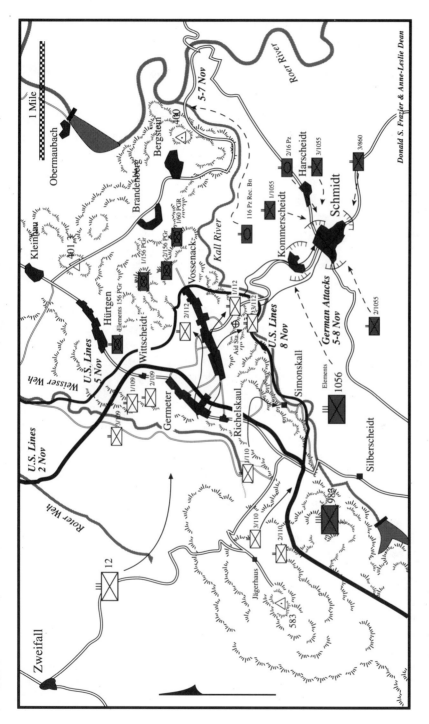

Map 3. 28th Infantry Division: Schmidt/Vossenack, 2–11 November 1944

Donald S. Frazier & Anne-Leslie Dean

progress. Company K gained only a few hundred yards on the east side of the Germeter-Hürtgen road (a stretch of the Simmerath-Düren road, now highway B-399) before it hit part of a large minefield the Germans called *Wilde Sau,* or "Wild Pig," emplaced in the woods north of Wittscheidt.

Four men from Company I, moving on the left (west) side of the road, found a path through some of the mines, but when no other men would follow, they decided to return to Wittscheidt. The group had 15 German prisoners with them, 5 of whom were killed by their own mines on the trip back. Heavy machine-gun and sniper fire pinned down the company's 3d Platoon for hours. It cost an estimated 40 casualties, including the company commander, to gain 300 yards. When 1st Lt. William Pena took temporary command, he could locate only about 30 men out of about 100 in the rifle platoons who had started the attack. One platoon had only a dozen men and two officers.[5]

The Germans had problems as well. Though General Schmidt lost no time in launching a counterattack to contain the American penetration north of Germeter, the 275th Division suffered high losses and managed only to slow, not stop, the 109th. On 3 November, just before the start of a counterattack by elements of the 253d Engineer Battalion supported by the 60th Panzergrenadier Regiment, artillery fire, some of which was probably German, killed or wounded about half of the engineers.[6] The survivors regrouped and attacked a 1st Battalion, 109th Infantry, observation post (OP). The losses were so heavy that Hauptmann Paul Brückner, commander of the engineer battalion, had to help supply parties carry the rations and ammunition. His reserve consisted of two teenage messengers. The constant artillery fire prevented recovery and evacuation of the wounded and dead.[7] The Americans held their fire "until the Germans were right on top of them." They had to stop firing more than once to remove the bodies piling up in front of their foxholes.[8]

The S-2 of the 1st Battalion, 109th, 1st Lt. Charles Potter, later told an interviewer that "the tree bursts were the worst thing we had to contend with. . . . the trees in this place were so thick that it was impossible to see more than thirty yards in any one direction. In many places they were not over four feet apart. . . ."[9]

On 3 November, Maj. Howard L. Topping, commander of the 3d Battalion, 109th Infantry, had left Company K on the east side of the Germeter-Hürtgen road while he sent his other companies to flank the Wilde Sau. Progress was very slow, and the confusion inherent in battle led to one of several very tragic events that plagued the "Bloody Bucket" division during its encounter with the Hürtgen Forest. While Hauptmann Brückner's counterattack bore down on Major Ford's battalion, Major Topping received an order to change the direction of his attack to the west to assist. Topping could hear the sounds of artillery and mortar fire coming from the direction of the 1st Battalion and thought this must be the reason for the change in plans. He ordered Companies I and L to assist the 1st Battalion.[10] About noon, when Lieutenant Pena and his men reached the area, they reportedly saw four German tanks firing directly into 1st Battalion positions. Company L encountered several dozen—if not a hundred or more—German riflemen. To the GIs, every tree seemed to shelter an enemy soldier.[11]

The commander of the 109th, Lieutenant Colonel Strickler, had in fact issued no order to Topping. No one ever determined the reason for the order,[12] and the change served little purpose other than to separate the rifle companies and weaken the strength of the push up the Germeter-Hürtgen road.

Meanwhile, the Germans had managed to swarm into a gap between Companies C and F. The gap was the result of the problems of maintaining control of formations in the forest. The commander of the 2d Battalion wanted to push his companies north behind the 1st Battalion, but Company F ended up in the line to the left of Company C. The other rifle companies of the 2d Battalion, E and G, ended up to the east of the 1st Battalion, along the west side of the Germeter-Hürtgen road, in the gap left by Companies I and L.[13]

By the time the regiment was able to renew its attack to the north, the Germans had thrown together a tight cordon that kept the regiment from making any significant gains during the rest of the operation. The final positions of the companies is indicative of the problems the regiment was having by the end of 3 November. From west to east, the lineup was Companies F and L, then the 1st Battalion, and then Companies E, G, I, and K. The regiment was not properly tied in with the adjacent 112th Infantry on the right or with the 294th Engineer Combat Battalion on the north.[14]

The 2d Battalion assumed the main effort on 4 November. The casualties were high, and progress was limited; for example, there were only four survivors in Company E's 2d Platoon after an attempt to cross a minefield. Because evacuation parties crossing open ground during daylight were often the targets of German artillery and mortar fire, it was impossible to recover all the dead, and several bodies remained in the area for days. When a patrol from the company later established an OP on the Germeter-Hürtgen road, the Americans noticed a German patrol digging in a few yards away. An American recalled, "The Jerries were calling us names as we were working. The next morning we exchanged hand grenades and rifle fire."[15]

Company L gained a few more yards on 6 November, but it had to stop when it came under a concentration of artillery fire. The riflemen scrambled for cover, and the leaders lost control of the situation. It took the personal efforts of Major Topping and several others to reorganize the company and get it back to its starting point. But German soldiers were already there, and the battalion spent valuable time clearing the enemy from the area. When the Germans withdrew, they captured some of Company L's walking wounded.[16]

A 30-year-old Michigan native attached to Company D later said, "The days were so terrible that I would pray for darkness, and the nights were so bad I would pray for daylight."[17]

THE DRIVE ON SCHMIDT, 2 NOVEMBER

At 9:00 A.M. on 2 November, Lt. Col. Theodore S. Hatzfeld's 2d Battalion, 112th Infantry, supported by elements of the 707th Tank Battalion, launched an attack to seize the Vossenack Ridge. It was an example of what was possible when the Americans could operate in relatively open terrain, but it was not an example of a "typical" tank-infantry attack during the battles in the Hürtgen Forest. Most such operations were not nearly as successful.

Two companies of infantry (F and G), supported by seven medium tanks from Company C, 707th Tank Battalion, moved through the outpost line in Germeter and reached the open ground between Germeter and Vossenack. One tank accidentally strayed from a cleared path through an American minefield and hit a mine. Then the platoon leader's tank mired in the soggy earth and blocked the cleared path. Capt. George S. West, Jr., the tank company commander, picked up the platoon leader and continued in his own tank to direct the company.

Company G, meanwhile, emerged from Germeter and headed north of Vossenack. Small-arms fire wounded the lieutenant in charge of the supporting machine-gun platoon from Company H. About the same time, a member of Company G's headquarters section stepped on one of the countless mines in the area. A machine gunner went to help. He also stepped on a mine, which killed him and set off at least five other mines. When the debris and mud cleared, 12 of 27 men who had been in the area lay wounded or dead. Company G pressed on, however, and entered Vossenack about 10:00 A.M.

Company F, with three tanks in support, also attacked at 9:00 A.M. First Lieutenant Eugene S. Carlson's 3d Platoon headed southeast on the ridge, moving in the tracks of the supporting tanks to avoid the mines. Carlson kept a hand on the rear of a tank for the first 500 yards of the advance.

Fire from a German machine gun bypassed by Carlson's men decimated the 1st Platoon until the platoon leader knocked out the machine gun with a grenade. He reorganized his men and continued into Vosse-nack. The 2d Platoon reached Vossenack with relative ease, but once in the town, German fire killed the platoon leader and wounded the platoon sergeant. The company commander, 1st Lt. Eldeen F. Kauffman, had a tank fire on the building suspected of housing the enemy. He and his runner cleared the building by themselves. They captured a German officer who told them to expect a counterattack.[18]

The remainder of the 2d Battalion had meanwhile reached the eastern end of the ridge and set the stage for one of the most tragic events in the Hürtgen campaign. During the planning for the attack, Generals Gerow, Cota, and Davis decided that the 112th Infantry needed to put "at least one battalion on the high ground E. of Vossenack"[19] to provide security for the attack on Schmidt. While no one could debate the need for securing the flank of the 112th Infantry, there was no reason for the men to remain in these positions around the clock in full view of German artillery observers located on the Brandenberg-Bergstein Ridge. Unfortunately, that is what happened. Some of the riflemen were eventually withdrawn to Vossenack during daylight without endangering the battalion because the buildings were near enough to the foxholes to allow the soldiers to react swiftly to any threat. Evidently, a staff officer at the regiment or division level drew arbitrary locations for the positions on a map overlay, and no officers in the battalion successfully challenged the reasoning. Within a few days they would wish they had. On 2 November the 2d Battalion, 112th Infantry, began ninety hours of needless exposure to German fire.

Maj. Robert T. Hazlett's 1st Battalion, meanwhile, had attacked at noon. This was the main effort of the regiment and division. The objective was to clear the area southeast of Richelskaul, enter the Kall River Valley, and take Kommerscheidt and Schmidt from the south. But the lack of troops to commit to this attack (only one battalion), which was made through some of the most difficult ground in the forest, brought only failure. Capt. Clifford T. Hackard (Company B) lost his 1st and 3rd Platoon leaders to German fire. A wall of bullets stopped the 2d Platoon cold. Hazlett and the commander of the regiment, Lieutenant Colonel Peterson, decided to stop the attack and pull the company back to a less exposed position.

Peterson did not call for tank or artillery support, though the enemy had stopped only one company, and he did not commit the 3d Battalion. Hazlett also did not press the issue and commit one of his two remaining companies. General Cota did not release the division's reserve battalion. It is possible that Peterson compared the 1st Battalion's difficulties with the ease of the 2d Battalion's attack on Vossenack and recommended to Cota that he allow him to shift the direction of the attack to the north. In any event, the 1st and 3d Battalions would move through Vossenack against Schmidt the next day.[20]

The 110th Infantry's costly attack on 2 November failed to clear the area between Richelskaul and the Todtenbruch. The regiment had made detailed plans that included tank support from the 707th, but officers did not conduct a proper reconnaissance. Time had a part to play in this, but the cost was high. For example, the 2d Battalion hit a nest of bunkers that the men simply could not capture. Artillery slammed into the 1st Battalion's assault positions before the attack began. (H-Hour was 7:00 A.M.) Companies B and C lost several key NCOs and experienced riflemen. The 3d Battalion encountered bunkers protected by double-strand concertina wire and a deep antitank ditch. Every attack ended with the survivors stumbling back to the LD. A second attack on 3 November also failed, and Cota released the reserve 1st Battalion back to Colonel Seeley's control for an attack to flank the strongpoint.[21]

GERMAN DEVELOPMENTS

A map exercise sealed the fate of the 28th Infantry Division. Field Marshal Model convened the previously scheduled exercise at Schloss Gut Shlenderhan, near Cologne, on the morning of 2 November. The exercise, which began about the same time as the American attack, was under the direction of General der Panzertruppen Hasso von Manteuffel. The Germans intended to develop the best response to a theoretical American attack on either side of the boundary between the 5th Panzer Army and the 7th Army. By a remarkable chance, nearly every senior German officer who might play a role in countering an attack in the Hürtgen Forest was present. The attendees included Model, Brandenberger, Gersdorff (7th Army chief of staff), Köchling (Schack's replacement at LXXXI Corps), Straube (LXXIV Corps), Waldenburg (116th Panzer), Engel (12th Infantry), and Lüttwitz (XLVII Panzer Corps).

Model learned of the attack from Straube's chief of staff. He ordered Straube to return to his headquarters and direct the battle from there; he also ordered the exercise to continue, based on the actual situation then developing near Schmidt. Model ordered Waldenburg's 116th Panzer Division, in conjunction with Bruns's 89th Division, first to halt the Americans and then to counterattack to destroy their penetration. The ultimate objective was to restore the defensive line in the woods, where American artillery and air power would have little impact on the defending troops.[22]

A captured document from the 89th Division dated 9 November noted, "The men, who since the beginning of the battles for the Westwall had repulsed the enemy with heavy losses . . . experience a sudden change of

Soldiers of Company E 110th Infantry move on the Raffelsbrand Road Junction south of Germeter, 2 November 1944. Probably none of the riflemen in this photo survived the battle. (Courtesy National Archives, #111–SC–334992)

mind. Gone are the thoughts of rest and relaxation, gone is the hope for an eventual furlough. Hard necessity requires new commitment."[23]

THE AMERICANS CAPTURE SCHMIDT

At the 112th Infantry Regiment CP on the evening of 2 November, Capt. Bruce M. Hostrup (Company A, 707th Tank Battalion) learned from Lt. Col. Albert Flood, commander of the 3d Battalion, 112th Infantry, that his company would support a daylight attack on Schmidt, spearheaded by Company K (Capt. Eugene W. O'Malley). Other tanks and Company B, 112th Infantry, would support the attack by fire.[24]

The temperature was just above freezing when Company K, supported by a heavy machine-gun section from Company M and Hostrup's 3d Platoon, passed through Vossenack en route to Schmidt. About two hours after the attack began, the lead elements of Company K reached the Kall River and began working their way up the steep east bank of the valley, pulling themselves along, tree by tree. Following 400 yards behind were Companies L and I. Fire from tanks at Vossenack roared over the infantrymen and exploded in Kommerscheidt, where the GIs captured eight German soldiers. Scouts from the 1st Platoon of Company K went ahead and reached the edge of Schmidt about 2:00 P.M. They reported no resistance. The 112th Infantry had achieved nearly complete surprise.

O'Malley split his company into two groups. He sent one through the center of Schmidt and the other through town to the southwest.[25] There was no significant resistance, but Lieutenant Randall Patterson, probably the first officer to enter Schmidt, thought the attack had been "too easy." Patterson's men surprised and captured a few German soldiers (89th Division) who were riding bicycles through the town. Patterson's platoon sergeant, T.Sgt. John M. Kozlosky, stopped a horse-drawn ammunition wagon. When the driver found that Kozlosky could speak Polish, he jumped from the wagon and kissed Kozlosky on both cheeks.[26] The soldier was a "volunteer" from Poland.

Artillery fire hit Company L, which was behind Company K, during its advance from Vossenack to the woods bordering the Kall Valley. There was little resistance on the ground, however, and the company passed the Mestringer Mühle, a mill (now a restaurant) beside the Kall River, a few hours behind Company K.

At Kommerscheidt, Flood instructed Capt. Jack Walker, the commander of Company L, to have his men continue to Schmidt, where they arrived about 4:00 P.M. The riflemen worked through some sniper fire and reached the eastern part of town before dark. Company I entered Schmidt next and took positions on the open ground on either side of the Kommerscheidt-Schmidt road. Darkness later forced the wet, chilled, exhausted riflemen to stop their search for snipers. Many of the GIs took shelter in the buildings rather than dig foxholes, which they were simply too tired to do.[27]

Capt. Guy T. Piercey's Company M (the battalion's weapons company, armed with .50-cal. machine guns and 81mm mortars) reached the outskirts of Schmidt after dark, and the men did not complete digging in their weapons until after midnight. Piercey's men were also too tired to dig individual foxholes.[28]

Schmidt was a large area for one battalion to defend adequately, and the perimeter, such as it was, stretched in a roughly square pattern of about 900 yards on each side. Company L's 3d Platoon blocked the road leading southeast to the settlement of Hasenfeld. The 2d Platoon was to the left of the 3d, and the 1st Platoon blocked the road leading northeast to Harscheidt. Company K went into positions on the south and west of town, with one platoon across the road to Strauch and the Monschau Corridor.[29]

Lieutenant Colonel Flood and his S-3 also reached Schmidt after dark. Flood located Captain Walker and instructed him to keep his men in their present locations for the night.[30] Apparently Flood did not want the battalion to expand its perimeter and overstretch an already thin line. Walker followed Flood's orders, but he (and probably all the other company commanders also) failed to dispatch any reconnaissance patrols. This left the battalion without any way to collect information regarding German troop dispositions.

Just as critical, the battalion had no antitank or tank support, and the prospects of getting such support were slim. Flood was under the impression the battalion would get tanks that night, but the only route for tanks to use in crossing the Kall River Valley was the virtually impassable trail between Vossenack and Kommerscheidt. Because the 3d Battalion, 112th Infantry, had crossed the Kall a few yards south of the trail, it is likely that Flood had not seen it. If he had seen the trail and still entertained thoughts about prompt tank support, he greatly underestimated the road requirements for tanks. The trail was barely passable for a wagon, and at the time the infantry was clearing Schmidt, the attached engineers had not started work to improve it. (Engineer officers had reconnoitered it in the late afternoon and for some reason had determined that the trail would accommodate tanks.)[31]

A supply convoy of M29 Weasels (small, tracked cargo carriers) was able to negotiate the trail and reach Schmidt late in the night of 3 November with ammunition, rations, and 60 antitank mines. The exhausted infantrymen were unable to dig the mines in—they simply placed them on the roads leading into town and made no effort to camouflage them.[32]

Events by this time were moving in favor of the Germans. About dark, a soldier from Company L reported seeing "haystacks" moving around on a distant hill. Others thought he was nervous, but as one soldier later noted, "We found out differently the next day."[33]

Lieutenant Patterson also thought he saw enemy tanks. He believed the enemy was preparing to counterattack, and he sent a written message to Flood describing the activity. He also asked for an artillery observer. Several years later, Patterson found that his warning, for whatever reason, had never made it past regiment.[34]

Lt. Leon Simon, the 3d Battalion's assistant operations officer, was the liaison officer to regiment. He arrived at Flood's CP, located in a bunker between Kommerscheidt and Schmidt, about 8:00 P.M. Simon told Flood the engineers assigned to work on the Kall trail were under artillery and mortar fire. Flood told him to find Lieutenant Colonel Peterson and emphasize the need for tank support.[35]

As the events noted above were unfolding, the regiment's 1st Battalion was also moving on Schmidt. Companies A, C, D and the battalion head-quarters had departed Germeter about noon on 3 November. Company B remained in Richelskaul. The straight-line distance between Vossenack and Schmidt was less than two miles, but progress over the difficult terrain was slow, and it was 4:00 P.M. before Company A entered Kommerscheidt. Later in the afternoon, the division chief of staff sent Peterson a message directing him to send the 1st Battalion into Schmidt. This was in accordance with the original plan, but for reasons still unclear, the 1st Battalion did not move past Kommerscheidt. Peterson probably disregarded the instructions because he did not want to lose two battalions should the Germans make a successful counterattack at Schmidt.[36]

He had good reason to think along these lines. Losses had been heavy, particularly in junior leaders. The troops were physically tired from negotiating the forested hills, and there was no possibility of armor support at the critical objective of Schmidt. Resupply was difficult because of the nearly impassable main supply route. There were no reinforcements. He could only pray that the Germans were as weak as his men.

Despite these problems, the mood that night in Cota's headquarters—a two-story stone gasthaus in Rott—was one of celebration. As far as anyone there knew, the Keystone Division was ready to complete an assignment that had eluded the Americans for weeks. This was not true, but Cota received no messages to the contrary (that is, he received no messages stating the actual condition of the troops). Had he had liaison officers with the battalions, he might have had a better view of the actual situation. Instead, his staff accepted the glowing reports from the front without question—and at that point there was nothing to lead one to believe that the reports were anything but an accurate estimate of the events across the Kall.

Cota received congratulatory messages from several division and corps commanders and he "was beginning to feel like 'a little Napoleon.'" Brigadier General Davis, the assistant division commander, also thought that the operation to that point had been "extremely successful."[37] Schmidt was in American hands. Things appeared to be going well. To the north, the 109th Infantry had elements just south of Hürtgen. To the south, the 110th Infantry was pushing slowly to the Kall River near Simonskall. Unfortunately for Cota and the nine battalions of infantrymen involved, this was the last good news anyone in the division would receive for several days to come.

THE KALL TRAIL

The change in the direction of the attack on Schmidt from the south to the west made the narrow, muddy trail across the Kall Valley critically important to the 28th Division. This cart track was the main supply route for a regiment making the main effort of a corps. There was a drop on one side of the trail, and a steep hill with rock outcrops on the other. Only the start and end of the trail were visible on aerial photographs, and until they passed through the area, the Americans did not know for sure that the trail in fact traversed the entire valley.

On the afternoon of 3 November, two officers from the 20th Engineer Combat Battalion, 1171st Engineer Group, reconnoitered the trail as far as the river and reported that the trail and a stone bridge across the Kall appeared to be capable of supporting tanks. The estimate about the bridge was correct, but it was certainly anything but accurate regarding the muddy trail leading to it. At any rate, this was the report Captain Hostrup and Lieutenant Colonel Ripple received late that afternoon.[38]

Hostrup led the 1st Platoon out of Vossenack a short time later. He stopped the column at the head of the trail and continued in his command tank. Just before he reached the rock outcrops, the side of the trail crumbled; according to Hostrup, "We nearly went into the gorge. Only the fact that my tank driver was alert and reversed the motor, kept us upright."[39]

Hostrup had his driver back the tank up the trail, and he informed Lieutenant Colonel Ripple by radio that the trail was impassable. Ripple passed the news to division headquarters and instructed Hostrup to remain in place until engineers arrived to work on the trail. Ripple also told Hostrup to have his company ready to move at daylight on 4 November.[40]

The 20th Engineer Combat Battalion was in Vossenack on the afternoon of 3 November. Part of Company A had already set out for the trail, but artillery fire drove the men back to Vossenack, where they remained for several hours. Engineers with mine detectors eventually left Vossenack, but their mission was only to clear the trail east of the river. Captain Hostrup, still with his tanks on the trail, was later dismayed to see Company B arrive with only hand tools to use against the rock outcrops. A bulldozer arrived about 2:30 A.M. on 4 November, but it snapped a cable shortly after it began work. The result of the engineers' work was less than satisfactory.[41]

Early on the morning of 4 November, Hostrup, who was anxious to get his tanks to Schmidt, ordered Lieutenant Fleig's 1st Platoon to move down the trail. It was clear to Fleig that the engineers had accomplished little. By carefully following the bank of the trail, Fleig managed to get his tank past the rock outcrops, but his tank struck a mine a few minutes later. He turned the recovery operation over to his platoon sergeant, S.Sgt. Anthony Spooner, and took another tank across the Kall and up the opposite side of the valley. Spooner used tow cables to anchor Fleig's

Ray Fleig, platoon leader in Company A, 707th Tank Battalion, in 1945, after his promotion to captain. Fleig led the first tanks across the Kall River early on 4 November. (Courtesy R. Fleig)

remaining tanks to the damaged tank and he managed to guide three more tanks around the damaged one. Things for a few minutes were looking up until one of these tanks threw a track. The recovery process continued.

Fleig reached Kommerscheidt about 8:00 A.M. He reported to Major Hazlett, who told him about a German counterattack and ordered him to "get out there and stop those tanks." Infantrymen pointed in the direction of Schmidt and told Fleig there were "lots of Germans with tanks over that hill."[42]

DISASTER AT SCHMIDT

In conjunction with the orders issued during the map exercise near Cologne, the 116th Panzer Division's reconnaissance battalion had moved to the Kall Valley during the night of 2–3 November. The division's 16th Panzer Regiment (equipped with MK IV and MK V Panther Tanks but, contrary to American reports, no Tigers) moved to Harscheidt, a village about half a mile from Schmidt. The rest of the division followed the next night. The 1st and 3rd Battalions of the 89th Division's 1055th Infantry Regiment, already in the area, took up positions on either side of the Harscheidt-Schmidt road. The 2d Battalion assembled near the Strauch-Schmidt road. Elements of the 341st Sturmgeschutz Brigade entered Harscheidt the same evening.[43] The Americans were unaware of the German activity.[44]

Artillery fire began to hit the Americans in Schmidt shortly after 7:00 A.M. on 4 November. For at least 30 minutes, the shells systematically worked back and forth among the American positions. A 3d Battalion NCO later said, "It was so powerful, so loud, and so continuous that it seemed to form a background that you got used to. We were so tired that we didn't even hear the shells when they landed close."[45]

A soldier from Company L saw a flare shoot up from the direction of Harscheidt. "Oh! What a sight!" he later said. "There was a long line of Jerry [one of several epithets for Germans used by the Americans] tanks coming down the same road we had used to get to our platoon position."[46]

Moments later, the stunned Americans saw dismounted German infantry supported by tanks approaching from the direction of Harscheidt. The Americans opened fire. Captain Walker (Company L) called for mortar fire. Soldiers reported seeing one enemy tank simply detour the mines they had placed on the road the night before and continue toward the foxholes. More infantry supported by some eight tanks and four assault guns attacked from the direction of Strauch.

Lieutenant Tom Lyga's 1st Platoon, Company L, was astride the Harscheidt road. At 8:30 A.M. he reported that his men were under heavy attack and could not hold out for long. When one man hit a German tank with a bazooka round, the tank stopped for a few seconds, left the road, and then lumbered through a muddy field as if nothing had happened. One German tank destroyed two foxholes—and the soldiers in them—with point-blank hits. Lyga ordered his men to pull back. Soldiers in a bazooka team dug in with Company L's 2d Platoon fled their foxholes without firing a shot and ran toward the rifle squad positions, "yelling that tanks were coming right at them." The bazooka men were "jabbering away," and when German mortar fire hit, the "whole [rifle] platoon took off."[47]

The attack from the direction of Strauch hit a platoon each of Companies I and K. The Company I commander ordered his men to try and get to the houses in the northwest part of Schmidt. The intense German fire, however, diverted them toward Kommerscheidt. "It was quite a sensation to see your buddies killed alongside of you and also to see our bazooka shells bounce off the . . . tanks," recalled a survivor.[48]

Company M mortars fired on German infantry moving across the open ground from the direction of Hasenfeld. This fire temporarily broke up the infantry attack, but according to one soldier, "the tanks . . . had smashed through the two forward company positions and broke them all to hell . . . the situation was bad."[49]

By this time several German tanks were in Schmidt, roaming at will, searching for the American positions and pouring fire directly into them.

Several dozen men fled to the woods southwest of Kommerscheidt. The Germans eventually trapped about 200 Americans in the area. Three men reached friendly lines on 7 November and reported that the others were without food and water. On 8 November, the 89th Division reported the capture of 133 Americans, probably the only survivors.[50]

The defenses in Schmidt were crumbling. O'Malley and Walker tried to organize a stand in the center of town, but they had lost control of their men. A few company aidmen remained behind to treat the wounded. The battalion made no attempt to recover the dead.[51] The first rounds of American artillery did not fall on the attackers until nearly 9:00 A.M., about the time the regimental staff received its first word that Schmidt was under attack from at least two directions.

Regiment and division headquarters remained uninformed about the events at Schmidt until well into the morning. Positive reports from the 112th Infantry regarding strength and combat effectiveness were incorrect, but Cota had no other way to assess the regiment's condition. This led him to order the regiment to undertake patently impossible tasks. For example, Lieutenant Simon returned to Kommerscheidt with orders for the 3d Battalion to continue its attack as soon as it had the situation back under control. When Simon and his party departed for Schmidt, they nearly ran into a German tank. "We dug our noses into the ground and remained there for about ten minutes," he said.

Simon later found the 3d Battalion operations officer "in a retching condition . . . out of touch with things." Lieutenant Colonel Flood told Simon to return to regiment and get tank support. Fleig's tank was the only tank in Kommerscheidt, though others would arrive soon.[52]

Simon arrived at the 112th Infantry CP a few hours after the German attack commenced. Lieutenant Colonel Peterson told Simon to take him to Kommerscheidt.[53] Peterson needed to get an accurate picture of the events at Kommerscheidt and Schmidt, but it would be some time before he had the correct story. Peterson had already sent his executive officer, Lt. Col. Landon J. Lockett, Capt. Hunter Montgomery (the S-2), and three others to determine the situation. They did not reach Kommerscheidt. A German patrol ambushed and captured everyone but the S-2.[54]

Meanwhile, the 3d Battalion's forward aid station had moved into a abandoned log dugout beside the Kall trail. By 10:00 A.M., the casualties began to stream in. Soldiers of Company A, 707th Tank Battalion, saw groups of seemingly dazed men heading pell-mell for Vossenack.[55] Hundreds of men who were sick, tired, and isolated from their comrades had endured all they could. The unexpected ferocity of the enemy attack had caught the GIs unprepared both physically and mentally.

KOMMERSCHEIDT

It took every available man from the 1st Battalion to stop the demoralized men fleeing Schmidt. Some of the survivors who stopped in Kommerscheidt took up positions to augment the 1st Battalion's defenses. S.Sgt. Frank Ripperdan (Company L) recalled seeing men whose "spirits were pretty well shot."[56]

About 2:00 P.M. at least eight MK IV tanks from the 16th Panzer Regiment and about 200 infantry from the 1056th Infantry Regiment attacked Kommerscheidt. The tanks remained out of bazooka range and poured shells into the town.[57] Ray Fleig's tanks there were all that stood between the riflemen and the enemy.

Fleig's crew accounted for two enemy tanks, and S.Sgt. Spooner's crew knocked out a third. Fleig relocated his tank and spotted a MK V about 300 yards away. He fired first and scored two hits. Unfortunately, the rounds were high explosive (HE) instead of armor piercing (AP), and they did not destroy the tank. The frightened Germans abandoned the Panther anyway. Fleig then realized that his remaining AP rounds were stored in the hull, not accessible unless he traversed the turret. During the frantic seconds it took Fleig to get the AP ammunition, the Germans realized their error, climbed back into their tank, and returned the fire.

The round missed and gave Fleig's crew a few seconds to chamber and fire a round of AP ammunition that miraculously sliced off part of the Panther's gun tube. Three more rounds destroyed the tank.[58]

The weather was gradually improving, and P-47s were by this time overhead. They helped a bazooka team finish off another German tank. American artillery shells were also landing dangerously close to the infantrymen. One man later said, "Our artillery is better than the Germans. I know. I caught plenty [near] Kommerscheidt. . . . It has a lot more concussion than the German shells."[59]

It was afternoon before General Cota received reports of the events at Schmidt and Kommerscheidt. He then sent General Davis to investigate. Davis arrived at Kommerscheidt about 4:00 P.M. and met with Peterson, Flood, and Hazlett. He saw "a number of soldiers who seemed dazed and puzzled by the day's happenings, including the 3d Battalion CO of the 112th." Davis ordered Fleig to keep his tanks in Kommerscheidt and not to withdraw them under any circumstances—he was afraid the infantry would abandon the village if they thought the tanks were withdrawing. Cota finally received his first accurate account of the events when Davis returned to the division CP.[60] Nearly 12 hours had passed since the beginning of the German attack. The 3d Battalion, 112th Infantry, had been virtually destroyed, and the 1st Battalion was under tremendous pressure and might not hold Kommerscheidt.

THE KALL TRAIL, 4–5 NOVEMBER

Adding to the confusion at division headquarters was word that the Kall trail was clear, though neither the 112th headquarters nor division had sent an officer to assess the situation in person. The trail was in fact blocked by the disabled tanks, and it was not ready to support the size of the force needed to avert disaster at Kommerscheidt. Only smallwheeled vehicles or Weasels had any chance at all of negotiating it.

Captain Hostrup had spent most of the morning and afternoon coordinating the efforts of his own men and the engineers. Captured German Teller mines (the most common type of German antitank mine, activated by pressure), and later explosives, failed to blow off the rock outcrop, and the engineers decided not to use any more explosives for fear of causing more damage to the nearby disabled tanks. The commander of the 1171st Engineer Group, Col. Edmund K. Daley, sent the commander of the 20th Engineer Combat Battalion, Lt. Col. J. E. Sonnefield, to take charge of the work on the trail.[61]

Maintenance crews from the 707th Tank Battalion tried throughout the evening to recover the damaged tanks. That night, the battalion S-4 delivered to Hostrup a message stating that General Cota "wants to give you all the time possible to retrieve your vehicles, but that main supply route must be open by daybreak. If necessary, you will roll your immobilized tanks down the slope and into the draw."[62]

Hostrup's men could not do the impossible. About 2:30 A.M. on 5 November, they drove or pushed them from the trail.[63]

The Germans temporarily cut the trail not long after Hostrup's men cleared it. Elements of the 3d Battalion, 1055th Regiment, contacted elements of the 116th Panzer Reconnaissance Battalion about a half-mile northeast of the Mestringer Mühle, but the Germans were unable to commit enough troops to keep the trail closed.[64] A convoy of five M29 Weasels carrying rations and ammunition later reached Kommerscheidt without incident. Two platoons of M10 tank destroyers (893d Tank Destroyer Battalion) and the 3d Platoon of Company A, 707th, also arrived in Kommerscheidt before noon on 5 November.[65]

KOMMERSCHEIDT, 5 NOVEMBER

The defenders at Kommerscheidt repelled an early morning attack by the 16th Panzer Regiment and 1055th Infantry Regiment. The enemy regrouped and tried again a few minutes after 9:00 A.M. During the attack, a survivor of Company K's fight in Schmidt raced 100 yards over fire-swept ground to set out aircraft recognition panels when he saw that American planes were about to bomb and strafe friendly positions. A few minutes later the same man took a bazooka from a dead soldier and engaged two German tanks moving toward his company. He fired from a range of only 25 yards and put one tank out of action. He was never seen again.

A soldier assigned to Company L recalled seeing two American tanks pull up on either side of Kommerscheidt's overcrowded aid station and fire at the German tanks lumbering toward the terrified, wounded GIs. A round from one of the tanks hit the back of the aid station; according to one soldier, "I don't know what happened to the wounded men back there, but some of the men with me got more shrapnel. Immediately after that, all walking wounded were told to get out—quick. We had to move, walk, and run across a half mile of open but downhill space, the artillery still thundering into Kommerscheidt."[66] The Germans made probing attacks throughout the afternoon, but for the most part, they remained in Schmidt, content to sit 900 yards from Kommerscheidt and fire down into the American positions.

On 5 November, Lieutenant Simon was again in Kommerscheidt, having led Company B, 112th Infantry, to the woods west of the town. Lieutenant Colonel Peterson had asked Simon to bring Flood and Hazlett back to discuss the plight of the regiment. Simon found Flood's executive officer, Maj. R. C. Christensen, and Major Hazlett working together to direct the defense of Kommerscheidt. According to Simon, Lieutenant Colonel Flood was "pretty well exhausted." Simon took Flood to Peterson; Christensen took command of the 3d Battalion, and Major Hazlett took overall control of the Kommerscheidt defense.[67]

Throughout the day, walking wounded from Kommerscheidt made their way to the log aid station set up along the Kall trail. Pfc. Delmer Putney, assigned to the regimental medical section, set out from Kommerscheidt for the aid station with 27 walking wounded. On the way the soldiers met German medics, who forced them to carry a wounded soldier as far as the river. The Germans disappeared, and Putney's group reached the aid station about midnight on 5 November. Putney met either the 1st or the 3d Battalion surgeon, a captain, who told him there was room at the aid station for only the most seriously wounded. Putney led the walking wounded to Vossenack, where he explained the situation to the regimental surgeon early the next morning.

About 4:00 A.M., a German patrol stopped at the aid station, and the patrol leader offered to share rations and any supplies the Americans might need. He told the medical officer in charge that as long as the aidmen and assistants remained unarmed, the Germans would permit them to remain in the dugout.[68]

TASK FORCE RIPPLE

Before daylight on 6 November, Maj. Richard A. Dana, the 112th Infantry's S-3, received a message from division headquarters directing the 112th Infantry to retake Schmidt. To assist the infantry, Cota provided a newly formed task force under the command of Lieutenant Colonel Ripple. The so-called Task Force Ripple consisted of Lt. Col. William Tait's 3rd Battalion, 110th Infantry (about 350 men); the tanks and TDs already in Kommerscheidt; and Company D, 707th Tank Battalion. The formation of TF Ripple is another example of the division's continuing lack of appreciation for the situation at Kommerscheidt. It indicates that either Davis failed to understand the nature of the events he had seen or that he had failed to make Cota understand what was happening.

The Germans prevented TF Ripple from using the trail to cross the Kall Valley, and the infantry did not reach the 1st Battalion until midday. Meanwhile, at the 112th Infantry CP, Ripple, Tait, and Peterson met with the TF unit commanders and attempted a reconnaissance of the unfamiliar terrain. Snipers seriously wounded Tait and several others. Dana recalled that "everyone was on edge." Ripple and Peterson decided they could not attack without additional armor support.[69]

The survivors of the 1st and 3d Battalions, 112th Infantry, remained in their foxholes throughout the day, in full view of the enemy, never daring so much as to lift their heads above ground. Many soldiers could not leave their positions to relieve themselves.

Lieutenant Colonel Peterson tried to calm the men with a demonstration by the tanks and 1st. Lt. Turney Leonard's TDs. The demonstration did not go as planned. When the tanks left their positions the tank destroyers remained motionless. They did not move when Leonard exposed himself to enemy fire in an attempt to lead the vehicles into firing positions. An officer later determined that the TDs had bellied on hidden tree stumps. Fleig last saw Leonard "lashing a tank destroyer that was bellied up . . . with a riding crop. His left arm looked like it had been mangled by artillery, and his uniform was covered with blood." Leonard was last seen alive at the Kall trail aid station.[70] He was awarded a posthumous Medal of Honor for this and other acts of heroism at Kommerscheidt.[71]

The Germans attacked again on the morning of 7 November. The artillery preparation was so heavy that Major Dana counted about 50 explosions in one 90-second period. A tank-infantry force composed of elements of 1st and 3rd Battalions, 1055th Regiment, and 2d Battalion, 860th Regiment, with armor support from the 518th Tank Battalion and other units, followed the artillery barrage. A tank put a shell directly into the CP of Company A, 112th Infantry, and fired on individual 1st and 2d Platoon foxholes. At a range of only 30 yards, a TD knocked out a German tank rumbling toward the center of the village. Another TD accounted for three more German tanks. Captain Hackard of Company B knocked out a tank with a bazooka.[72]

The Germans "would fire repeatedly on one hole until it was knocked out, and then shift to another one, systematically eradicating each man. This was hell on the men, and after seeing a number of nearby holes shot up, some of them took off and others followed. They streamed back toward the rear," recalled Major Dana. The remnants of Companies A and B and the survivors of the 3rd Battalion, now thoroughly demoralized and intermingled, fled to the Company C positions inside the woods north of Kommerscheidt.[73]

Lieutenant Colonel Peterson and Major Dana dragged the wounded commander of Headquarters Company, 1st Battalion, into the CP dugout. Ripple was there and told them that he had spotted German soldiers only 50 yards away and that an assault gun was even closer. A moment before the CP received a hit from either artillery or the assault gun, Ripple and the others "ran like hell" toward their alternate CP, located in the nearby woods. Hazlett moved from foxhole to foxhole encouraging the beleaguered defenders, but the men pulled out when a company of German infantry occupied the southeastern part of Kommerscheidt.

M-10 Tank Destroyers of the 893d Tank Destroyer Battalion, probably on Road W west of Germeter, on 4 November. Medal of Honor recipient Lt. Turney Leonard was a platoon leader in the 893d. (Courtesy National Archives, #111–SC–197366)

Staff Sergeant Ripperdan saw burning TDs and tanks and a German soldier standing at the entrance of the combined 1st and 3d Battalion CP. Nearby were the surrendering battalion staffs.[74]

Captain Piercey's men were "getting jittery." He recalled that for some time he was not aware that the soldiers on the right flank had withdrawn. The riflemen started to run when a German tank appeared, but Piercey and several others forced the men back. Piercey said that there was "one tank and two machine guns firing point-blank at us. . . . I saw one shell from the tank blow one man straight up into the air. We managed to get up into a sunken trail . . . with the 88 fire zipping along just over our heads. The men got out by infiltration. One or two at a time would take off. . . . the field was soft and it seemed like a lifetime to cross it."[75]

Peterson received a written message that afternoon directing him to return to the division CP in Rott. Ripple took command when Peterson, determined to make Cota aware of the situation east of the Kall River, departed. Peterson never questioned the authenticity of the message, though he probably should have, because he was aware that Col. Gustin M. Nelson was due to replace him.

On the return trip, Peterson and two escorting soldiers ran into German patrols near the Kall River. One soldier who had volunteered to lead the others soon outdistanced and eventually abandoned them. Small-arms fire killed the soldier with Peterson. Mortar fragments wounded Peterson in both legs, and Peterson was convinced he would die from wounds and exposure unless he reached American lines. He crawled and limped back and forth across the ice-cold Kall River looking for friendly troops while trying to avoid German patrols operating on both sides of the river. Two Americans finally appeared and evacuated him to Rott.[76]

After Peterson departed, Ripple had ordered Company C, 112th Infantry, to move to Kommerscheidt, but the company commander and his men were "in an absolute daze incapable of taking or carrying out that order." Ripple told them to remain in the woods west of Kommerscheidt. By this time, the Germans had knocked out two tanks and three TDs. Two of the remaining tanks threw a track when they left Kommerscheidt. Only two M10s and one M4 reached the tree line.

Major Christensen, the 3d Battalion executive officer who had replaced Lieutenant Colonel Flood after his breakdown, told Captain Walker (Company L) to organize a defense in the field north of Kommerscheidt, but the morally and physically tired soldiers fled to the woods. Christensen turned and walked alone to Kommerscheidt. At 11:25 A.M., Ripple informed 28th Division headquarters that the town was lost.[77]

The bright prospects for success at Schmidt evaporated within a few hours on the morning of 4 November 1944. There were several reasons for the failure of the 28th Division, and some of them will be discussed at the end of the next chapter, but comments by Ray Fleig in 1989 go a long way in explaining the disaster: "Those poor devils of the 112th were loaded down with a wool overcoat that was saturated with rain; they had a full field pack, carried extra ammunition and rations, had struggled up the near-vertical side of the Kall Gorge, then advanced two more miles uphill under intense artillery and mortar fire to attack the town of Schmidt. I saw men die under artillery fire because they were so tired that they were only able to scratch the outline of a foxhole in the dirt."[78]

6
Disaster at Vossenack

During the hours of panic at Schmidt and Kommerscheidt, another disaster was in the making at Vossenack. The problems there arose because of poor staff planning. There, as in Schmidt, the first phase of the attack went well. But it took every ounce of will on the part of the troops dug in on the exposed ridge to remain in their positions. There were no reinforcements, and for the first two days no one permitted the riflemen to take refuge in nearby buildings. The German fire never let up.

The 2d and 3d of November went relatively well for the 2d Battalion, 112th Infantry. But on the 4th, the German fire became "fiendish and unnerving. . . ." The Germans were bold enough to continue the fire even when American fighter-bombers were overhead searching for the firing positions.

The riflemen had no place to escape the constant artillery, mortar, and direct fire pouring into Vossenack from the surrounding high ground. The fire began whenever the weather cleared, and it ended only at night or when the Germans decided to save ammunition. Lieutenant James Condon, acting commander of Company E, decided to have as many of his men as possible remain in the houses during daylight. He kept one man per squad on the ridge. Condon said the Germans "would single out an individual foxhole and fire at it until they scored a direct hit, and then shift their fire to the next." Sometimes the fire followed a man if he left his foxhole. Dirt from explosions covered one NCO six times. Some of the men were becoming so exhausted by the strain that in some cases platoon leaders and NCOs had to order them to eat. And any soldier who entered the line during the day was either killed or a combat exhaustion case by the evening.

The artillery fire covered nearly every foot of Vossenack, methodically working its way up and down the main street in a deadly pattern. The shell fire also set the Company E CP on fire. The next day, German fire set the new Company E CP ablaze. The company also listed four men missing after a barn in which they took shelter caught fire. Dozens of men rushed to rescue them, but the four were trapped in the barn, where they died under hundreds of pounds of burning hay.

The situation grew worse by the hour. Just before dark, shell fire obliterated three Company G foxholes. Nothing remained of the occupants.[1] Some of the men sought refuge in buildings, but this left an undefended gap in the center of the Company G line. A few men cried when officers saw the danger and ordered them to return to the foxholes. The battalion commander, Lieutenant Colonel Hatzfeld, also succumbed to combat exhaustion, and Capt. John Pruden, the executive officer, took command of the battalion. In spite of these events, the regimental situation reports stated that the 112th Infantry was in "excellent condition."[2] There is no evidence that any division staff officers questioned the reports.

Morning came on 6 November without the usual shelling. Just after Clyde R. Johnson, a Company G lieutenant, remarked to a sergeant that this was unusual, a burst of small-arms fire broke the nervous silence. Seconds later Johnson heard a man scream. It was quiet until a dozen artillery explosions broke the uneasy silence. More small-arms fire erupted from the wooded draws to the front of the infantry. This was the breaking point. The men could endure no more. A few soldiers grabbed frantically for their gear and ran toward Vossenack. Someone said they saw German soldiers moving through the gap in the Company G line. More and more men began to flee from the open ridge. The Company G commander reported an enemy attack.[3]

The Company F commander, Lieutenant Kauffman, realized that Company G's abrupt withdrawal threatened the security of his own company. He ordered his men to pull back to the buildings. A few men stopped when they reached the first buildings, but most kept on running. Captain Pruden said that the men began to flee the exposed ridge because "they had just had too much. Their endurance could stand no more of such concentrated shelling."[4]

Officers at the CP tried to stop the panic-stricken men. Condon saw men "pushing, shoving, throwing away equipment, trying to outrun the artillery and each other . . . in a frantic effort to escape. They were all scared and excited." He saw badly wounded men lying where they fell, screaming for medics, but ignored by the other soldiers.

First Lieutenant Melvin Barrilleaux, the Company E commander, was by this time back with the company after returning from a pass. He and Condon realized that it was impossible to hold the temporary line near the Company E CP. Barrilleaux ordered the men to withdraw further into Vossenack. The mortar squads of the heavy weapons company also pulled back. Artillery fire caught these men in the open and caused several casualties.[5] The situation was chaotic, with no one in effective control of the battalion. The Americans in fact were in the process of losing Vossenack. Pruden called for tanks to cover the withdrawal, but the panicked rush of the infantry left the supporting tanks (Company C, 707th Tank Battalion) and TDs, which were then in the eastern part of town, without protection.

As the events described above unfolded, a platoon of tanks from Company B, 707th Tank Battalion, moved from Germeter through Vossenack under a prearranged plan. But the tanks were firing over the heads of the infantry, and this only added to the confusion. The tanks originally present in town withdrew soon after the Company B platoon arrived. The withdrawing platoon, from Company C, left behind a damaged tank, and the leader of the newly arrived Company B platoon misinterpreted a message that instructed him to evacuate the crew of the disabled tank. He evidently decided he was also to pull his platoon out of town rather than simply rescue the crew and remain in place. Captain West, the Company C commander, intercepted the platoon and tried to get it back to the open end of the ridge, but German artillery drove the tanks back to the center of town.

When the situation with the tanks stabilized, Captains Granger (Company B, 707th) and West (Company C, 707th) met to discuss the situation. As both officers stood in the turrets of their tanks and tried to talk over the noise of the battle, a mortar shell hit the hull of West's tank. The concussion tore away part of the commander's hatch and killed West instantly. Granger was stunned but uninjured. He arrived in town shortly before 11:00 A.M. and, after meeting with Pruden, withdrew his remaining tanks to the line set up near the church.[6]

Meanwhile, Pruden and his command group went into the street running through the center of Vossenack and tried to halt the fleeing riflemen. "A few of the men were rational, but all were shocked," said Pruden. He and his S-1, Capt. James T. Nesbitt, took the 60 or 70 men they had gathered and formed a new line at the battalion CP, located just west of the town church. American artillery had by that time joined the action, but a few rounds fell short, hit the near the CP, and killed or wounded several soldiers.[7]

The evidence indicates that there was no German attack prior to the flight from the foxholes outside Vossenack. No American reported seeing German soldiers during the minutes immediately preceding the flight from the ridge. The Germans were in fact planning to attack Vossenack, but bad weather on the evening of 5 November disrupted the preparations of the 156th Panzergrenadier Regiment. The German commander delayed the attack until after daylight, and his soldiers did not enter Vossenack in force until after the 2d Battalion, 112th Infantry, had departed the ridge. The Germans followed the Americans as far west as the town church before noon.[8] Waldenburg recalled after the war that the Germans had not planned to shell the village that morning because they wanted to make a surprise attack. This obviously had an unanticipated effect on the Americans.[9]

The experiences of one German soldier give an interesting view of the battle. On the way to Vossenack, Manfred Otten, a German infantrymen, saw "bloody and moaning soldiers, a shell-torn forest made impassable and bombed fields." Otten passed wounded soldiers he had no time to help, entered Vossenack, and reached a house where he found an American soldier's breakfast still on a table. By noon he was as far west as the church. Through a hole in a wall, he saw an American tank 40 yards away. He fired a panzerfaust and missed the tank. A second round also missed, as did one fired by a sergeant. Seconds later, an American rifleman killed the sergeant. Otten knew it would be suicide to fire again. He hid in the church, hoping the Americans would not search it. He later made his way to a nearby house, where he fell asleep. The Americans later took him prisoner.[10]

THE RECAPTURE OF VOSSENACK

General Davis turned to the 1171st Engineer Combat Group for help in restoring the Vossenack defenses. The group commander, Colonel Daley, alerted Lt. Col. Carl J. Isley's 146th Engineer Combat Battalion, then working at the back-breaking task of road maintenance, for movement to Vossenack. Daley and Isley also met with Pruden, who told them that his men needed help badly. The battalion CP itself was at the front line. Davis meanwhile met with Daley's operations officer and told him to get a company moving to Vossenack as soon as possible. "Go in," urged Davis; "drive the enemy out of the town. Move. Get going."[11]

Some of the engineers were still wearing their mud-covered hip boots when they arrived at Vossenack and headed for the rubble that was the church. The engineers knew little about the situation; the Company A commander issued his platoon leaders their orders while their men were still on the move. Soldiers of both sides were intermingled in the town. Troops later killed a German soldier in a house next door to the 2d Battalion CP.

Davis went to Vossenack that night and met with Isley. He told the engineer battalion commander that his mission in Vossenack was to defend the MSR to Kommerscheidt. He went to a map and pointed to a location, telling Isley to put some men "out here." Pruden reminded Davis that this was the exposed former location of the 2d Battalion, 112th Infantry. Davis, who probably had never before seen the Vossenack Ridge, then told Isley he could determine the exact positions. Company A set out after dark for the open part of the ridge, but the 112th Infantry guides became lost. The men could neither evade the enemy nor get to the desired location, and the company commander led them back to Vossenack, using the light of the burning buildings as a guide. The Germans had effectively isolated Vossenack from the Kall trail.[12]

A firefight meanwhile raged throughout the night in and around the church. The building changed hands several times; on one occasion, the Germans occupied the tower and basement while the American engineers held the main floor.[13]

An artillery preparation on the morning of 7 November signaled the start of the engineer's attack to retake Vossenack. Company A moved on what remained of the church. One man at a time fired through the church's main door and then rushed inside, not knowing what awaited him. The engineers killed several Germans, took 16 prisoners, and cleared 20 more enemy soldiers from adjacent buildings. In one building, the Germans had either failed to notice or did not try to use two boxes of American hand grenades abandoned the day before.

When the supporting tanks reached the end of the main street, they began to receive fire from enemy tanks or self-propelled guns located on the Brandenberg-Bergstein Ridge. The tank platoon leader requested an air strike. Two P-47s bombed Vossenack by mistake, and one of the crewman from a mine-disabled tank was killed.[14] By the end of the day, the Americans held the town except for a section at the eastern outskirts. It would be another four weeks before they retook this part of town, which became known as the Rubble Pile.

THE END NEAR KOMMERSCHEIDT

Another indication of the 28th Division staff's lack of understanding of the conditions east of the Kall River was the formation on 7 November of Task Force Davis, the successor to Task Force Ripple. TF Davis consisted of the 1st Battalion, 109th Infantry; 1st and 3d Battalions, 112th Infantry; the 3d Battalion, 110th Infantry; Companies A and C, 707th Tank Battalion; Companies B and C, 893d Tank Destroyer Battalion; and supporting units. The troop list was impressive, but with the exception of the battalion of the 109th Infantry, no unit was close to full strength. The mission was to retake Schmidt.[15]

To prepare for the attack of TF Davis, Major Topping, the commander of the 3d Battalion, 109th Infantry, received orders on 7 November to secure an escape route for the survivors of TF Ripple. The 4th Division's 12th Infantry had replaced the 109th Infantry north of Germeter effective at 12:50 P.M. (the activities of this regiment will be outlined later in this chapter), and Topping's battalion was now available to enter the battle east of the Kall. There was no time for proper reconnaissance, and of course neither Topping nor his staff and commanders were familiar with the terrain. He had to depend on a guide supplied by regiment to get the battalion to its assembly area while he reconnoitered the proposed route of attack. He then returned to the assembly area to wait for the battalion. It did not arrive. He soon learned that it had become lost and dug in by mistake behind the 1st Battalion, 110th Infantry, near Richelskaul. It remained in place until the next day.

Task Force Davis, therefore, never got under way on 7 November. The next morning, General Davis and Colonel Nelson, the 112th Infantry's new commander, led Topping's battalion to the west bank of the Kall, opposite Kommerscheidt. Company L crossed the river, but in a three-hour firefight, it lost two platoon sergeants, a squad leader, and at least ten other soldiers. It lost even more men during its withdrawal to the west bank of the river, including Major Topping, who was wounded.[16]

Lieutenant Colonel Peterson meanwhile had arrived at the division CP after his harrowing journey across the Kall River. Cota could hardly believe his eyes when he saw the wounded, exhausted Peterson lying on a stretcher. He knew of no message calling for Peterson's return, and Cota thought he had abandoned his men. At that point, six days of tension took its toll on the division commander, and he passed out. Although much has been made of this incident, a recent biography provides new information about Cota's health. In a postwar physical, doctors found that Cota was slightly diabetic. It is possible that diabetes, coupled with the stress of the Schmidt operation, played a role in Cota's reaction to the unexpected appearance of Peterson. Cota recovered and returned to duty. He retired as major general and died in the 1970s. Peterson was medically retired and entered private business after the war.[17] An officer who knew him said that he was "still bitter, and perhaps considered himself a failure—broken." Peterson died a few years later.[18]

After the encounter with Peterson, Cota on the afternoon of 7 November asked General Gerow for permission to withdraw the men remaining east of the Kall River. It was apparent that the attack had failed. Gerow called Hodges, who would not approve the request without first talking with Davis, a man who Hodges knew and trusted. This was a professional slight to Gerow and Cota, but Davis convinced Hodges to permit the withdrawal.[19] The second battle for Schmidt was drawing to a close.

Davis put Colonel Nelson in charge of the withdrawal,[20] which would begin on 8 November. At dusk, the tank and TD crewmen disabled their remaining vehicles, and the infantry quietly booby-trapped and disabled their weapons, vehicles, and antitank guns. Volunteers prepared the litter cases for the journey through the Kall Valley. An NCO from Company M, 112th Infantry, remembered, "There were over 60 litter cases. We had to get rid of all weapons and side arms. . . . No one knew exactly how we were to go, but general orders were to follow a road to the rear and try to contact the 109th Infantry. It was snowy and muddy, and we practically had to drag the litter cases."[21]

The litter bearers and walking wounded reached the Kall River bridge, where they found four German guards. The Germans agreed to let the Americans pass unharmed.

Nelson intended for those evacuated from the woods outside Kommerscheidt to dig in with the 109th Infantry in positions west of the river. He organized the remnants of the 112th Infantry into a provisional company under the command of Captain Walker. Ripple led about 80 soldiers, and Hostrup and Fleig led another group of about 50. They could use no lights. To keep contact, they had to hold on to the shoulder or the belt of the man in front. On the way out, German mortar fire scattered the Hostrup-Fleig column and separated it from the group under Walker. Ripple fell about 20 feet down a slope but was not injured and managed to lead some of his men to the location of the 109th Infantry. Only a few men were still with Nelson when his group reached friendly lines.[22]

Fleig and six exhausted men arrived at the assembly area near Vossenack about midnight. "The actual move was a nightmare," he recalled. "It was right at the freezing point and rainy, darker than the inside of your hat; we were under mortar and artillery fire. The hillside was muddy and covered with broken trees."[23]

It was early morning, 9 November 1944. The second attack on Schmidt was over.

THE AID STATION

Though it now held positions west of the Kall, the 3d Battalion, 109th Infantry, made no attempt to provide security for the aid station located on the trail. It is impossible to determine whether or not this was because of neglect or whether it was from failure to understand the tactical situation and to realize that German troops were in the area. It is also possible that because of his wounds, Major Topping, the battalion commander, was unable to direct his men properly.

The Germans in control of the trail made periodic checks of the aid station but did not interfere with the treatment of the wounded. The medical personnel had enough supplies to treat the litter cases, but many others had to lay outside, covered by blankets and overcoats, exposed to the cold rain and snow. Medics directed the walking wounded to Vossenack.

German fire on 8 November turned back five attempts by personnel from the division's medical battalion to reach the aid station. An officer from the battalion also made an unsuccessful attempt using the Simonskall road. Neither regiment nor division acted on earlier requests by Major Berndt, surgeon of the 112th Infantry, for a truce to evacuate the wounded from the Kommerscheidt woods line.

The division surgeon organized a convoy of 13 Weasels that set out for the aid station during the night of 8 November. The drivers could not locate the start of the Kall trail, and German fire turned back the column. Another convoy of four Weasels departed Vossenack after dark. The Germans opened fire because they could not see the Red Cross panels displayed on the vehicles. Another attempt to evacuate the wounded shortly before daylight on 9 November met with more success. Medical personnel working at the aid station used trucks and jeeps that had been left on the trail a few days before to evacuate most of the litter patients to the edge of the woods below Vossenack. Abandoned vehicles there blocked the trucks, but a Weasel with five patients did manage to reach Vossenack.

Major Berndt was still interested in a truce. He had already discussed the possibilities with division G-4. A short time before the events described above, he went on foot as far as the Kall River, where German soldiers appeared and told him the vehicles at the aid station could leave with the wounded. Berndt then returned to Vossenack to report the situation. In the early afternoon, another convoy of ambulances, protected from observation by the snow and fog, reached the aid station. Medics loaded the wounded, and the vehicles returned without incident to Vossenack. The Germans, however, did not permit the surgeons and chaplains to leave.[24]

Two days later (11 November) a German doctor named Stuttgen, accompanied by a medic, met with the Americans at the now-damaged stone bridge. They stood in the swirling snow and discussed terms for a truce to evacuate the dead and wounded. "It was worse than we thought," recalled a German officer. "Between abandoned and shot-out tanks and vehicles lay the dead and wounded of both sides. Friendly and enemy lumped together, fully soaked through and starved in their foxholes."[25]

Artillery fire crashed down a few minutes later and interrupted the gruesome work of recovering the casualties. The commander of the

1056th Regiment ended the operation a few hours later. The Americans were attacking north of Vossenack, and the Germans had to return to the business of war.

"The dream and reality of a peaceful meeting between both sides was over," said a German witness. The standoff continued for a few more days until the Americans abandoned the aid station.[26]

REINFORCEMENTS

The failure of the 28th Division to hold Schmidt and Vossenack prompted Hodges to direct the 4th Infantry Division's 12th Infantry Regiment (then in Luxembourg preparing to move north with the 8th and 22d Infantry Regiments to participate in the VII Corps attack) to move immediately to the Germeter-Vossenack area. Colonel James S. Luckett, Jr., the commander of the 12th Infantry Regiment, arrived at General Cota's headquarters in Rott late on the afternoon of 6 November, where he learned his regiment was to relieve the 109th Infantry, which would move to Germeter, that night—unit for unit, foxhole for foxhole. There was no time to alter the dispositions that the 109th Infantry had secured after several days of close-in fighting. The regiment's 2d and 3d Battalions relieved six companies of the 109th Infantry west of Germeter. Companies I, K, and L took positions near the Wilde Sau minefield; Companies F and G dug in to the north; and Company E faced the Weisser Weh Valley. The 1st Battalion was about a mile to the west, across the valley. After the relief, the 12th Infantry would attack to reduce a salient located in the Weisser Weh Valley and manned by troops of the 275th Division.[27]

The 7th of November passed uneventfully, and the 1st Battalion attacked at midday on the 8th to cut the base of the salient. The first two hours of the attack went well, but in the early afternoon, Companies B and C ran into booby-trapped wire obstacles covered by automatic weapons. The Americans did not breach the wire, and Luckett called a halt to the attack at dusk. The battalion withdrew to its original positions the next morning.[28]

Shortly after the 12th Infantry jumped off the next morning, the 116th Panzer Division launched an attack against the 2d Battalion. German artillery fire set off mines, causing several American casualties and forcing Company F to withdraw. This move exposed Company E, and as it also began to pull back, an estimated 100 German infantrymen followed the Americans into their old positions. The Germans managed to separate Companies E and F and surround the 2d Battalion command post, where Lt. Col. Franklin Sibert, the battalion commander, took personal charge of the defense.

Things also went badly for the 3d Battalion. In preparation for the attack, the battalion commander withdrew Company I, which was separated from Company K by the Wilde Sau minefield, to a new location adjacent to Company K. Luckett moved a reserve platoon into Company I's former position. This left Company L, in effect the battalion's reserve company, responsible for more than 800 yards of thick woods. The attack stopped in the late afternoon.

At the end of the day, the three line companies of the 3d Battalion had just over 200 men left—less than half the authorized number. The regiment was now separated into five groups, and Luckett's problems with command and control were enormous. Companies I and K were in positions near the Germeter-Hürtgen road. Fifty men from Company L occupied foxholes a few hundred yards away. Companies F and G, with a platoon of Company L, were west of Germeter, cut off from the rest of the 2d Battalion. Company E was still in its original location. The 1st Battalion had made no progress either.

The 12th Infantry reverted to 4th Division control at 7:00 P.M., and Maj. Gen. Raymond O. Barton, the division commander, permitted Luckett to halt operations and reorganize his regiment. Ironically, this caused even more casualties. In some cases, when GIs arrived at their old positions, they found them occupied by German soldiers. Supply parties also could not move forward, and that night, the cold, hungry soldiers of Companies F and G scavenged for food among the bodies surrounding their positions. The Americans used recovered 109th Infantry supplies and six captured German machine guns to overcome shortages of ammunition and weapons.

There were still problems on 11 November. The Germans counterattacked and surrounded Companies A, C, F, and G. Luckett's headquarters was out of contact with these units for the rest of the day. The 3d Battalion was at less than 50 percent strength in the line companies. Barton and Luckett decided it was time to consolidate the separated companies and halt the attack.

On 12–13 November the regiment began withdrawing to a new line west of Germeter. Colonel Sibert later said, "God, it was cold. We were hungry and thirsty. . . . That night we really prayed. . . . In the morning, we found out that God had answered all our prayers. It snowed during the night, and the whole area was covered with fog—perfect for getting out. . . . The supply line was littered with dead. The men that came out with me were so damned tired that they stepped on the bodies—they were too tired to step over [them]."[29]

The regiment received replacements and regrouped. Between 7 and 15 November, the 12th Infantry suffered 562 casualties in the rifle battalions out of an original strength of about 2,300.[30] The attack failed to accomplish its intended goal, and the regiment lost about twice as much ground as it took in its furthest advance. Cota and others probably considered these to be only local attacks to straighten a line, but this rendered the 12th Infantry Regiment virtually combat ineffective on the eve of a major attack.

What had happened to the 12th Infantry? The same thing that would have happened to any other regiment—veteran or new to combat—which received the same mission. The terrain of the Weisser Weh Valley separated the companies from the possibility of mutual support. Only on 13 November was Colonel Luckett able to regroup the companies on a consolidated front. The logistics problems were nearly insurmountable. Armor support was nonexistent. In short, the 12th Infantry fought a type of battle for which it was simply not prepared.

BETWEEN GERMETER AND VOSSENACK

After the withdrawal of the units east of the Kall River, limited operations to clear the west bank of the valley continued. Major Ford, the commander of the 1st Battalion, 109th Infantry, was killed in Vossenack on 7 November. Two days later, Lt. Col. Harmon Williams took command of the battalion and led it on 10 November to support the attack of the 12th Infantry. German artillery caught Company A in a clearing and forced it to fall back to Vossenack and reorganize. Company B meanwhile encountered no opposition and dug in on what its commander thought was the objective. It was actually the wrong position, but it still was the deepest penetration made to date between Vossenack and Hürtgen. Reinforcements could not reach the company, and it spent several days with little food, water, or ammunition, isolated from the rest of the battalion.[31]

Company C was to follow Company B to the battalion's objective. A replacement private recalled, "When we crossed the small stream . . . and went up into the woods, we became aware of the fact that most of the tops of the . . . trees had been blasted off from artillery bombardment. . . . At the crest of the hill were four U.S. litter bearers [who had been] carrying a wounded soldier who were crunched in a heap (all dead) frozen in place, apparently victims of a . . . mine."[32]

Cota and the new commander of the 109th Infantry, Col. Jesse Gibney (formerly of the 60th Infantry), sent Lieutenant Colonel Strickler, now the regiment's executive officer, and six other men into the woods on 11 November to locate the widely separated companies of the 1st Battalion, 109th Infantry, and get them to the battalion's objective. Strickler and his group dodged German patrols, and it took hours to find the scattered elements of Companies A and C. "How I ever got out of that deal, I don't know," Strickler later said. The next morning, the Germans laid mines around the 1st Battalion CP.[33]

On 13 November, a patrol from the German 89th Infantry Division located Company B, still occupying the ground it took on 10 November. The Germans returned in force the next day. The Americans were running low on ammunition, and it took two and a half hours to get artillery support. On 12 November, the Germans turned back an attempt by Company C to reach Company B. By this time there were only 75 men remaining, most of whom were suffering from trench foot. The men took turns kneeling in the water-filled foxholes—it was too painful for them to stand. The company was out of food and water.[34]

Two days later, the 1st Battalion executive officer was killed during an attempt to relieve the isolated company. The survivors of the German attack that followed some time later reached Company B the same day and finally were able to organize its evacuation.[35]

The 7th Army chief of staff, Generalmajor von Gersdorff, later said, "The 89th Infantry Division considered the ejection of this force to be a point of honor, but they were never able to dispose of them. This typically confused example of forest fighting may be likened to a game of 'cat and mouse.'"[36]

THE COST

After the 31 enlisted and 2 officer survivors of Company K, 112th Infantry, withdrew across the Kall River, they traveled to the division trains area southeast of Roetgen. The company received 56 replacements during 9 and 10 November. The Red Cross supplied beer, and the next day the men had pancakes for breakfast. General Cota spoke to the men that afternoon, and the division band held a concert. The Red Cross supplied coffee and doughnuts. On 12 November, more replacements arrived, and the men received three hot meals. Company K began its move to a rest area in Luxembourg two days later.[37]

The 110th Infantry also paid a high price. The 1st Battalion, for example, on 13 November could count fewer than 75 men in the line companies, including replacements. The battalion executive officer said, "We left a hell of a lot of our best men up there."[38] It would take weeks of training and integration of the replacements before the regiment would again be ready for battle.

Cota later told the division: "I am *very, very* proud of the fight that you men have put up and of the results you have accomplished. It cost us heavily in killed and wounded. You who have come through this fight know full well the hardships and heartaches that the soldier must endure during battle. It has been rough and tough. History will record that you men of the 28th Infantry Division can take it and hand it out. I congratulate you on a job WELL DONE!"[39]

The 28th Infantry Division suffered appalling casualties during the first two weeks of November, as there were approximately 5,684 battle and nonbattle losses. Supporting units lost another 500 men. Of the figures listed, the 112th Infantry lost 232 men captured, 431 missing, 719 wounded, 167 killed, and 544 nonbattle casualties, all from an original strength of about 3,100. The matériel losses, which were equally high, included 16 of 24 M10 TDs in the 893d Tank Destroyer Battalion and 31 of 50 M4 tanks in the 707th Tank Battalion. German matériel losses are more difficult to assess, but personnel losses were about 2,900 from all causes.[40] During the third week in November the division went to Luxembourg, where it rested, took in more replacements, and conducted training and patrolling. It would perform well less than a month later during the Ardennes counterattack.

The battle for Schmidt was a risky operation that failed to accomplish its objectives. Hodges would have to be satisfied with a south flank for the main effort of the mid-November attack resting on the Kall, not the Roer. This meant that when the V Corps entered the battle, it would again have to contend with woods teeming with the enemy, the "B-B Ridge," and even stronger defenses than those it faced in early November.

The 110th Infantry took Simonskall, but not the northern reaches of the Monschau Corridor. The 112th Infantry succeeded in taking and holding Vossenack, but the regiment managed that only with the assistance of a battalion of engineers. The 12th and 109th Infantry Regiments failed to secure a LD for use later in November. Ironically, the 28th Division succeeded very well in its mission of drawing German reserves from the VII Corps front.

There were several reasons for the division's failure. The terrain itself was decisive in terms of its impact on logistics and on the morale and physical capabilities of the troops. Plans based on map reconnaissance only called for the Kall trail to serve as the MSR for the 112th Infantry. A historian assigned to V Corps in 1944 called this the "single greatest factor" in the outcome of events at Schmidt. He was correct.

Sickness—and foxholes dubbed "artesian wells"—caused a significant number of casualties without the Germans firing a single shot. German fire along with the weather caused irreparable damage to the division's command and control capability and contributed to Cota's inability to shape events. Other reasons were the Americans' failure to neutralize the Brandenberg-Bergstein ridge and the unexpectedly strong German reaction to the attack. The Americans expected and planned for an infantry battle, especially at Schmidt. The Germans did not oblige them.

Cota admitted that the battle revealed "certain weak links in the training of the Division, both tactical and command and staff." He and his staff lost control of the situation early in the battle and never regained it. Problems later cited by General Gerow included the following: the artillery commander did not keep close enough contact with the artillery battalions and was not always aware of the situation with the infantry; the division staff failed to give Cota the recommendations and estimates he needed; and the staff accepted without apparent question erroneous reports from the combat units. One interesting example is a false report that on 12 November Company A, 110th Infantry, had surrendered. The circumstances were different, though unclear even to those on the ground. Evidently, a German attack had routed the few surviving riflemen, and several Americans had been captured. The surrender was reported through regiment to Cota (and the V Corps G-3, who happened to be at the division CP), without verification by the battalion. The G-3, Col. John G. Hill, called army headquarters, and Hodges had the false report within minutes.

Commanders at all levels failed to coordinate properly with attached units. Before the attack, the division sent no patrols in the direction of Vossenack and Schmidt. No one discovered the Wilde Sau minefield before the attack, and the division engineers failed to provide terrain intelligence to the attached corps engineers.[41]

Any division would have had problems at Germeter and Vossenack. The 28th Division had some very experienced and capable leaders and soldiers, but they did not compensate for the difficult mission and the problems noted above. General Gerow acknowledged as much soon after the fight.

The Hürtgen Forest was an equalizer of combat power. As long as the Americans insisted on fighting there without aiming for the Roer dams, they were throwing away—with no good reason—every advantage they had over the Germans. The doctrine of combined arms was difficult to apply effectively in the forest, and the Germans had only to remain in their defenses and wait for the virtually unsupported infantry attacks.

By mid-November, the battle had no important long-term goal. Although the Americans eventually expressed some concern about the Roer dams, it was almost as if the Americans were banking on enemy weakness to allow them to take the entire forest area at their leisure. German reaction to the 28th Division's attack should have made it plain that it was too late for that.

There was a lot riding on the next offensive, now set to begin on or about 10 November. An officer in a tank battalion attached to the 4th Infantry Division reported that General Eisenhower told a group of unit commanders the attack would be "the big push of the war to break the

Germans' back. It is entirely conceivable that the war will be over by Christmas if this attack is successful."[42]

New York Times correspondent Harold Denney summed up the thoughts of the front-line soldier: "Our men in the cellars and foxholes are steeling themselves to a winter campaign, but they are praying—rather than hoping—for an earlier finish to the war."[43]

The big First Army attack failed to answer their prayers.

7
The November Offensive

G eneral Hodges's plan for the November attack called for the VII Corps to make its main effort in the Stolberg Corridor, the most direct route to Rhine crossings near Cologne. The supporting attack would be in the Hürtgen Forest. The veteran 1st Infantry Division, with the attached 47th Infantry Regiment (9th Division), would spearhead the attack with a push toward Langerwehe and Jüngersdorf, both located about 10 miles northeast of Stolberg. The remainder of the division's zone of attack was south of the steep hills marking the boundary of the Hürtgen Forest with the Vicht Creek Valley.

The 1st Division's 16th Infantry (Col. Frederick W. Gibb) would seize Hamich and Hill 232 and maintain contact with the adjacent regiments on either flank—the 26th Infantry on the right and the 47th Infantry on the left. German observers on Hill 232 could spot American troop movements as far south as the edge of the forest, and those on the other hills had commanding views of the Roer plain near Eschweiler. The other important hills were 207 and 203, both south of the Wehe Creek, in the fringe of the forest. Both offered views of the Roer plain and Stolberg Corridor.[1]

Meanwhile, the 47th Infantry would take Gressenich, push north, and maintain contact with the 104th Infantry Division. Col. John F. R. Seitz's 26th Infantry would sweep the northern reaches of the forest and maintain contact with the 4th Division's adjacent 8th Infantry Regiment. The 3d Armored Division's CCB (Boudinot) would support the 1st Division by taking the villages of Werth, Köttenich, Scherpenseel, and Hastenrath. The attacking regiments had to gain maneuver space quickly to allow commitment of the 1st Division's reserve regiment, the 18th Infantry (Col. George A. Smith, Jr.), against Hills 207 and 203 and Langerwehe.[2]

The 4th Infantry Division, on the VII Corps' right, would attack

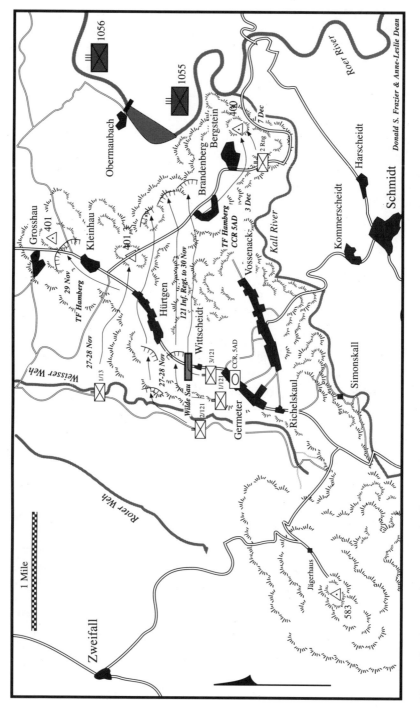

Map 4. The Capture of Hürtgen, Kleinhau, and the Brandenberg-Bergstein Ridge, 21 November–7 December 1944

1056

1055

Obermaubach

Roer River

Brandenberg
Bergstein
400
7 Dec
2 Rng
400
3 Dec
TF Hamberg
CCR 5AD
Vossenack
Kall River
Harscheidt
Kommerscheidt
Schmidt

Grosshau
401
Kleinhau
401
29 Nov
TF Hamberg
27-28 Nov
1/13
Hürtgen
121 Inf. Regt. to 30 Nov
27-28 Nov
Wilde Sau
Wittscheidt
3/121
1/121
CCR. 5AD
2/121
Germeter
Richelskaul
Simonskall

Weisser Weh

Roter Weh

Zweifall

1 Mile

Jägerhaus
583

Donald S. Frazier & Anne-Leslie Dean

through the forest to gain Roer crossing sites south of Düren—the original objectives of September. En route, the division was to capture the northern section of the Simmerath-Düren road where it passed through Hürtgen, Kleinhau, Grosshau, and Gey. The 4th Division's requirement to secure the flank of the 1st Division while at the same time clearing a large part of the forest led General Barton to place Col. Richard G. McKee's 8th Infantry on a narrow front just east of Schevenhütte. This left the 22d Infantry (Col. Charles T. Lanham) responsible for a three-mile front, one much too wide for a regiment operating in forested terrain. Because Kleinhau and Grosshau were initial objectives for this regiment, Barton ordered Lanham to concentrate two battalions in the northern half of his regiment's zone of attack. This would ease problems with command and control and would put more troops against key objectives, but it would also give the regiment a dangerously exposed flank. It would also be difficult for it to establish contact with Colonel Luckett's 12th Infantry to the south, which would renew its attack in the Weisser Weh Valley.[3]

The 104th Infantry Division went into the line on the VII Corps left. This division would push through the Stolberg Corridor while maintaining contact with the Ninth Army's XIX Corps on the left and the 1st Infantry Division on the right. The 104th would take the northern reaches of the Eschweiler urban area west of the Inde River and seize crossings over the Inde near the town of Pier.[4] Because most of the 104th Division's sector lay north of the Inde, its activities are not discussed in this book.

GERMAN UNITS FACING THE FIRST ARMY

The senior commanders in Army Group B knew they stood little chance of regaining the ground lost to date in the Aachen-Hürtgen area. The Germans would have to limit offensive actions to local counterattacks intended to prevent the Americans from pushing through the woods and reaching the Roer and Düren. Field Marshal Model and his commanders expected an attack in mid-November. Indeed, the intelligence reports suggested little other than an imminent American move. But the Germans did not think the Americans would commit a sizable force to the center of the forest when the most important objectives were the dams in the south and the Roer plain in the north.[5]

Generalmajor (as of 1 November) Engel, commander of the recently redesignated 12th Volksgrenadier Division, thought the Americans would try to seize Merode and Langerwehe in preparation for an attack south against the Schwammenauel Dam.[6] General der Infanterie Friedrich J. M. Köchling, General Schack's replacement as commander of the LXXXI Corps, also did not believe the Americans would make their main effort in the forest. "A push possibly south and north of the forest . . . would have brought the German troops fighting in the Hürtgen Forest into the danger of being locked up," he said.[7]

Köchling thought the Americans would instead aim for the Roer plain. He assembled a small reserve and had the troops build a second defense line about a thousand yards behind the main defenses. About a third of the available troops occupied the first line, and the remainder remained in the more protected positions in the rear.[8]

Two field armies shared responsibility for the defense. On 15 November, General der Infanterie Gustav von Zangen's 15th Army (XII SS and LXXXI Corps, with the army group reserve XLVII Corps) replaced the 5th Panzer Army. The LXXXI Corps' 12th Volksgrenadier and 3d Panzergrenadier Divisions faced the VII Corps north of the Hürtgen Forest. The 47th Volksgrenadier Division would relieve the 12th Division, slated for participation in the Ardennes offensive, on 18 November.[9] Köchling appears to have been reluctant to commit the new division, and he probably did not think he would need to as long as the Americans made their main effort well north of the forest. However, the events of 16 November changed his plans.

There were parts of four infantry divisions and one panzer division (LXXIV Corps) in the sector opposite the 4th Division and the neighboring V Corps: the 275th, 272d, and 89th Infantry Divisions and the 116th Panzer Division.[10] The 275th Division's 985th Infantry Regiment, with the XVIII Luftwaffe Fortress Battalion, the remainder of the 275th Fusilier Battalion, and two infantry battalions, held Grosshau and part of the salient in the Weisser Weh Valley. A collection of miscellaneous engineer, police, and infantry battalions held the area southwest of Hürtgen to the boundary with the 89th Division north of Vossenack. General Schmidt also had nine battalions of artillery, 23 antitank guns, and 21 tracked assault guns. He later recalled, "The spirit of the troops was surprisingly good. . . . [They had held] in spite of all the inclement weather, the exhaustion, poor clothing and equipment, . . . but the division was at the end of its strength."[11]

The 89th Division's 1055th Regiment held the area around Vossenack. The 1056th Regiment's sector followed the line of the Kall River south to the boundary with the neighboring 272d Division. The 116th Panzer Division served as a mobile reserve for the LXXXI Corps.[12]

OPERATION QUEEN

The artillery preparation for the First Army attack would begin at H-Hour minus 60 minutes and continue for over an hour. In addition, the combined air staffs of First Army and 12th Army Group devised, at Bradley's request, an air support plan called Operation Queen, the ETO's largest air attack in support of ground troops. This was not a close air support attack. To prevent the high number of friendly fire casualties that had occurred during Operation Cobra the previous summer, and to avoid making the ground impassable, the bomb line was far to the rear of the front-line German positions. Few of the attacking troops would see any direct results of Queen. Prisoners from one German division later estimated casualties at less than 5 percent.[13] It is difficult to estimate the impact of the decision to move the bomb line far to the rear of the front-line positions on the outcome of the fighting and the numbers of American casualties. The dilemma for the planners of Operation Queen is obvious. They had to weigh the virtual certainty of American casualties through "short bombing" against the risk of leaving a significant number of front-line German soldiers unscathed by the air strike. The planners chose in favor of avoiding American casualties. Ironically, they may have paid the same bill in combat after 16 November.

The 8th Air Force, the RAF, the IX Bombardment Command, and additional fighter-bombers from the IX and XXIX Tactical Air Commands (TAC) participated in the operation. Maj. Gen. Elwood R. "Pete" Quesada, commander of the IX TAC, told Hodges, "Our airplanes will be there with them [the ground troops] if we have to crash land every one of them in a field."[14]

The planners of Operation Queen devised elaborate measures to indicate front-line positions to the pilots. Ground troops placed three large white panel markers paralleling the First Army left boundary. The first went in near Liège, the second panel was northeast of Aachen, and the third was about two and a half miles behind the front-line positions. Troops also placed a line of orange-colored panels a quarter mile apart and 500 yards behind the front-line positions. The RAF placed eleven low-altitude, barrage-type balloons 4,000 yards behind the front-line, perpendicular to the aircraft line of approach.[15]

Four batteries of 90mm antiaircraft guns would fire red smoke shells set to explode in a line of eight simultaneous bursts every fifteen seconds 2,000 feet below the approaching aircraft. Other precautions included an order for commanders to "immediately cause all personnel . . . to provide themselves or be provided with suitable foxholes or other dug-in cover."[16]

Because of the importance of air support, Lt. Gen. Carl Spaatz, Eisenhower's air commander, had responsibility for designating the day the attack was to begin. The first four days of the operations window, 10–13 November, brought overcast skies with intermittent rain and snow, and Eaker postponed the attack. Hodges had responsibility for designating the start date during the period 14–16 November. The weather turned colder, and prospects still looked bad on 15 November. Hodges postponed the attack, but he was determined to get it underway on the 16th—good flying weather or not.[17]

At the breakfast table on 16 November, Hodges looked out a window and joked to the army and army group staffs: "Just look at that ball of fire—that's the sun." Bradley and the rest laughed, but Hodges cautioned them not to "look at it too hard, or you'll wear it out and chase it away!"[18] The attack would begin at 12:45 P.M.

At 11:00 A.M., only broken clouds remained at 1,500 feet. Above 8,000 feet, visibility improved to two miles in a light fog.[19] Troops of the 1st Division entered their covered positions at 11:25. At 11:32 A.M., the division artillery OPs reported, "Bombers dropping their loads. So far, actually see them. Fighter-bombers bombing around [map grid] 985432. Think the heavies are out around Düren."[20]

Several bombs fell "close enough to throw shrapnel" around the positions of the 2d Battalion, 16th Infantry. Five minutes later, the 47th Infantry reported, "Last bombing came in close. Clouded over with smoke. Can't tell exactly what's happening. None of it was short."[21] The 16th Infantry reported being attacked by friendly fighters. "No one was hurt except one man who hurt himself when diving into a hole."[22]

There were few casualties from friendly fire. In all, the 8th Air Force used 1,204 heavy bombers to drop 4,120 tons of fragmentation bombs, with a loss of four planes over Langerwehe, Eschweiler, and Weisweiler. More than a thousand RAF heavy bombers dropped 5,437 tons of bombs on Düren, Heinsberg, and Jülich, with excellent results. The bombs leveled the center of Düren and damaged the railroad marshaling yards. Craters and debris blocked every road leading to the city. Little remained of Jülich. In photos of Dürwiss, located a few miles northeast of Aachen, it was difficult to determine where some of the buildings once stood.[23] The devastation resembled that sustained by cities such as Nürnberg, Hamburg, and Dresden, with the difference that the devastation wrought by Operation Queen occurred in one day.[24]

The next phase in the battle for the Hürtgen Forest and Roer dams began officially at 12:45 P.M., 16 November 1944. It would be every bit as grueling as those fought by the 9th and 28th Divisions—but it was on a much larger scale.

The following statement by a member of Company E, 16th Infantry, sums up the fight at the foxhole level: "The two weeks which followed are acknowledged by almost everyone to be the roughest battle of all, next to the beach on D-Day. It was the drive through the Hürtgen Forest. . . . The sun never shone through the trees, and the men were without overcoats and blankets for the first three days and nights in the cold, wet woods. . . . There was no rest or warmth, and casualties mounted."[25]

8
The Battles in the North

A few days before the beginning of the First Army's November attack, Hitler bestowed the designation "Volksgrenadier" on the 12th Infantry Division. Generalmajor Engel, the division commander, told his troops, "The Führer wants to express thanks and admiration [for] the extraordinary fighting qualities and accomplishments" of the division since September. Engel added that "just as we have upheld our proud history, we shall know how to conduct ourselves in the future. With pride and joy we learn that the excellent reputation of our division has reached [Berlin]. We pledge to uphold this honor in the future!"[1] After 16 November, any GI who fought near Gressenich or Hamich would have taken Engel's exhortations very seriously.

The 47th Infantry had remained with VII Corps when the 9th Division went to V Corps for rest and refit after the first battle for Schmidt in October. Now, for the first time since September, the 47th Infantry, attached to the 1st Division, was about to break free of the wooded confines of the Schevenhütte area and head north into the Stolberg Corridor.

Not long after the roar of the heavy bombers had subsided at midday on 16 November, a TOT (Time on Target—the fires of several different artillery units synchronized to hit a target simultaneously) fired by five battalions of artillery slammed into the village of Gressenich, located less than two miles west of Schevenhütte. The simultaneous explosions of rounds fired by some 60 cannon was a prelude to the attack of the 1st Battalion (Lt. Col. James D. Allgood), 47th Infantry. But the dazed members of a battalion of Oberst Wilhelm Osterhold's 48th Grenadier Regiment who survived the TOT reacted quickly. They poured fire into the formations of olive-drab-clad riflemen as they rushed from the woods opposite the town.

Allgood's men had a toehold in the south edge of Gressenich by the early afternoon, but a house-to-house fight raged for several hours. The Germans withdrew only after they recognized that progress by the 3d Armored Division to the north and the 16th Infantry to the east would cut them off from the rest of their regiment. The Americans spent the rest of the day and night clearing the burned and shell-battered buildings. The Germans lost a key position blocking entry into the Stolberg Corridor, but their defense cost the Americans a day they did not want to waste.[2]

Success was much more elusive a mile away at Hamich, another farming village located along the fringe of the forest. Hamich was the objective of the 1st Battalion, 16th Infantry (Lt. Col. Edmund F. Driscoll).[3] The defenders of Hamich itself were the 14th Company, 48th Grenadier Regiment. The Regiment's 5th Company occupied the woods in front of the Americans. Lieutenant John B. Beach, leader of the 1st Platoon, Company C, remembered being told to go forward "regardless of casualties. . . . If we were hit by artillery shells, we should leave our casualties where they lay, and keep on moving." Medics would attend to the wounded. Beach also remembered, "When we finally came face to face with [the Germans] where they had dug themselves in, the fighting became bitter and personal." The Germans allowed the Americans to come close to their positions before they opened fire. Not long after Company C moved out, fire from a log bunker began to rip into Beach's platoon. Beach, who carried a Thompson submachine gun, joined another soldier using rifle grenades against the German position. The Germans surrendered.[4]

Unfortunately for the Americans, such local success meant little in the larger picture of getting to Hamich. The combination of enemy resistance and the shattered forest had caused the usual disorganization and losses, despite the best actions of squad and platoon leaders. The attack of the 1st Battalion, 16th Infantry, was now a matter of soldiers in twos and threes trying only to survive.

It took hours for the battalion to work past the first line of German defenses, and there is some doubt whether the Americans even penetrated the main German line, though there are accounts of a few 1st Battalion soldiers reaching Hamich. "There were dead bodies all over the place," remembered Beach.[5]

Lt. James H. Wood's 2d Platoon, Company C, meanwhile, had suffered very high casualties (losing at least 30 of the approximately 40 men with which it had set out on the 16th) and had only 6 unwounded men when it was hit by a counterattack. The platoon sergeant, T.Sgt. Jake W. Lindsay, was one of the wounded who had remained with Wood. Lindsay's Medal of Honor citation reports that he drove off the attack with well-aimed fire. A few minutes after this, he saw some Germans setting

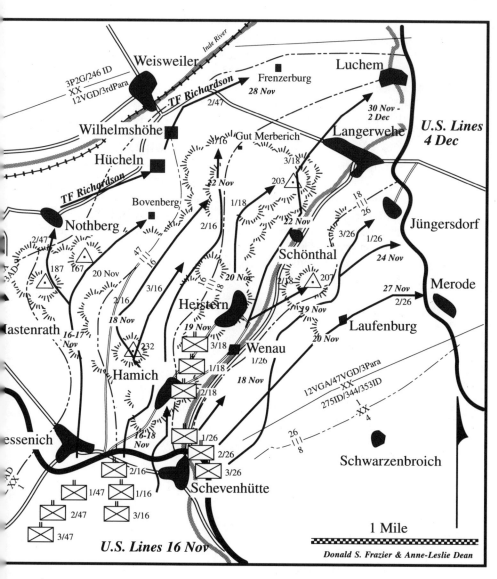

1st Infantry Division, November–December 1944

Donald S. Frazier & Anne-Leslie Dean

up a machine gun in the same location where he had earlier destroyed two machine guns. He fixed his bayonet, ran 50 yards across open ground, and took the German position. Lindsay later received the Medal of Honor before a joint session of Congress. He was the 100th infantrymen of the war to receive the award.[6]

Colonel Driscoll wanted Companies A and C to carry the attack into Hamich, but by the time they were ready to do so, it was getting late in the day, and the Germans had already begun local counterattacks. These attacks probably were not well coordinated, but they did prevent Driscoll's battalion from reorganizing. Even if a few men were in Hamich, the battalion was unable to reinforce them. It also could not disengage and consolidate into better, more defensible positions in the woods. The German artillery fire had also cost the attached Company A, 745th Tank Battalion, two tanks, and several more had bogged down along the muddy trails and had not reached the infantry.[7]

That night, after Colonel Gibb ordered Driscoll to continue the attack the next day (17 November), Driscoll visited the rifle companies to make a personal assessment of the situation. He came away convinced that it would be impossible for his battalion to take Hamich without assistance. Company A had lost about 60 men, and Companies B and C had lost nearly 100 men each. Driscoll later told Gibb's S-3, "After checking C and B Cos. the situation doesn't look too good. . . . The enemy are within 20 feet [of Company C]. The enemy has just stopped, and were not driven off. I was up there myself so I know what the situation is. . . . B Co. had practically a platoon wiped out there."[8]

Then, shortly after midnight (16–17 November), another enemy counterattack came close to punching a hole through the weakly held line of foxholes. Driscoll asked Gibb, "Send me some more litter bearers"; they were unable to keep up with the flow of casualties.[9]

Several men had to remain where they had fallen earlier in the day. "We are using the Germans' half-track . . . [to] evacuate the wounded," he added later.[10]

Later in the morning intense artillery, small-arms, and direct fire led Gibb to tell Hubner that the men were "taking a terrific pounding."

"Keep shoving and wiggling. Either we are going to break or the Boche is going to break. I am not going to bother you. Go whenever you can," Hubner replied.[11]

This remained Driscoll's intent until about 15 minutes later, when he received a message telling him to "take assigned objective at once."[12]

Of course, this was easier said than accomplished. For example, three of the battalion's supporting light tanks got lost late on 16 November and still had not reached the infantry as late as 8:49 P.M. on the 17th.[13]

These events prompted Gibb to change his original plan for the 1st

Battalion to take Hamich, even though the battalion finally gained some tank and TD support soon afterward. Hubner ordered the 3d Battalion (Lt. Col. Charles T. Horner, Jr.) to move on the village. The 2d Battalion would take Hill 232, and the 1st Battalion would hold in place.[14]

The 48th Grenadier Regiment grudgingly gave up Hamich under the steady pressure of the 3d Battalion's attack, which began on the morning of 18 November. The Germans withdrew from one building to the next by using tunnels connecting the basements. It was common for the Americans to own the upper floors and the Germans to hold the cellars of even the demolished stores and homes. The 3d Battalion that afternoon reported sharing Hamich with enemy tanks and a half dozen artillery pieces.[15] The Americans and Germans dug in opposite one another, with only a narrow street between them.[16]

Not long after Colonel Horner finally reported the town secure, about 9:25 P.M. on 18 November, some 200 Germans supported by several armored vehicles hit the two rifle companies in the town (K and L, 3d Battalion).[17] The executive officer of Company K, 1st Lt. Karl Wolf, remembered: "I received a radio message that a German tank had penetrated the platoon positions and was on its way back to our [CP]. I made our personnel keep quiet and extinguish all lights for fear that the tankers might put a round in our cellar [the location of the CP]. After about 15 minutes we heard an explosion and saw flames and then a German officer came running down the steps screaming."

A bazooka man from Company K had entered the upper floor of a house opposite Wolf's CP and fired on the tank. The German officer had been severely burned and evidently was the only survivor of the tank crew.[18]

Hamich was by then little more than a pile of debris. "The situation up in Hamich is not too good. . . . People are screaming for bazooka ammunition and bazookas," reported Horner.[19]

And Company I, which was still outside Hamich, was "ready to crack. . . . The people will have to be held [by the hand]. . . . Two officers [from Company I] are here [the 3d Battalion CP], and they [medics] are giving them morphine."[20]

"We can't get food in or the wounded out," reported the battalion commander.[21]

Hamich was rough: by daylight on 19 November, Company A had about 100 men remaining; Companies B and C were at platoon strength, and Company I had about 90 survivors. Medical personnel had evacuated at least 491 men for battle and nonbattle injuries such as exposure and trench foot. Between 120 and 125 men had been killed in action. "I am hurt for leaders," reported Gibb.[22] Leaders by this time meant any trained soldier of any rank who had enough experience to train replacements.

The battle for Hamich took place within only half a square mile. A few hundred well-protected defenders decimated much of the fighting strength of the 16th Infantry Regiment in a period of about 48 hours. Here, as much as anywhere else during the first days of the November attack, was an indication that there would be no easy victory in the northern reaches of the Hürtgen Forest.

THE CAPTURE OF HILL 232

The fight for Hamich was still raging on the afternoon of 18 November when the 2d Battalion's Company F (7 officers and 175 enlisted men), reinforced with a platoon each of light and medium tanks and a platoon of TDs, assaulted Hill 232 (= the Hamich Ridge). This fight is a good example of what could happen when the conditions were right for the Americans to follow their combined arms doctrine.

The company commander, Capt. John G. W. Finke, was talking with Lieutenant Colonel Driscoll in a damaged house near Hamich when a 15-battalion TOT smothered the hill's defenders, the 12th Fusilier Battalion. Driscoll told Finke that he had his battalion's "fire support and its sympathy."

The attack began on time and without incident. The M4 tanks lumbered from the woods near Hamich, stopped briefly to let the infantry dismount, and then started to follow them. Minutes later, however, one tank stopped without orders and began to lob shell after shell into some buildings on the hillside. The tank then stopped firing and remained in place, though there was no return fire from the hill. Captain Finke thought the attack was falling apart. He was about to run to the tank when a lieutenant arrived to inform him that the assault infantry platoon had moved in the wrong direction and was now in some buildings outside Hamich rather than approaching the ridge as it should have been doing. Just as Finke turned his attention to this incident, the commander of the nearest tank opened his hatch. Finke tried without success to yell over the noise of the artillery. He even tried throwing rocks at the tank. Aiming too high, he bounced a rock off the tanker's helmet and sent him back into the turret. The tank commander then evidently realized that he was not under fire. He reappeared, saw Finke, and jumped to the ground. They resolved the problem and the attack continued.

The tanks moved to within about 200 yards of the base of the hill to cover Company F with fire. This helped the infantry secure Hill 232 that afternoon at a cost of five men killed and five wounded. Company E followed a short time later. The GIs found several dead and wounded enemy, and those still alive appeared to be in shock from the pounding of the artillery. The riflemen hustled the Germans from the hill and began to dig in.

That night, German shells fell with uncanny accuracy among the Americans, catching a rifle platoon in the open as they completed digging in. Another shelling caught Company G when it reached the hill a few hours later.[23] The Americans now held the highest ground in the area; the Germans wanted it back.

GERMAN REACTIONS THROUGH THE NIGHT OF 18–19 NOVEMBER

To meet the latest threat in the Hürtgen Forest, General von Zangen, the commander of the 15th Army, late on 16 November canceled the planned withdrawal of the 12th Volksgrenadier Division and made plans to use its scheduled replacement, the 47th Volksgrenadier Division (recently arrived from Denmark), as a reserve for LXXXI Corps. He evidently did not direct an immediate counterattack, planning instead to do that later. But this was not a strong enough response for Field Marshal Model. He believed the resistance to the enemy attack north and east of Aachen warranted more effort, and he directed the 47th Volksgrenadier Division to enter the line east of Gressenich and take responsibility for the Schevenhütte-Eschweiler sector. This allowed Model to concentrate his forces against what he believed was the main American effort—the attack of the Ninth U.S. Army.[24] He put the 47th Volksgrenadier Division in the southeast sector because he did not want to commit the new division against the Ninth Army.

The division commander made plans to retake both Hamich and Hill 232 before daylight on 19 November. A kampfgruppe from the 116th Panzer Division would support. Only a few days before, he had ordered: "All guns will fire to the last shell, and once the last shell is expended, the gun crews will fight as infantry. Only when there is no longer ammunition for the infantry weapons will an order be given to destroy the guns. Even if such an order is given, an investigation to determine if it was necessary will be conducted. If it is found that the order was not absolutely required, appropriate action will be taken against the responsible persons."[25]

Though the Germans had expected the attack, they still had to work at scraping together enough men to reinforce the existing defenses and replace casualties. There were not enough troops to make large-scale counterattacks, though the men available did allow for local efforts such as those at Hamich and Hill 232 (described below). The key to success for Field Marshal Model was to delay the First Army and hold the Simmerath-Düren road.

About 5:30 on the morning of 19 November, a company of the 47th Volksgrenadier Division's 104th Grenadier Regiment managed to slip to within a few yards of the American foxholes on Hill 232. At a prearranged signal, they showered grenades on the Americans and then rushed the hilltop positions. Hand-to-hand fighting began immediately. Automatic weapons blazed in the early morning darkness. A few Germans managed to pour into a gap between two platoons of Company F, 16th Infantry. It was "a deadly affair of darkness with grenades coming out of nowhere . . . and fire being poured in all directions by both sides." Foxholes changed hands again and again. The victor was often the first soldier to throw a grenade or thrust a bayonet into another form in the darkness. Soldiers stumbled into the craters of the earlier artillery shelling; the muzzles of small arms flashed.[26] The battle continued for hours, until daylight revealed that the Americans had kept the key to the southern reaches of the Stolberg Corridor.

The other half of the 47th Volksgrenadier Division's two-pronged thrust fell apart. This was the attack on Hamich described above. The German lieutenant in charge of this column became confused in the darkness, took the wrong road outside of Hamich, and accidentally ran into positions occupied by the survivors of the 1st Battalion, 16th Infantry. The Americans opened fire, and the lieutenant, who was unaware of the actual strength of the defense, ordered his men to withdraw and use another route. This road led directly into Hamich, and it did not take the lieutenant long to realize that he had made another serious mistake. He tried but failed to get his men turned around. A few minutes later, the 16th Infantry reported, "The attack has reached a climax. Tanks are in the center of the town, estimate enemy strength of ten tanks and 200 infantry."[27]

The Americans then resorted to their perennial ace in the hole. The Germans never had a chance against the 15 battalions (180 tubes) of artillery that pounded Hamich a few minutes later. The confused lieutenant was the only prisoner taken by the Americans.[28]

The 16th Infantry later continued its efforts to widen the division's sector by driving to the north and northeast. The 3d Battalion pushed through the corridor formed by the Hamich-Heistern road on the right and the Bovenberger Forest on the left, and by 23 November it was in control of a piece of high ground topped by a castle called the Rösslershof, located south of the Aachen-Düren railroad. The 3d Battalion later moved to an assembly area near Heistern where it went into regimental reserve until December.

"A lot of my older veterans cracked under the strain of the Hürtgen Forest," said Lieutenant Colonel Horner, the battalion commander.[29]

The 16th Infantry spent three weeks in and near the Hürtgen Forest. The regiment ended the battle on east bank of the Inde River near Luchem—more than two miles from the Roer River. Its next major fight would be during the Ardennes counteroffensive.

HILLS 167 AND 187 AND BOVENBERG

With Gressenich secure, the 1st Battalion, 47th Infantry (Allgood), next moved on Hills 167 and 187, located near Nothberg. Germans on the hills could observe movement by the 104th Division to the north, the 3d Armored Division in the central part of the Stolberg Corridor, and the 1st Division in the lower reaches of the corridor. The resolute defense of these hills further delayed the 1st Division's fight to clear the eastern part of the Stolberg Corridor and the 104th Division's push along the Inde River. This led Collins to order the massing of 20 battalions of corps and division artillery against Hill 187.

The artillery "killed all the Krauts on the hill, except a few who came out screaming and moaning; they were more than tired of the war at that point. . . . It just literally made the ground bounce," said Allgood. The Americans did not occupy Hill 187 until 22 November—and not long after (and not surprisingly), the Germans also evacuated Hill 167. The 1st Battalion, 47th Infantry, withdrew from the area eight days later.[30]

On 20 November, the 3d Battalion, 47th Infantry (Lt. Col. Donald C. Clayman), meanwhile faced the task of clearing a small patch of woods between Hill 232 and Nothberg. This area was a thorn in the side of the units moving on Nothberg and Wilhelmshöhe, and its capture would aid the attack then underway on Hills 167 and 187.

Colonel Clayman's battalion passed through the hard-won positions on Hill 232 and on the morning of 20 November headed for the Bovenberger woods. By 10:00 A.M. elements of Company K were well inside the woods and progress had been deceptively easy. When the commander of Company K stopped to radio a progress report to Clayman, several surprised German soldiers stood nearby and watched him go about his work. He and his radio man soon found themselves in a firefight with the confused Germans, who melted into the forest without disrupting the pace of the American attack.[31]

Lieutenant Chester H. Jordan of Company K remembered that he was "walking through open woods and just walked smack-dab into the Krauts. One of my BAR men fell almost immediately, and I grabbed his gun, gave the ammo to my runner, and started shooting up the woods. . . . I shot up Germans, trees, bushes, and anything that looked like it might hold a Kraut. . . . Artillery shells started falling all around. There was nothing to get under so I lay down next to a small fir tree. I was lying on my back looking at the tree tops and praying."[32]

Company K surged ahead on the heels of the Germans. But the artillery and mortar fire had picked up and the GIs stopped to reorganize. Then, a column of German infantry appeared at the rear of Company K. The Americans reacted quickly and took several prisoners, who informed them that they were some of the same soldiers who had first spotted Company K when the commander stopped to radio Colonel Clayman.

The Germans, meanwhile, had successfully delayed Company L, which was now out of direct contact with Company K. It was late afternoon before the GIs had reestablished contact, and Colonel Clayman decided to halt the attack. He did send a patrol to contact elements of the nearby 16th Infantry, but the Germans drove the patrol back. Later that night, when the battalion's ammunition and pioneer platoon swept the battalion's supply route for mines, they used mess kits to cover the mines. It was easy to see the metal mess kits in the darkness, and it was too dangerous to dig out the mines.

The attack resumed on the morning of the 21st, and the battalion progressed as far as the edge of the woods, where the riflemen encountered a dairy surrounded by thick stone walls. The Germans brought down artillery and small-arms fire from three directions. Grazing fire from automatic weapons located in cellars hit several GIs. Soldiers on the upper floor of one building simply dropped their grenades on the Americans. The Germans cut off one platoon in a stand of trees, and when the Americans evacuated the area under cover of a smoke screen, only six men remained unwounded. They dragged out as many survivors as possible.

The Americans could not bypass the dairy. There were several outbuildings dotting a cleared meadow cut by a narrow stream. A barbed wire fence covered by thick brush also blocked the area.

The supporting tanks withdrew and left the infantrymen thinking that "the entire weight of the German Artillery Corps was massed on their small patch of Bovenberger woods." Colonel Smythe ordered the attacking companies to withdraw. But the woods offered no safety, because "practically every round coming in was a tree burst from which there was no cover." GIs were in the woods, trapped in the meadow and in the stream bed, and probably hugging the walls of the dairy as well.

The commanders of Companies I and L decided that the best bet was to get to the buildings. At the time the fire from there was not nearly the threat the tree bursts were. But the men were reluctant to reenter the open ground, and in Company L only a few men were firing their rifles. A few tried to move out, but the Germans opened up with their machine guns, which had been temporarily silent. Some of these men did reach the wall.

The commander of Company I signaled a tank for support, but he found this tank was already knocked out. German armor had by now entered the battle. A few tanks or assault guns were evidently firing from Hill 167 or 187. Others were firing from the railroad embankment behind the dairy.

The 1st Division artillery refused to fire in response to Clayman's requests, on the grounds that the targets were too close to the 16th Infantry's positions near Heistern. It was about noon.

Company L had fewer than 40 men left, and the executive officer was now in command. He could not find the artillery observer, and the mortar observer was dead. He called for tank support, but the tank platoon leader was "completely shaken and incoherent. When Colonel Clayman ordered him to take his tanks down to the farm again, the officer became hysterical." The platoon leader was wounded a few minutes later.

Soon afterward the battalion executive officer arrived with a group of cooks and clerks who would evacuate the wounded that night. The casualties for the day were 20 officers and 335 men killed, wounded, or missing.

Colonel Smythe ordered Clayman to withdraw the remnants of his companies. Smythe decided the answer to the problem of the Bovenberg dairy lay in firepower. A rifle company moved through the 104th Division's zone near Nothberg to seal off the dairy from reinforcement. The 47th Infantry then received the assistance of 8-inch guns from corps artillery. Twenty-six hits from the big shells were enough to convince the Germans to evacuate the dairy.

A major reason for the German resistance at the Bovenberg dairy was, according to one officer, poor coordination between the 47th Infantry and the 1st Division. On 21 November, the day the Americans encountered the dairy, the division (with the attached 47th Infantry) was supposed to have made a coordinated attack at 8:00 A.M. However, the 16th Infantry did not attack, and apparently no one informed Smythe that this was the case. His regiment moved as scheduled, but without the 16th Infantry on its right flank. Had the 16th Infantry attacked and threatened Heistern, the Germans could not have placed such heavy fire on the 3d Battalion, 47th Infantry. Another problem was coordination between the attached tank platoon and Clayman's battalion. The tank platoon had never before operated with the 3d Battalion, 47th Infantry. This no doubt led to a lack of confidence between the tankers and the infantrymen. Also, the thick woods prevented the riflemen from properly protecting their flanks.[33]

The Bovenberg woods and the dairy are one example of the hard fighting throughout the northern fringe of the Hürtgen Forest. An even more interesting example follows.

HUCHELN AND THE FRENZERBURG CASTLE

Because the 104th Division's fight went easier than that of the 1st Division, late on 22 November, Collins changed the VII Corps plan. The

Timberwolf Division would continue the attack across the Roer as soon as it had cleared the river's west bank. The 1st Division (with the 47th Infantry) would now seize the Langerwehe-Merode-Schlich line.[34] To assist the 104th, Collins would use CCA, 3d Armored Division, reinforced by infantry, to take Hucheln, Wilhelmshöhe, and the 104th Division's Inde River crossing sites.

Operating nearby the 104th Division in the area of Nothberg and the Inde River was Maj. Lewis E. Maness's 2d Battalion, 47th Infantry, which entered Nothberg on 23 November. The route of attack toward Hucheln concerned Maness. Railroad tracks 500 yards apart canalized the route and would force the men to move across an open beet field. Enemy observers on a nearby slag pile would see every move the battalion made. Maness had no aerial photos, and patrols were unable to determine the exact location or strength of the enemy defenses between the towns. He had to rely on his best guess as to where the enemy might be, and Colonel Smythe told him to halt the attack if enemy resistance became too difficult to overcome. As Maness noted, however, "you can't dig in and get protection on an open field."[35]

Things did not go as Maness had planned. Supporting artillery fire fell 400 yards long and inflicted little damage on the enemy. Maness had his battalion's 81mm mortars fire high-explosive and smoke ammunition to cover the infantry, but the Germans were well protected in their system of zigzag trenches, and the first burst of machine-gun fire killed five men in Company E. The tanks were by that point too far behind the infantry to support the attack with their machine guns, though they did use cannon fire against suspected positions. The enemy artillery fire disabled radios, and Maness, watching the attack from a house in Nothberg, for a time had no way to contact his companies. He called the attack off. Another attack the next morning also failed to seize Hucheln.[36]

TF Richardson (Lt. Col. Walter B. Richardson), composed primarily of CCA's 3d Battalion, 32d Armored Regiment, received the mission to reinforce the attack. It moved to Nothberg late in the morning of 24 November. During a renewed attack that afternoon, several tanks bogged down in the muddy fields, and antitank fire disabled another tank. Mines finally stopped the tanks altogether, and engineers had to be brought in to clear a path before the tanks could continue. Companies E and F, 47th Infantry, finally seized Hucheln late in the day from elements of the 12th Division's 27th and 89th Grenadier Regiments.[37]

Wilhelmshöhe fell the next day, but the tanks once again had trouble in the muddy fields along the Weisweiler-Langerwehe road (Highway B-264).[38] Maness ordered Company E to bypass the enemy positions and move on the Frenzerburg, a castle estate reminiscent of a Middle Ages fortification, which blocked the flat, open approach in the 47th Infan-

Company E, 47th Infantry, and tanks of TF Richardson attack near Nothberg, 25 November 1944. (Courtesy National Archives, #111–SC–334947)

try's zone of attack toward the Roer south of Julich, about 3½ miles away. "The brass were on me to get moving," he said.[39] (Postwar construction claimed the remains of most of the estate. All that remains are the outbuildings—today the area is the site of a farmhouse.)

German fire battered the Americans almost as soon as they moved out, and within minutes, Company E suffered 10 men killed and 15 wounded. The 35 survivors withdrew to their original positions.[40]

On 26 November Colonel Smythe reinforced the 2d Battalion with the 3d Battalion's Company K (now with 1st Lt. William L. McWaters in command) and had Maness send it northeast along the Aachen-Jülich railroad cut to protect the 2d Battalion's left during the attack on the Frenzerburg. Two rifle platoons from Company F mounted tanks and moved toward the Frenzerburg. Company E and two TDs remained at Wilhelmshöhe as a reserve. (The 1st Battalion occupied a blocking position a few hundred yards northwest of Langerwehe to prevent the enemy from escaping.)

German antitank fire knocked out two M4s before they advanced even a hundred yards. The infantry scrambled for cover and returned to the LD under intense enemy fire. The plan began to fall apart. Company K meanwhile was acting under its original orders and continued to move toward the railroad cut under heavy shelling.[41]

"When we got down to the fields we found they were planted in sugar beets. Between the beet fields and the rail line was a deep, wide drainage ditch filled with small trees, brushes, weeds, and some water," recalled Chester Jordan. He and McWaters were looking for cover for the company when they noticed a nearby stand of woods that appeared to surround the Frenzerburg. With nowhere else to escape the murderous fire, Jordan and several of the surviving riflemen ran to the trees. From there, they would head for the Frenzerburg.

According to Jordan, running across the beet fields was like "running on loosely packed bowling balls."[42] Company K took several prisoners at the woods.

The sequence of events from here becomes confusing, but probably developed as follows. It was not in the original plan for Company K to assault the Frenzerburg, but that was what was happening. About a company's worth of defenders from the 89th Grenadier Regiment were between Company K and the castle.[43] So far, they had not discovered the Americans, but they soon would, and they had no safe route of withdrawal. McWaters believed the men had no choice but to get to the relative safety of the castle's outbuildings. He ordered Jordan's men to rush the castle.[44]

Maness meanwhile was with his S-3 NCO, using a high-powered artillery telescope to observe the attack. They spotted a German artillery observer in a castle window. Maness had a supporting TD fire on the window. According to Maness, "This was the end of artillery fire on the approaches to Frenzerburg."[45]

McWaters and the rest of the company remained in the woods near the castle while Jordan's platoon jumped a hedge near the trees and overran another group of Germans. The Americans shot two Germans and dragged the wounded of both sides to the castle. At the outbuildings, the Americans found that a stone gatehouse and a water-filled moat about 20 feet wide separated them from the castle itself. They took the prisoners to a cellar and left them under guard.

Jordan saw that the only way to enter the castle was through a heavy oak gate facing the courtyard. He told Pfc. Carl V. Sheridan to fire his bazooka at the gate. If the gate fell, Sheridan was to wait for the rest of the platoon.[46] Sheridan ran from cover toward a nearby stone wall, but his ammunition bearer fell wounded. As Sheridan ran to pick up a few bazooka rockets, enemy soldiers in an upper floor window spotted him and threw down grenades at him. The grenades missed, and Sheridan fired two bazooka rockets at the gate. After firing his last rocket and seeing that the gate did not fall, Sheridan jumped up and yelled to the rest of the men, "Come on, let's get 'em!" He sprinted ahead, only to fall mortally wounded a few feet from the gate. Sheridan was awarded a posthumous Medal of Honor.[47]

The Germans counterattacked and cornered a squad of Jordan's men. They surrendered when a German pointed a panzerfaust at them. The Germans then released the prisoners captured at the hedge.[48]

The American troops remaining in the outbuildings amounted to no more than an outpost with no chance of rescue unless they received reinforcement. They had no artillery support because no one outside of the Frenzerburg was sure of their precise location. The situation was in doubt throughout the late afternoon.

Help came about dusk when Maness brought up four tanks and Companies E and F. To avoid losses from a frontal assault during daylight, Maness had waited until late in the day to send the tanks against the castle. Of the three that tried to enter the grounds, one bogged in the mud, and another sustained hits from antitank fire. The third tank wandered into the moat.

Maness ordered the reinforcing companies to move against the western approaches of the castle. But maneuver room was limited, and the Americans could not prevent German reinforcements from entering the area.[49]

Late on the 26th about 60 German paratroopers from the 15th Engineer Battalion, 9th Parachute Regiment, received orders to reinforce the defenders of the castle. Early the next morning, the leader of the engineers, a former Luftwaffe pilot grounded because his unit had no fuel, met an army officer who told him the Americans had already passed the Frenzerburg. He objected to the use of his engineers as infantry, but his regiment backed the orders he received from the army officer. "I gave my orders. Widely spread out, my company advanced in the direction of Frenzerburg, firing to all sides."[50] The engineer officer, Oberleutnant Ludwig Havinghorst, ran with the German version of a bazooka into a large hall in the castle. As he was about to fire, an American tank put a round into the room, blasting plaster around the Germans. Havinghorst and three of his men ran into another room and positioned the bazooka to fire. "We carefully took aim," he remembered, "a damp report of the anti-tank weapon, followed by a hollow boom signalled that the Sherman had received a killing blow." The crew escaped.[52]

Maness believed that his men had spent enough time, effort, and lives to take the castle. He decided to burn out the remaining Germans. He obtained two 155mm self-propelled guns from corps artillery and had them brought within direct-fire range of the castle. He also had his heavy weapons company fire white phosphorous shells on the German positions. "This worked fine," he recalled, "and we set the castle ablaze."[53] Some of the Company K riflemen remaining there had to tunnel their way out to avoid some Germans covering a door. The fighting continued until about 3:00 P.M., when a truce to evacuate the dead and wounded interrupted the struggle.

Havinghorst remembered the incident. He recalled meeting an American officer who spoke fluent German. The American told Havinghorst that he had been born in Nürnberg and had emigrated to the United States in 1935. He told Havinghorst that he was not fighting Germans, but rather their Nazi system. He offered the Germans excellent treatment if they surrendered and gave the German a pack of Chesterfield cigarettes. He did not induce Havinghorst and his men into surrender, though Havinghorst offered the American a shot of schnapps. The American replied that his men would storm the German positions. Havinghorst countered by telling the American the engineers would have a "delightful reception" waiting for them when the battle resumed. Not a shot was fired for several minutes, and possibly for as long as two hours.

The Germans used the truce to evacuate the castle.

During the morning of 28 November, Company G entered the castle and found that the Germans had withdrawn a few hundred yards to new positions. The 30 or so survivors of Company K also withdrew, though Companies F and G were involved in heavy fighting for two more days. The battles of Hucheln and the Frenzerburg Castle cost the 2d Battalion, 47th Infantry (plus Company K), some 200 men wounded or killed.[54] The Americans were still 3 miles from the Roer.

The 47th Infantry Regiment's experience with the Hürtgen Forest ended temporarily, three months after it had first entered Schevenhütte. During that period the regiment had gained only about 5½ miles. The regiment would return to the area in early 1945 and take part in the final fight for the Urft and Schwammenauel Dams.

THE FIGHT FOR THE WEHE CREEK VALLEY

By 19 November it was apparent to Hodges and Collins that the attack would not achieve a decisive rupture of the German line, and Collins did not hesitate to let Hubner know that he was dissatisfied with the progress of the 1st Division. The fight at Hamich had taken far longer than anyone had anticipated. Even Gressenich was costly in both time and lives. Hill 232 fell to a coordinated tank-infantry assault, but the Germans had managed to gather enough men to launch a strong counterattack against it.

Hubner decided he had to commit his reserve regiment, the 18th Infantry, in the once-picturesque Wehe Creek Valley to put more power behind the attack. He could no longer afford to keep a quarter of his force in reserve. The regiment originally designated to take Langerwehe and Jüngersdorf, the 26th Infantry, gained the new objective of Merode in addition to Jüngersdorf.[55]

The 3d Battalion, 18th Infantry, attacked the village of Wenau, located in the shadow of the steep hills marking the northeastern limits of the Hürtgen Forest, on 19 November. Wenau controlled the parallel Schevenhütte-Langerwehe and Hamich-Heistern roads. Company I put a roadblock on the south edge of Wenau, but a confusing situation later developed when the battalion incorrectly reported that Wenau was clear of the enemy. The Germans, in fact, held most of the town. Nearly an hour passed before correct word of the situation reached Colonel Smith, and it was early the next morning (20 November) before the Americans were actually in control of the settlement.[56]

The German resistance picked up on the 20th. Hubner told Smith not to hesitate using artillery and to "shove off [to Heistern] as fast as you can. [If you] run into resistance, bypass it and go around."[57]

Hubner's orders led to a two-company frontal attack (Companies K and I supported by a platoon of tanks) that by dusk put the Americans into the center of Heistern.[58] The commander of the 104th Grenadier Regiment, 47th Volksgrenadier Division, then launched a two-company counterattack at 3:30 A.M. on the 21st. Five battalions of American artillery broke up the attack. The Americans took more than 100 prisoners, including the German regimental commander, and killed an estimated 250 of the enemy.[59]

General Hubner remained impatient. Prodded by Collins, Hubner told Smith to commit the 2d Battalion against Langerwehe. But Hill 207 stood in the battalion's way. The casualties in attacking it were heavy, and the casualties of both sides littered its slopes when Company E finally cleared it on 23 November.[60] Warren B. Eames, who at the time was a nineteen-year-old first scout in Company G, later recalled the fighting in the area: "Nights in the foxholes were spent lying in seeping water. In the mornings, iced over, no less. . . . Along with the water, earthworms would be wiggling all around the edge of the foxhole when you awoke in the morning. They began to weigh on my mind. I had the feeling that I might be killed and they would eat my body, so I methodically smashed them with my rifle butt. Mornings came when I was immersed in water up to my chest, all frozen on top, and I would have to break the ice to get out of my hole."[61]

The Germans on 23 November shifted their defenses south of Langerwehe to a line between Hill 203 and Schönthal. At the same time the attack on Hill 207 was underway, the 18th Infantry's 1st Battalion engaged in a bloody attack to take Hill 203, the northern tip of a rectangular

To
Major Ed Miller
With kind
regards,
Warren B. Eames

photo:
Paris –
Summer
1945

Warren B. Eames in Paris during the summer of 1945. Eames, a 19-year-old scout in Company G, 18th Infantry, fought in the vicinity of Hill 207 and the Wehe Creek valley. (Courtesy W. Eames)

patch of woods about 1,500 yards by 750 yards in size, which dominated the southwestern approaches to Langerwehe. On 22 November, the battalion was on a northwest-southeast line about halfway through the woods south of the hill, operating without close armor support. Here, the GIs hit the enemy's main line of resistance, a series of log-covered bunkers covered by automatic weapons, wire, and riflemen in trenches nearby. Company C sustained some 50 casualties and withdrew 150 yards to reorganize. Company A's attack also failed, and Smith alerted a company from the 3d Battalion to assist. That evening, two battalions of artillery kept up a wall of fire to prevent the Germans from forming for a counterattack.[62]

Company B, now supported by M4 tanks, by late afternoon of 23 November had managed to inch its way closer to the settlement of Kämmerbusch, located on the hill, where a mortar observer spotted a German antitank gun just as the lead tank neared a house. The observer tried to get the tank to halt, but he could not make himself heard over the noise of artillery and small-arms fire. Two quick shots from the antitank gun knocked out the tank. A few riflemen reached positions a hundred yards from the top of Hill 203 not long afterward. (An officer also reported reaching the crest of the hill but leaving when he found himself alone.) But the stalemate continued until the 27th. A reinforcing battalion of young German paratroopers might have spelled disaster for the Americans, but U.S. artillery decimated the Germans while they were en route to the hill.[63]

A report noted that most of the prisoners were "17; a fair number are only 16. Only a few have started to smoke, and one razor would satisfy all the prisoners." An interrogator asked a prisoner if his parents had given them permission to enlist. "No, I was drafted," was the reply.[64]

Today, the wooded summit of Hill 203 is topped by a religious shrine. The only other evidence of the bitter fight for the hill and the surrounding woods are the remains of trenches and foxholes. But in 1944, Hill 203 cost the 18th Infantry an estimated 400 men. The regiment cleared Langerwehe on 28 November and finally left the forest in early December. Yet the trials of the 16th and 18th Infantry Regiments were nothing like those of the 26th Infantry to the south, at the village of Merode.

MERODE

At the same time the 47th and 16th Infantry Regiments were inching their way northeast through the Stolberg Corridor and the 18th Infantry was moving slowly on Langerwehe, the 26th Infantry Regiment (Col. John F. R. Seitz) struggled within the forest against an enemy who had been relatively untouched by the Operation Queen bombardment. The regiment's initial objectives were a group of wooded hills located in the northwestern fringe of the forest. The hills dominated the Schevenhütte-Langerwehe road and could threaten the attack of the 18th Infantry. The division's (and regiment's) zone of attack was so narrow that the first priority was for the lead 2d Battalion to gain enough maneuver space to allow the commitment of additional troops. The regiment failed the first day to gain that space, and when Hubner asked Seitz if he could get another battalion underway, Seitz replied, "There is no point in getting it forward, as there is no place to commit it." Though Seitz was determined to "kick [the enemy line] through" on 17 November, the regiment made no progress.[65] An officer from the 3d Battalion said the situation was "pretty sticky," with "lots of fire, mortar, and high velocity coming in."[66] The 1st Battalion finally entered the battle on 18 November. The Germans fell back a few yards, but the outpost positions of both sides remained less than 100 yards apart throughout the night.[67]

The difficulty of fighting in the Hürtgen Forest held no weight with higher headquarters. Review of S-3 journals indicates a natural impatience on the part of the division and corps commanders for progress, but also perhaps a lack of understanding of the problems faced by the troops fighting deep in the woods. General Hubner told Seitz's S-3 that General Collins was "raising heck" because of the regiment's slow progress. "Got to take a few chances and get going," said Hubner.[68]

The 3d Battalion (Lt. Col. John T. Corley) passed through the 2d Battalion on 19 November to take Hill 272. The next day, the Americans took the remains of a Middle Ages castle called the Laufenburg.[69] (Today the restored estate boasts a restaurant.)

The same day, elements of the 115th Regiment, 47th Volksgrenadier Division, brought the 2d Battalion's advance to a halt. An estimated 20 enemy soldiers fell in front of a BAR gunner in Company G, Pfc. Roland Littlejohn, who kept firing his weapon, even though he was wounded in the stomach.[70] Pfc. Francis X. McGraw, a machine gunner in Company H, remained at his position during an hour-long German artillery barrage. When enemy infantry approached, McGraw poured fire into their ranks and eventually halted the attack. When the Germans brought up a machine gun, McGraw stood up in his foxhole and fired, knocking out the weapon. The concussion from a German shell knocked the BAR from McGraw's grasp, but he picked the weapon up and silenced a second machine gun. He also made several trips to get ammunition before he was hit by the enemy fire. He then returned to his foxhole and resumed firing. After another shell sprayed mud and debris on the weapon, McGraw cleaned it and drove off another attack. Then, after running out of ammunition, he killed one German and wounded another with his carbine before a burst of machine pistol fire cut him down. McGraw was awarded a posthumous Medal of Honor.[71]

If the infantrymen believed the battle was drawing to a close because they were near the edge of the Hürtgen Forest, they were wrong. On 22 November, German fire pinned down two companies near the eastern edge of the forest. "Jerry reacted violently to our attack east," Seitz told Col. Richard G. McKee, commander of the 8th Infantry. Elements of the 1st Battalion, 26th Infantry, remained within hand-grenade range of the German positions for the next two days.

Help with the mission of maintaining contact with the 8th Infantry came from elements of the 4th Cavalry Group. This allowed Seitz to direct the 2d Battalion against Merode and the 3d against Jüngersdorf, which fell on 28 November.[72]

"What do you think of taking a crack at Merode?" Hubner asked Seitz on the evening of 28 November. When Seitz replied, "I think we can do it," Hubner promised all necessary artillery support. The attack would begin at 10:00 A.M., 29 November.[73] The results, however, demonstrated what could happen when the Germans cut off American infantry from its supporting arms.

Lieutenant Colonel Daniel, commander of the 2d Battalion, used two companies, E and F, for the attack. Sidney Miller, a platoon leader in Company F, recalled fighting an enemy who "came popping out of bunkers, foxholes, [and] culverts, and it became a situation like you were hunting rabbits back in the States." In an earlier incident, his men shot and wounded two German soldiers walking in the woods to the front of the platoon positions. Because no one dared venture from a foxhole after dark, the Germans remained where they fell. The next morning the Americans found both men dead. They had attempted to bandage one another's wounds.

Miller noted that "it was extremely difficult to keep the men's morale up, as it seemed like we would never get out of the forest. We had one [soldier] shoot himself in the foot on purpose . . . in the height of despair."

With an eye out for snipers, the squad leaders got their men moving shortly before 10:00 A.M. on 29 November. German artillery caused several casualties. The company commander told Miller to take charge of the disorganized 2d and 3d Platoons and get them into the town.[74]

Just before 2:00 P.M., the commander of Company F called for artillery fire east of town. An air strike was ineffective, and Lieutenant Colonel Daniel reported to Seitz that the planes might have hit American positions. By this time, supporting tanks had arrived. No sooner did two of them reach the edge of Merode, however, than German fire knocked one out. Two others halted for a moment, but their commanders, concerned with the German fire and lack of infantry support, backed away. An artillery shell hit one of the tanks, and it blocked the trail. Calls for a recovery vehicle brought no results until the next morning, and it was too late by then to do any good. At any rate, the M32 recovery vehicle did not remove the tank. When an NCO requested additional tanks from the 1st Battalion, an officer from the regimental operations section overturned the request on the grounds that the 2d Battalion had not adequately used the tanks already assigned to it.[75] As daylight faded on the 29th, Lieutenant Colonel Daniel was desperate to reinforce the men in Merode, but he could do little in the face of the constant artillery fire. Seitz reported that the rifle companies "hit a lot of artillery. Pretty heavy stuff. Coming from quite a range."[76]

The German fire formed a wall between the Americans in Merode and those in the woods trying to reach them. "We had no support that we knew of, but I thought that surely as long as we had occupied a part of the village of Merode that additional support would be sent," recalled Miller.[77] Unfortunately, the only road into Merode was so choked with mud and disabled equipment that not even a jeep could reach the edge of the forest, much less the town.

A counterattack ended any hope that the Americans could hold Merode. Tanks prowled the narrow streets, hunting down the Americans. Lieutenant Miller asked an NCO what he thought about the situation. There appeared to be little they could do, he replied.[78]

About midnight, the battalion CP received a last, weak transmission from Merode. A few minutes later, Seitz reported to Hubner, "This is probably as tight a position as we have been in since the operation started. I am afraid the men in the town are going to take a beating, but there is nothing we can do about it. Our casualties were heavy today and are still coming in."[79]

A patrol attempting to contact the men in Merode drew heavy machine-gun and mortar fire. The regiment's S-3 told division that it would take a battalion to rescue Companies E and F. Hubner alerted the 16th Infantry to prepare a battalion for "possible movement and possible employment."[80]

The regimental S-3 responded, "Can't say that we need a battalion right now. What is in town may be annihilated now."[81]

The sounds of the battle in Merode quieted after daylight on 30 November, but the German artillery fire never lessened in intensity. Four men from the 2d Battalion who escaped reported seeing only seven other Americans alive.

Seitz reported, "We are trying to get communication with the town and are combing the woods to see if we can find anyone else from 'E' or 'F' Co. I feel that 'F' Co. is still in there."

"Can't imagine a whole company getting gobbled up," said Hubner.[82]

On 30 November the 26th Infantry listed 165 men missing in action.

Not until the second week of December did Merode fall to the 9th Division.

The 1st Battalion, 26th Infantry, also had its share of problems. The operations officer, Capt. Thomas W. Anderson, reported being told at 3:00 A.M. on 29 November that the commander of Company B could not find two of its platoons. "In the rain and darkness, the enemy had simply moved in and appropriated the men's positions," said Anderson. He added, "In this type of fighting, high ground did not make any difference, and there wasn't much sense striving for it, because when you got it, you usually couldn't see much for the trees anyhow."[83]

On 2 December, the 1st Infantry Division received word to withdraw from the forest. The 9th Division was the replacement. The 1st Infantry Division and the attached 47th Infantry suffered an estimated 3,993 battle casualties during the November attack. The 26th Infantry alone sustained 1,479 casualties, including 163 killed and 261 missing in action. The 18th Infantry suffered 899 casualties for the month of November, most of them after the 16th.

The division fell far short of its objectives. It took three weeks of hard fighting to gain about four miles of muddy forest and emerge on the Roer plain—three miles short of the Roer River. The final positions were on a line running roughly from Luchem to Langerwehe, then along the edge of the forest near Merode, then south for about two miles.[84]

Colonel Smith called the Hürtgen Forest "a month . . . that had no equal as far as intensity of fighting, physical hardships and heavy going was concerned."[85]

Marlin Brockette, a platoon leader in Company C, 26th Infantry, called the Hürtgen Forest "the worst, toughest, and most miserable of all that was my experience [in the war]."[86]

The veteran 1st Infantry Division had joined the procession of units being decimated in the dreary, shell-torn forest. Its experiences demonstrate that when the infantryman was able to fight in good terrain and with adequate support, things generally went well. Even a veteran unit—and this label in time became a misnomer because the losses were so high ("veteran" came to mean one who had survived a few hours of combat)—had problems if it fought for extended periods in the forest. By the time the "veterans" had reached places like Hill 203 and Merode, they did not have the strength to go on.

At the same time the events described in this chapter were unfolding, the factors noted above also combined to halt the 4th Division. It began the attack at a disadvantage—namely, its 12th Infantry had suffered substantial losses early in November near Germeter. The 4th Infantry Division had been part of V Corps for several weeks and had spent

Capt. Don Warner, commander of Company A, 22d Infantry Regiment. Warner
started the November attack as a platoon leader and ended it as a company commander. This photo was made in Luxembourg on 16 December, the first day of the
Battle of the Bulge. (Courtesy D. Warner)

September and October in eastern Belgium and the Schnee Eifel hills north of Prüm, Germany. It became part of Collins's VII Corps during the first week of November and went into the line west of Schevenhütte.

"We were there to be killed, and the sooner you realized it, the better. Lord knows, they were dropping like flies," recalled Donald Warner, then a rifle company commander in the 4th Division.[87] This division would complete the destruction of the 275th Infantry Division and capture a few miles of forest. It would also fail to gain the Roer.

9

Stalemate in the Center

The Germans were ready for Col. Richard G. McKee's 8th Infantry Regiment. The regiment jumped off on 16 November from positions in the Wehe Creek Valley and was to seize Roer crossings near Düren. The first significant objective was a ruined monastery called Gut Schwarzenbroich, located deep in the forest, about a mile and a half east of Schevenhüte. Between the Americans and the monastery, however, was a two-mile-thick belt of enemy defenses on the high ground east of the Wehe Creek.[1] There would be no chance of envelopment here—the regiment would have to conduct a frontal assault. This led the division commander, Major General Barton, to decide against a pre-attack artillery bombardment in favor of trying for surprise.

The 2d Battalion (Lt. Col. Langdon A. Jackson, Jr.), with Companies E and F abreast, pushed through very intense artillery fire and then reached an immense obstacle constructed from logs and railroad ties. Layer upon layer of concertina wire stood to the front of the barrier. Dug-in automatic weapons guarded the approaches, and the forest floor was filled with antipersonnel mines. One soldier finally succeeded in placing a bangalore torpedo next to the wire, but the charge was too wet to explode.[2]

First Lt. Bernard J. Ray, a platoon leader in Company F, went back to his battalion's ammunition supply point for more blasting caps. Meanwhile, the Ammunition and Pioneer Platoon that night made one breach in the obstacle, but on the morning of 17 November, machine-gun fire stopped three attempts by the riflemen to get through the breach. Lieutenant Ray, now back with the blasting caps, evidently decided that while the Germans could fire on a single gap in the wire, they might not be able to cover a second. He volunteered to try to blow another gap. Ray placed some blasting caps in his pockets, wrapped a length of primer cord around his body, and ran alone toward the wire. The Germans singled him out for special attention. Mortar shells crashed down around him, yet he somehow managed to place a charge under the wire. He was ready to set the charge off when he was severely wounded by a shell fragment. Ray perhaps thought the wound was mortal. At any rate, he connected the primer cord still wrapped around his body to the blasting caps he took from his pocket. His stunned fellow soldiers watched him set off the charge, which did blow another gap. Ray sacrificed his life, but the fire still prevented the 2d Battalion from exploiting the breach. He was awarded a posthumous Medal of Honor.[3]

Companies F and G withdrew to reorganize (the 2d Battalion suffered nearly 200 casualties on 16 and 17 November). Colonel McKee next ordered the 1st Battalion, with attached light and medium tanks and TDs, to take over the attack the next morning. It made little progress.[4]

The 8th Infantry made no significant progress on the 18th. It renewed operations on the 19th. The story of Company C provides a good example of the fighting. As Company C (Capt. Robert D. Moore), supported by tanks, moved through the obstacle, the riflemen could hear the muffled crack of exploding antipersonnel mines set off by the tracks. They followed close behind the tanks, walking in the muddy ruts made by the tracks. The first stages of the 1st Battalion's attack went well, because the log obstacle marked the outer shell of General Schmidt's defenses. The GIs picked their way across several hundred yards of fallen trees and waterlogged ground until a tank hit a mine cased in wood or plastic that the engineer's mine detectors did not find. Not long after this, Moore's men reached a clearing that was about 250 yards square and covered with the limbs of trees that had evidently been removed by the Germans to use as barriers elsewhere. No one by that time had seen a German, but Moore was convinced they were nearby. He ordered patrols to reconnoiter the flanks of the clearing and had the attached light tanks move up.

Just as he prepared to radio the battalion commander, "the air became saturated with small-arms and high-angle fire," which Moore later described as "sudden, overwhelming . . . devastating." Two platoon leaders and several other men were wounded. "There was no cover anywhere from the rain of death," he added. It took the company a half hour to reorganize. Fortunately for Company C, a P-47 arrived and strafed the enemy position. The company picked itself up and moved again until it hit yet another shrewdly constructed wood and wire obstacle. This one prevented the light tanks from accompanying the riflemen. Moore sent the 15-ton tanks back to the woods. His riflemen were now alone—just the way the Germans wanted them.

"The positions which the Germans had prepared were extremely well dug-in emplacements for machine guns. To the rear of them there were

Pfc. Maurice Berzon, S.Sgt. Bernard Spurr, S.Sgt. Harold Lessler, 8th Infantry Regiment, in the forest northeast of Schevenhütte, 18 November 1944. (Courtesy National Archives, #111–SC–196619)

communication trenches and fire trenches. These emplacements had been dug along the north and east sides of the field. Back in the clearing behind these defensive positions we found troop shelters that were partially dug-in log cabins covered with three layers of logs and mud and that furnished very substantial protection even against fire and were quite well camouflaged and concealed from observation," said Moore.

The company had to dig in and reorganize before it could go further. Moore had to adjust his plan to account for the loss of the tanks. He had lost 2 officers and 63 enlisted men out of an original strength that morning of 5 officers and 165 men. The enemy artillery fire was picking up, shell after shell slamming into the nearly unrecognizable forest. The wounded who could not walk or who were suffering from shock lay where they had fallen. Searchers listened in the darkness for their moans. Even if a medic could get to one of the wounded men, his chances of survival still were not necessarily good. The injured man faced a torturous journey of about 1,800 yards, and about a third of that distance required the litter party to pass through known or suspected minefields.

The paths had not been marked, and the only safe route was through the tracks made earlier in the day by the tanks. This situation made it equally difficult to bring up supplies.

The artillery and mortar fire picked up again at daylight (20 November). Moore recalled that "by 8:30 A.M., seldom did a period as long as five minutes go by without a concentration falling on the clearing. . . . It began to appear as if the enemy had some supernatural being directing its fire, since it was so accurate."

The fire killed or wounded all the scouts, and the lead platoon sustained several casualties. Moore, now the only officer remaining in the company, later wrote, "For the remainder of the day the longest period that we were not under fire did not exceed 20 minutes. We dug in around 1530. We were so close to the enemy that we were unable to construct overhead shelters, for if any man stuck himself up high enough to cut logs . . . the Jerries would fire small arms at him."

Including replacements, only 45 enlisted men now were able to fight. Moore disbanded his 60mm mortar section and used the crewmen as riflemen. The company headquarters section by then consisted of only the first sergeant and a radio operator. One rifle platoon had 17 men and another had 16, less than half their full strength. The foxholes started filling with water almost as soon as the men tried to dig them. They were forced to spend the night without even the cover of a bedroll. Finally, on 21 November, the company withdrew with a strength of one officer and 35 men.[5] It had failed to achieve its objective, though it did gain about 1800 yards. The company lost 148 men. Its table of organization strength was 187 enlisted men and 6 officers.

The 2d Battalion, 8th Infantry, meanwhile was also facing the special hell of woods fighting. The battalion commander, Maj. George L. Mabry, Jr., knew that to get the inexperienced replacements to move at all, he would have to lead them by example. The same day, while forward with a rifle company, he single-handedly located a path through a minefield covered by automatic weapons. He later disconnected explosives attached to a wire obstacle. Then he cut a path through the wire. Mabry next captured three Germans and led an assault against three log bunkers. At one, he clubbed an enemy soldier with the butt of his rifle and bayoneted another. His scouts assisted him in a hand-to-hand fight with eight others. Mabry and some riflemen then took six prisoners at another bunker. He finished the day leading the battalion under fire across 300 yards of open ground. For such valor he was awarded the Medal of Honor.[6]

On 22 November, the 8th Infantry was still a thousand yards short of Gut Schwarzenbroich. In other words, in six days of fighting, the regiment had managed to gain only about a mile.

THE 22D INFANTRY REGIMENT

The experiences of the 22d Infantry are among the best documented of any regiment that fought in the Hürtgen Forest. The commander of the regiment was Col. Charles T. ("Buck") Lanham. He was a 42-year-old native of Washington, D.C., who had a reputation as a writer and poet. Before the war, he contributed frequently to the *Infantry Journal,* and his writings caught the attention of senior officers like George C. Marshall. Lanham also served on the War Department General Staff. He performed well in that capacity, but he wanted to spend time with troops in combat. He took command of the 22d Infantry in July 1944.

Lanham was the regiment's third commander since D-Day. When he arrived at the CP, the thin, graying colonel told one young officer, "I am Colonel Charles T. Lanham. I have just assumed command of this regiment, and I want you to know that if you ever yield one foot of ground without my direct order, I will court-martial you."[7]

On the morning of 28 July, Lanham was poring over operations maps in his CP when the S-3 announced the arrival of a war correspondent who would remain with the regiment until after the Hürtgen Forest. The visitor needed a shave, and he sported a worn uniform without insignia. The newcomer announced in a quiet tone, "I am a correspondent for *Collier's.* My name is Hemingway."[8] Following is the story of the 22d Infantry in the Hürtgen Forest.

Lanham planned to attack using battalions in column—the 2d, followed by the 1st and the 3d. The 2d Battalion would cross the LD (Roter Weh Creek) and drop a company off to secure the north flank of the regiment. The 1st Battalion would then pass through the 2d Battalion and continue to a wooded hill called Rabenheck, or "Raven's Hedge," Ridge. The regiment would then enter the Weisser Weh Valley and cut the important north-south road, designated MSR W, and head for Grosshau.

Companies E and G led with platoons in column at 12:45 P.M. on 16 November. The battalion did well, gaining about 600 yards before it met resistance from the German outpost line. Company G overran the Germans and reached the Rabenheck, but Company E ran into a German position that was protected with wire and mines. The Germans first delayed the company and then stopped firing altogether. The Americans continued, but they did not realize that they had only bypassed, not silenced, the German position, leaving several enemy soldiers between them and the remainder of the battalion. The GIs had no idea the Germans were in their rear until the regiment could get no supplies to Company E. They eventually took the enemy position from the rear.[9]

The 1st Battalion had meanwhile struck the flank of an enemy battalion and had to dig in. Security was the first order of business after closing into night positions, and Lanham ordered the Company A's 1st Platoon to fill the 600-yard-wide gap separating the 1st and 2d Battalions. The platoon leader placed his men 10–15 yards apart, but he ran out of men with 300 yards of ground still open to infiltration.

Later that evening, while only about 50 yards from their own foxholes, GIs on patrol literally stumbled across some sleeping German soldiers. The Germans were as surprised as the Americans, and the patrol drew no fire. On a second trip, the GIs found a German patrol thrashing about in the darkness. They let the enemy approach to within about 25 yards before they opened fire. One man stated that an infantryman hit a German soldier in the chest with a rifle grenade. The rest of the enemy fled without further contact. On one German soldier, the men found detailed maps of the 2d Battalion's positions.[10]

17–18 NOVEMBER

Friday, 17 November, dawned with promise for the regiment, but within a few hours, the situation changed for the worse and never improved for Colonel Lanham's beleaguered infantrymen. The 2d Battalion was unable to lead the regiment because of the supply problems noted above, and Lanham decided to send the 1st Battalion across the Rabenheck. He wanted it to swing to the east (on the left of 2d Battalion) and cut Road W. Lanham reminded the commander of the 1st Battalion, Maj. Hubert L. Drake, that the entire regiment would depend on how well his battalion performed.[11]

The Germans were well prepared. Their shelling began at daylight, disrupted communications, delayed the start of the attack, and fatally wounded Drake. The executive officer, Capt. Clifford M. Henley, took temporary command. According to Henley, "Everything was in a muddle. B Company had about 50 casualties at the top of a slope, and it was difficult to hand-carry [them] in litters to the forward aid station 1,000 yards away."

Lanham ordered Maj. George Goforth, the battalion executive officer, to take command of the battalion. Lanham told Goforth "not to get in the same hole as Captain Henley. We [have] lost too many officers already. . . ." Lanham later ordered, "Have [1st Battalion] fight like the devil on its present direction, [and not] turn off until the situation is settled."[12]

Four light tanks from the attached 70th Tank Battalion were available, and though Lanham was reluctant to commit the tanks before the regiment had taken Road W, Henley had to have help. Unfortunately, two of the tanks hit mines on the way to the 1st Battalion, and it was some time before tanks would be of much assistance to the regiment. The problem of the unimproved trails and firebreaks was made worse because of the design of the light and medium tanks. The design had originated before the war, when engineer bridges then in use could accommodate only relatively narrow vehicles. The resulting ground pressure was so great, however, that the tanks tended to mire very easily.

The GIs, meanwhile, were passing through "woods . . . filled with dead Krauts."[13] On the north side of the road leading across the Rabenheck, Company A took one strongpoint consisting of six log-covered bunkers connected by shallow communications trenches. Company B, without flank protection, drove another 300 yards to a point near the Weisser Weh Creek, but when Company A proved unable to join it, Goforth withdrew it to better positions. The Germans followed and dug in only 200 yards away. The battalion could not cross the Weisser Weh and Road W.[14] That day, the regiment, including the reserve 3d Battalion, lost two battalion commanders, several company officers, and over a hundred enlisted men killed, wounded, and missing.[15]

The 1st Battalion finally got across the Weisser Weh on 18 November. Companies A and C crossed the creek first, while Company B distracted the Germans with small-arms and automatic weapons fire. During a firefight along a firebreak a few dozen yards west of the Weisser Weh, a soldier fired a rifle grenade that blew the head off a German and killed another with its concussion. After crossing the stream, one soldier said, "I never dried out, and neither did most of the rest of us for the next two weeks. The heavy mud caused most of the boys to throw away their galoshes, and the constant rain and sleet made us that much colder and wetter. Not so bad when you keep moving during the day, but not so nice when you sleep with your sopped shoes on in a foxhole which leaks."[16]

The radios were too wet to work properly, and a sergeant volunteered to return to battalion headquarters and report the crossing. Well behind his own lines, he killed a German with a grenade. Meanwhile, some distance up the east bank of the creek, Capt. William Surratt, the Company A commander, observed several Germans near the company objective. Surratt and three men from the company headquarters ambushed and killed the enemy soldiers.[17]

The 2d Battalion was also trying to get across the Weisser Weh. Machine-gun fire pinned down Company G, and Companies E and F ran into a dense antipersonnel minefield located on the reverse slope of the Rabenheck. The battalion commander, the S-3, and the communications officer were wounded. The executive officer took command and brought with him a new operations officer. Artillery fire hit the area a few minutes later, wounded the executive officer (the incoming commander), and killed the new S-3. Maj. Howard C. Blazzard, the regimental S-2, took temporary command. By the time he arrived, no original member of the battalion staff remained in action, and the attack had ground to a halt. Blazzard reorganized the battalion and led it across the Weisser Weh where it dug in before dusk.[18]

THE 22D INFANTRY HALTS ITS OPERATIONS

Colonel Lanham faced grave problems on 19 November. His three original battalion commanders had been killed or wounded. The regiment's casualties during the first 48 hours of the attack numbered over 300, including most of the company commanders and many key staff officers. The lack of adequate routes for resupply also worried Lanham. The accurate German shelling had prevented repair of a demolished bridge over the Weisser Weh, and badly needed replacements had to join hand-carry and litter parties to keep the rifle companies supplied.

The exhausted riflemen fought an unseen enemy. The first indication of contact was usually the sound of an exploding mine or of German machine guns spewing bullets through the broken trees. The regiment was operating on a 3,500-yard front with both flanks exposed. Some 3,000 yards separated the 12th Infantry from the open right flank of the 2d Battalion, 22d Infantry. On the north, 1,500 yards of trackless forest separated the 8th Infantry from the 22d Infantry.

Colonel Lanham notified Major General Barton at 7:00 A.M. on 19 November that the 22d Infantry could not meet the scheduled 8:00 A.M. start time for the 20 November attack. Barton reluctantly permitted Lanham to cease operations and use the remainder of the day to reorganize and resupply the regiment. The "enemy is fighting every inch bitterly," said Lanham. Barton replied, "Time for this engagement is growing short."[19]

General Barton's foe was Generalleutnant Hans Schmidt. His 275th Infantry Division was now little more than a kampfgruppe. Operation Queen and American artillery fire before noon on 16 November signaled the beginning of the American attack. Schmidt received the first word of ground action during the early afternoon, when the 985th Regiment reported contact with American infantry. His division held the Americans to limited gains on 16 November, but he had no reserves.

The picture brightened somewhat after Schmidt talked with General Straube. A kampfgruppe from the 116th Panzer Division would arrive soon and enter the line between the 12th Volksgrenadier and 275th Infantry Divisions. (The 116th Division had recently been released from its commitment at Schmidt.) Also, on the night of 19 November, two companies from the first regiment of the 344th Infantry Division, also en route to the forest, entered the line near Grosshau. Schmidt's elation at the reinforcements did not last long, however, because American artillery pounded the troops as they arrived. The survivors returned to the rear for reorganization. On 20 and 21 November, the rest of the 344th Division arrived and began relief of the nearly destroyed 275th Infantry Division.[20] Ironically, had the 4th Division been able to push ahead before the 344th Division arrived, it might have gained the edge of the forest. Unfortunately, the division was so weak it could not do so, and the Germans were able to complete the relief.

The 275th Infantry Division had performed admirably. It made the Americans pay a very high price for a few thousand yards of gloomy forest. On open ground a division thrown together in the manner of the 275th would have survived only a matter of days or hours against a combined armor, artillery, and infantry assault. It survived as long as it did because once in the Hürtgen Forest, the Americans sacrificed the advantages in mobility and firepower that had enabled them to reach the forest in the first place.

THE DRIVE TO GROSSHAU, 20–21 NOVEMBER

The 22d Infantry Regiment's 1st and 2d Battalions renewed their attacks on the morning of 20 November.[21] Elements of the 1st Battalion took 50 prisoners at a complex of bunkers that scouts thought was an enemy battalion CP. The 2d Battalion fought a meeting engagement, and its CP took fire from Germans bypassed by the rifle platoons.[22] Disturbing reports filtered into the regimental command post:

> [2d Battalion:] We have jumped off. . . . We are receiving mortar, MG, small-arms, and artillery fire. Making slow progress.
> [1st Battalion:] Need AT guns. [Lanham] says replacements today will be used as carrying parties [for supplies].
> [2d Battalion:] The Krauts jumped off the same time as we did. Lots of small-arms fire.
> [1st Battalion:] Advanced about 500 yards. Ran into pillbox, lots of mortars, and small arms.
> [2d Battalion:] Ran into a lot of rifle and burp-gun fire to the right of the CP.
> [22d S-3 to G-3:] The real problem is supplies and [casualty] evacuation.
> [Lanham to Barton:] Enemy not falling back. Don't think we'll be able to move tomorrow.[23]

Major Goforth reported that his lines were "pretty thin" and that if the regiment continued operations the next day, another battalion would have to attack in place of his.[24]

The same day, a bypassed German platoon that had closely watched the regimental CP for at least a full day and probably for two launched an attack that took Lanham and his staff completely by surprise. Hemingway fought beside the soldiers until the Germans melted back into the forest. "MG and mortar fire on Regt'l CP—constant mortar and artillery on Bns.—fire coming from SE. Five tanks in front of 'G' Co.," reported the S-3.[25]

At dusk, Barton told Lanham that "General Collins has used Colonel Lanham as a shining example to all the officers in his command," and "the performance of the 22d has been an inspiration to all."[26]

That day, the regiment lost 2 officers and 2 enlisted men killed, another 165 men wounded, 7 men missing, and 26 nonbattle casualties. The number killed to date was 23. There was an unusually high number of wounded (505) and other losses (77). The regiment had received 337 enlisted and no officer replacements.[27] Captain Henley later said of the period 16–21 November, "These five days so far were the roughest and bloodiest I have seen. It was a nightmare."[28]

On 22 November, after a demonstration by fire by Companies A and C, the 3d Battalion pushed 1,200 yards to reach new positions by Road X, about 600 yards from Grosshau. The Germans reacted quickly, however, and placed fire on the 3d Battalion elements outside Grosshau.[29] Scouts reported, "A lot of Krauts are seen moving about in Grosshau."

A radio message from Lanham to Barton told the story: "Blue [3d Battalion] is on its objective. Grosshau is filled with Krauts, and we are firing lots of artillery in town. White [2d Battalion] has suffered heavy losses."

The same day, the 2d Battalion had crossed Road Y and gained nearly 1,000 yards. Yet the mines were so thick on and near the road that supporting engineers refused to clear them. The commander of the 2d Battalion called for aid men and jeeps to evacuate the wounded. Lanham put 100 replacements in the line that afternoon to cover a dangerous gap in the battalion's front.[30]

The regiment continued to attack on 23 November to secure positions west of Grosshau. A few shells landed very close to the 3d Battalion CP, which was located in a concrete bunker. "We figured that this was probably registration for a shelling, so everyone climbed into his hole. When the shelling did not return, one or two of the battalion Hq. personnel started to come out of the CP but found that as soon as they popped their heads up, a machine gun started firing right over their holes," recalled the S-3. He added, "This placed all of us in a rather embarrassing position, as those inside could not leave, and no one outside could get in. Fortunately one of the Hq. wire men perceived the situation and shot two of the Jerries."[31]

There was no action on 24 November. The first assault on Grosshau, conducted in conjunction with an attack on Hürtgen by CCR, 5th Armored Division, began on 25 November. On the basis of information from the division G-2 indicating that Grosshau was lightly held, the 3d Battalion attacked across the open ground between the woods and the town; the 2d Battalion attacked from the southwest. "We practically ran ahead, assault firing as we moved," said the 3d Battalion S-3.[32]

After minefields caused delays that cost the regiment the element of surprise, German artillery and mortar fire knocked out four tanks and two TDs. The battalion fell back on the woods. The next day (26 November) the regiment conducted limited operations to clear the area west of Grosshau and prepare for a renewed attack.

THE 12TH INFANTRY RENEWS OPERATIONS

The 12th Infantry entered the November battle after having suffered a stinging defeat in the Weisser Weh Valley earlier in the month. The regiment had had only a few days in which to rest and reorganize from that action [it had made a limited attack on 13 November] before it attacked on 16 November.

One story will serve to describe the fighting. A former 2d Battalion commander identified the location and units involved. One evening, a machine gunner from Company G heard several men walking along Road W. He was about to throw a grenade when he heard an explosion. An American had lost part of a leg to a mine but lay conscious along the shoulder of the road. The wound bled very little because the explosion cauterized the arteries and veins. The Americans could not reach him because of the enemy fire; however, the Germans crawled to him; removed his personal possessions, field jacket, and helmet; and placed a booby trap under his back. The soldier remained conscious for about 70 hours—long enough to warn medics about the booby trap. Probably no one else displayed more courage during the battle in the Hürtgen Forest.[33]

The 12th Infantry had nothing but casualties to show for its efforts. The total battle and nonbattle casualties for the regiment during the period 7–21 November were 1,671. The regiment lost another 479 men through 30 November.

On 21 November, General Barton relieved Luckett; his replacement was Col. Robert H. Chance. In deference to the conditions under which the regiment fought, Luckett retained his rank and took command of another regiment. The 12th Infantry would remain in the forest for a few more days until relieved by elements of the 83d Division.[34] It went north the day after Luckett's relief to secure the zone between the 8th and 22d Infantry Regiments. Barton had intended the regiment to take Gey, but it was in no condition to do anything more than secure its own positions. It left the forest during the first week in December.

REPLACEMENTS AND COMBAT STRESS

"Being a replacement is just like being an orphan. You are away from anybody you know and feel lost and lonesome," responded a replacement soldier to a 1944 survey.[35] This book often cites the integration and training of replacements in combat units as contributing to the problem of implementing combined-arms doctrine in the Hürtgen Forest. The impact of the individual replacement on the performance of units in this battle therefore deserves some discussion.

The combat units faced a critical shortage of trained replacements. This quite naturally led to the desire to get the men to the foxholes as soon as possible after their arrival at a division. At the same time, there was a recognized need to integrate and train the replacements properly in order to help them survive their introduction to combat. Such trade-offs at the front-line units were just one of the issues facing the army's replacement system in 1944–45.

The army used a system of assigning individuals, not units, as replacements. The Replacement System, the agency responsible for the program in the ETO, was organized as a separate command under the Services of Supply (the logistic headquarters in the ETO) and supervised by the theater G-1.

The system was impersonal, and troops never developed a sense of belonging until they reached their final destination. When a soldier arrived in France, he went directly to a "reception" depot located near the port. He might stay there for anywhere between a few hours to overnight. There were no comforts there, usually just a roof and a cot. The next stop for a soldier en route to the First Army was a "stockage" depot, the 11th (which also supported Ninth Army), where he received a rifle and any missing items of equipment. He also received lectures in hygiene and might receive some additional training. The stay here varied from two days to much longer. The soldier next went to the 3d Replacement Depot, which supported the First Army, and later, to a forward battalion supporting a corps.

The soldier had a lot of time on his hands while he was in the replacement depots, and the impersonal nature of the system did little to relieve any anxieties he might have had. For example, transportation to the army depot, especially in the first few months after the invasion (to the late autumn), might be a railroad boxcar without provisions for proper sanitation. In addition, mail delivery was at best a hit-or-miss proposition while the soldier was in the "pipeline." He was left with only his own thoughts of what combat might be like. The only thing the infantry replacement had going for him (if this could in any way be considered positive) was that the urgent need for riflemen meant that they tended to move through the system a little faster than soldiers with other specialties.[36] One soldier expressed sentiments that many others no doubt shared: "I was in depots five weeks. . . . After so long a man doesn't know whether he's coming or going; he's unsettled and anxious and finally just doesn't give a good Goddamn."[37]

There is no doubt that had the system operated using units rather than individuals, the replacements would have entered combat as part of a team and with a sense of belonging. The result, instead, was often "confusion and anxiety for the individual replacement, [and] an additional hazard for the unit as a whole."[38]

For officers and NCOs retrained from another specialty, there were additional problems. These men had the responsibilities of combat leaders, but they had no training or experience. Some of the NCOs requested reduction in rank to private because they did not believe they were qualified to be in charge of men in battle. About 25 percent of the replacements assigned to the 1st Battalion, 22d Infantry, in the final stages of the regiment's fight in the Hürtgen Forest, for example, were reclassified cooks, clerks, drivers, and so forth. Many of them had just completed basic training.[39]

The sergeant major of the 121st Infantry, M.Sgt. Willard Bryan, told an interviewer after the regiment took the town of Hürtgen that the "biggest headache is that they [headquarters] send us men with high ratings who are airplane mechanics, radar operators, and cooks. Officer replacements . . . are staff men who don't know what to do in line outfits." He also noted that between 21 November and 5 December, the regiment had eleven court-martial cases involving men who refused to go to the front.[40]

An NCO in the same regiment's 3d Battalion said that "in most cases they [replacements] have had no more than 17 weeks training. . . . We try to work them in with older men and let them train them. We had no opportunity here [the Hürtgen]."[41]

From the perspective of the 4th Division staff, the heavy casualties made it "impossible to maintain the units at anything near Table of Organization strength. . . . the strength of all three regiments decreased steadily until at the end of the month, all regiments were very low in fighting strength." The division G-1 section sent as many as 650 replacements per day to the regiments. There was no way for units to integrate such numbers successfully into units while they were in the line.

When a regiment received replacements, the battalion adjutant or sergeant major led them to the company area, where a guide took them to the platoons. They traveled in groups of five "to avoid being wiped out by a few shells, to facilitate their . . . assignment, and to enable them to get into other men's foxholes if they did not have time to dig in" before dark. Officer replacements received briefings at the battalion CP before being assigned by the commander.[42]

"The U.S. bet you $10,000 you would not survive," said Don Warner, who would advance from platoon leader to commander of the 22d Infantry's Company A during the second half of November. "If a replacement lasted a day, it was fantastic," he added.[43]

Edward B. Phillips, then a platoon leader in Company H, 22d Infantry, recalls receiving replacements who were "about 18–19 years of age, straight out of basic training. This was criminal. [On one occasion], when I went out to find them in the early A.M. they were gone. I could hardly blame them."[44]

In Company I, BAR gunner Bob Moore's squad received three replacements a few minutes before it attacked on 23 November. Within minutes, the men were hugging the ground, head to foot, under artillery fire. Moore heard a man saying, "This is suicide. This is suicide." By dark, the replacements were dead or wounded. Moore remembers that later in the same action, mortar shells fell every time one of the wounded soldiers cried for help.[45]

"As tough as the regulars found the situation, it was even tougher for the inexperienced replacements. I recall two replacements sent to the 3d Platoon late one evening and given an assigned area for a foxhole and briefing of our position and mission as we knew it. Then in the night of the same evening after a heavy artillery barrage, they were heard crying and finally were returned to the company CP. I suppose we did not get the chance to know who they were," recalled former 1st Lt. Marlin Brockette of Company C, 26th Infantry.[46]

The new men who found themselves in the Hürtgen Forest in November had little time in which to learn the same survival skills as their predecessors did in September and October. They had to learn to recognize minefields. Digging in became an instinctive practice. The soldiers also received quarter-pound blocks of "plastic" C-4 explosive to use to blow a foxhole in the frozen ground. The problem of what to do with the blasting caps soon arose. If a shell fragment or enemy fire hit a blasting cap, the soldier might lose part of his body. One or two men tied the caps to the camouflage nets on their helmets with predictable results.[47] A survey made in France in August 1944 probably held true throughout the fall: common errors by new men included bunching up while under fire, talking or making noise at night, and shooting before they identified the target.[48]

Warren B. Eames, a member of the 1st Division's 18th Infantry, recalls thinking the division would hand out shoulder patches before going into action in November. Eames never received the patches: "Either they were too busy with more important things, or they figured we wouldn't last long enough in the lines to bother with it, and that proved to be the case. The whole division had turned over with replacements, it seemed, by the time they had fought their way through the forest."[49]

The main topic of conversation among the replacements, recalls Eames, was how they would react under fire. While everyone had some vague notion of how he would react, no one really knew. "It was both surprising and disconcerting to discover that our true character was a part of ourselves which we really didn't know well at all."[50]

He recalled that the men of his platoon shared three basic characteristics determined by the amount of fear they demonstrated while under fire. About 10 percent of the men appeared to lack fear other than that expected for their own safety. These few men formed the backbone of the company and were probably the ones who could best help the replacements. One even "seemed to derive real pleasure from the fighting and was constantly chuckling over the number of 'Jerries' that he had 'got' in the day's engagements."

The majority, about 80 percent, demonstrated varied reactions to combat, but their actions rarely interfered with the performance of their duty or caused a danger to others. The final 10 percent exhibited extreme fear, which caused anything from interference with the performance of duty to cowardice. Eames remembered one man in particular who had a conviction that "bad as the Germans were, we were far worse because of the fact that he was required to stay with us and fight . . . and implored our squad leader to shoot him immediately, as he would be required to do so later anyway."[51]

Combat stress is another issue that deserves some discussion. The subject relates to both new and older men. Capt. Clifford M. Henley of the 22d Infantry wrote a few days after the beginning of the November attack that "men are tired and sleepy and their nerves are about shot. Too much of anything is too much."[52]

Capt. William S. Boice, a chaplain in the same regiment, related the following incident in his postwar history of the regiment. Late on 23 November, a veteran mortar observer set out with his radio operator to take up a new position. A shell fragment killed the radio operator soon after they reached their position. The sergeant began to dig in when a machine-gun bullet tore away the handle of his shovel. He could not dig in. He spent 13 exhausting hours exposed to the artillery, counting hundreds of explosions in the immediate area. Not until 9:00 A.M. the next morning could the sergeant escape and make his way "toward the rear, eyes staring straight ahead, mind vacant, lips slightly drooling." He reached his company, and the first sergeant had him sent to the battalion aid station, where a medic "snapped his fingers a couple of times in front of the staring vacant eyes and wrote on the tag, 'Exhaustion.'" The sergeant eventually arrived at a hospital near Eupen, Belgium.[53]

Soldiers in the 121st Infantry who suffered from combat exhaustion received coffee, a shot of whiskey, and some sleeping pills. They were allowed to rest for a couple of days and then returned to the line.

"The constant pounding suffered by the older men served to condition some and weaken others, but the latter seemed to be a more general rule. Most of the men in the rifle companies agreed that it is far more trying on the nerves to sit motionless and try to get protection against artillery and mortar fire than it is to move forward in assault and be able to fire at where the enemy is known to be," said an officer. He added, "It is a wonder that the combat exhaustion figures were not higher." (Of all casualties in the 1st Battalion, 22d Infantry, 9 percent were due to exhaustion.)[54]

Lt. Col. William A. Hamberg, commander of the 5th Armored Division's 10th Tank Battalion (see chapter 12), recalled that his task force (composed of companies from his own and another battalion) had high morale before going into combat at Kleinhau. That changed after the task force had secured Bergstein. Hamberg refused to evacuate men for combat exhaustion. "The men were marched back to their units under guard, and the units were ordered to intercept future cases. This cured it as the word got around. (My surgeon was worried about repercussions, but nothing happened.)"[55]

Hamberg added, "When soldiers were slow to move under fire, the platoon sergeant would have to go around to the soldiers and get them moving. He would have to say something like, "You yellow SOB! Get out of my company! . . . Then the guy would start crying and moving to the rear. He got no sympathy until he reached a Medico [Medic] who would evacuate him. Once the word got around that no one was evacuated for CF [combat fatigue] until I or my XO had OKed it, we had no more trouble for the rest of the war."[56]

Regimental-level reports list the numbers of replacements (or, as they euphemistically came to be called, reinforcements) received each month, but they do not usually list replacements by name, thus making it impossible to determine with accuracy their survival rate. The same is true for cases of combat fatigue.

By late 1944 the army faced a serious shortage of trained replacement infantrymen. The problem in fact forced divisions to remain in the line until well after they were combat ineffective because there was no replacement division available. The army's policy of rotating units was more a system of taking them out of the line when they simply could no longer perform than it was a program of rest and retraining.[57]

The newcomers therefore faced tedious boredom in a replacement system geared more to administrative efficiency than to ensuring that men were ready to enter combat. When they arrived at the front, the men faced even more uncertainty than they had in the replacement pipeline. There was the possibility of a quick death, with little concrete prospect of relief. The units in combat were in urgent need of replacements, and there was a temptation to rush men into the line before they had received proper training.

It is difficult today to blame any one person or group of policy makers for the type of replacement system used by the army during the war. The bureaucratic inequities and impersonal nature of life in the replacement depots, however, is not justifiable. At a minimum the army should have better prepared the replacements for life at the front, whether the men arrived singly or in groups. The line units were not responsible for the conduct of training in the rear, nor for the problems with shortages of physically qualified manpower. However, they could have done a better job of integrating the new men—and commanders early on learned the hard lessons of not doing so.

Such factors as these, coupled with the inherent problems of fighting in the Hürtgen Forest, contributed to the lack of progress by VII Corps between 16 and 19 November. The 104th Division had gained less than two miles, the 1st Division and 47th Infantry held only Hamich, Hill 232, and Gressenich; and the 4th Division was still far from the open ground east of Grosshau. The poor results in the north led Hodges to send the V Corps into the attack. The mission was to help take some of the burden from Collins's corps by taking Hürtgen and Kleinhau. But if anyone entertained hopes that V Corps would be the decisive player in widening the scope of the First Army attack, such a belief proved misguided. The V Corps at best could only add more momentum to an attack already behind schedule and in danger of stalling.

10

The Capture of Hürtgen

The rested, full-strength 8th Infantry Division (Maj. Gen. Donald A. Stroh), nicknamed the Pathfinders, and CCR, 5th Armored Division, attached to the 8th Division effective at midnight on 19–20 November, received the mission of taking Hürtgen, Kleinhau, and the Brandenberg-Bergstein Ridge. This would bring the V Corps to the Roer and the southern approaches to Düren. The rest of the corps (9th (-) and 99th Infantry and the remainder of the 5th Armored Divisions) would remain available to exploit any success.[1]

Once again, the Roer dams were not stated objectives. Rather, the scope of the mission assigned to the 8th Division reflects the persistent attitude within the First Army that perhaps one more push would be enough to break through the forest and (by default) take the dams when the Germans evacuated the area.[2] An example of this attitude is contained in the V Corps field order directing the 8th Division's relief of the 28th Division. The order called for the battalion that would relieve the 1st Battalion, 109th Infantry, to be prepared to assist a CCR, 5th Armored Division, attack to secure the *entire* Hürtgen-Brandenberg area.[3] It ended up taking far more than a reinforced armored combat command.

THE V CORPS ATTACK BEGINS

General Hodges set the date of the 8th Division's attack as 21 November (at that time, the division's 13th and 28th Infantry Regiments and the attached 2d Ranger Battalion had already relieved the 28th Division in accordance with the corps' original timetable). The 8th Division's third regiment, the 121st Infantry (Col. John R. Jeter), was still in the process of moving north from Luxembourg, and it would go into the line north and west of Germeter to replace the 12th Infantry. There was no time to plan the relief properly, and ordinarily this might not have been an insurmountable problem. However, the pressure of time dictated that this relief be completed as soon as possible, much the way the 12th Infantry had replaced the 109th Infantry earlier in the month.

The original plan (as of 19 November) had called for the 121st Infantry to relieve the 28th Division's 109th Infantry by dark on 20 November. However, as Colonel Jeter later recalled, on the evening of the 19th, Stroh instructed him to move those battalions still in Luxembourg (107 road miles away) to the Germeter-Hürtgen area "at the earliest practicable time. That it was URGENT. No further explanation was afforded" (emphasis in original).[4]

That night, the assistant division commander, Brig. Gen. Charles Canham, along with Colonel Jeter and his battalion commanders and staff, attended a meeting at the 12th Infantry Regiment CP. There they learned the 8th Division would attack on 21 November to cut the Germeter-Hürtgen road near Wittscheidt and secure an LD for CCR. Jeter's hastily developed plan called for a partial envelopment of Hürtgen: the 1st Battalion would seize the woods line southwest of Hürtgen; the 2d Battalion would pass through the lines of the 12th Infantry and seize the woods line west of Hürtgen; the 3d Battalion would secure the edge of the forest south of Hürtgen. When the regiment was on line with the 22d Infantry (which was moving on Grosshau), CCR would pass through the 121st and take Hürtgen and Kleinhau. The 121st Infantry would then relieve CCR and prepare to follow the armor to the Brandenberg-Bergstein Ridge.[5]

The first problem for Jeter was assembling his separated regiment. Acting under the original plans, after daylight on 19 November, Maj. Wesley Hogan's 3d Battalion had moved to the Hürtgen Forest by truck convoy. The weather was near freezing, and most of the men rode in uncovered trucks. It was dark when the convoy halted in the Weisser Weh Valley, a few hundred yards southwest of Germeter. A grueling cross-country road march followed. The Germans detected the activity behind the American lines and "started throwing [in] mortar and arty. fire."[6] At least the battalion had time to rest before beginning the attack; this was not the case with the 2d Battalion.

This battalion was still in Luxembourg when Jeter received the change in orders. The battalion headed north late on 19 November, several hours ahead of the original schedule. Many of the GIs rode in uncovered cargo trucks. A steady rain changed first to sleet and then to snow. The convoy proceeded without anything more than maintenance halts throughout the night of 19 November and finally reached Roetgen on the afternoon of the 20th. The trucks then left the main road outside Roetgen and stopped deep within the forest. First Lt. Paul M. Boesch, a former professional wrestler from New York, and now executive officer of Company E, learned his company would conduct the passage of lines early the next morning (21 November) and make the attack as soon as possible thereafter. He also learned that the soldiers would receive a hot supper before the attack. Serving a hot meal so far forward in darkness meant that the soldiers had to pass through the serving line without using flashlights. Boesch recalled that he had no idea what the servers patiently doled into mess kits they could not see. A five-mile cross-country march to the Weisser Weh Valley was next—without any breaks or rests halts.[7]

Boesch remembered: "The rain pelted down with a fury. Several inches of sloppy mud covered the ground. The perspiration we had worked up on the march quickly dried and made us colder than ever. . . . It was a thoroughly miserable night. . . . Though we tried pulling the raincoats over our heads, this merely exposed more of our legs and feet. The coldness of the ground soon added to the other chill, so that our teeth began to chatter. . . ."[8]

Good news came before daylight. The company commander received orders to delay the relief and passage of lines until dawn. Later, in the gray early morning sky, Boesch and his men saw clearly the shattered trees, crumbled bunkers, and other debris from the battles of October and November. It was the same kind of scene the men of the 28th Division had faced a few weeks earlier—only worse. When the battalion finally reached its attack positions along Road W, deep in the canyonlike Weisser Weh Valley, the men found antipersonnel mines planted on the road, in a ditch on their left, and on the nearly vertical slopes of the hill on the right.[9]

The 21st of November dawned overcast and dreary. Round after round of corps and division artillery thundered over the heads of the weary infantrymen. Seven rifle companies attacked, and things went slowly from the start. The 1st Battalion gained only 200 yards. Artillery fire pounded Companies E and F on Road W, though a few men managed to reach a hairpin turn a few hundred yards from the LD.[10] This was a particularly difficult area. To the left of the road, there was a high, nearly vertical drop to the Weisser Weh. There was little ground in which to dig a foxhole on the steep ground on the right. German outposts dug in above the road could watch nearly every move the Americans made. There were reports of a rifle platoon and part of a weapons platoon disappearing without a trace. The men probably fell victim to a enemy reconnaissance patrol.

The 3d Battalion meanwhile pushed through the wooded, but relatively level stretch of ground near the Wilde Sau minefield. Company I fought past a line of enemy log bunkers "that extended almost without break across the entire front of the zone of advance" and was on its objective by noon. It had the distinction of being the only company in the division to reach its objective on 21 November.[11]

This was accomplished mainly through the efforts of S.Sgt. John W. Minick, who at 36 years of age was a rather elderly squad leader. When Company I moved out, Minick found a path through the mines and knocked out a German machine-gun position covering the road. A few minutes later, he single-handedly assaulted a group of bunkers and killed an estimated 20 of the enemy. Minick did not know it, but he had penetrated the outer line of the defenses between Hürtgen and Vossenack, something that the 39th and 109th Infantry Regiments had failed to do. He continued alone until he was within 30 yards of a German battalion CP. Nearby soldiers reportedly heard him shout, "Come on out! Come on out and fight!" just before hearing an explosion. Minick had stepped on a mine. He was awarded a posthumous Medal of Honor.[12]

22–23 NOVEMBER

The regiment continued to pound away at the defenses. The riflemen, usually fighting without armor and air support, demonstrated little desire to brave the thick minefields and close with the enemy. They had seen too many others die or lose limbs. There were other problems as well. Paul Boesch remembered that for some reason the Hürtgen Forest seemed to block the sixth sense for survival that an infantryman developed with experience. The men grew unable to "distinguish the various sounds of battle and recognize those that meant danger to him, but in the Hurtgen Forest we began to realize that the forest usurped this sixth sense. We [grew] slow and uncertain in our reactions. Uncertainty means delay, and sometimes the difference of a split second is all that separates life from death."[13]

No doubt such problems contributed to the losses caused by German mortar fire, mines, and artillery on 22 November. The 1st Battalion and Company L failed to make progress. Company E also ran into antipersonnel mines; Company F secured a few yards of muddy ground but withdrew because of losses. Though two squads from Company G's 2d Platoon moved unobserved up a branch of Road W, the platoon leader withdrew his men when he realized they were out of contact with the rest of the company.[14]

Thanksgiving Day, 23 November, was another day of limited progress and high casualties. Tanks could not reach Company A. Company B lost 50 yards to a counterattack. One platoon of Company G managed to cross the Weisser Weh, but enemy machine-gun fire stopped reinforcements. The riflemen had no place to escape the fire except for a ditch that turned out to be lined with antipersonnel mines. The frantic soldiers touched off the mines, and this in turn was a signal for the Germans to pour in artillery and mortar fire. The survivors fell back. According to an NCO, the company commander and another officer "just went berserk, crying and yelling." The regimental report of operations recorded that the men faced "stiff resistance with rain, mud, and fog . . . fighting was fierce with the use of hand grenades at close range."[15]

Another incident merits discussion as an example of poor decision making at higher levels. Commanders were also under orders to get a hot Thanksgiving meal to every soldier. To disengage units in close combat and withdraw them a few yards for the sake of serving a soggy turkey sandwich appears in retrospect to be a stunning failure of senior commanders to understand the conditions at the front. Yet they were determined to maintain the holiday tradition. The Company G kitchen delivered the food in insulated containers and the soldiers left their foxholes in twos and threes to line up for their food. During this process, a nearby TD fired on an enemy armored vehicle. Seconds later, the Germans shelled the Weisser Weh Valley and caught dozens of soldiers out of their foxholes. Several men lay wounded or dead, their sandwiches scattered on the wet ground. The company ceased operations for the day.[16]

The same day, Hodges, the First Army chief of staff, Collins, Gerow, and Stroh met to discuss progress of the attack. Hodges reportedly unleashed his temper on Stroh, telling him "in emphatic terms that he was not satisfied with the progress being made, that the minefields had not proved to be as much of an obstacle as people feared, and that the progress, or rather lack of it, made by the division showed lack of confidence and drive."[17]

To Hodges, this was a failure of leadership—not the failure of a plan or of the inability of his troops to fight under such conditions. Colonel Jeter replaced the commander of the 2d Battalion with Lt. Col. Henry B. Kunzig. He also relieved the 1st Battalion commander (and replaced him with the regimental executive officer) and two company commanders.[18]

2D AND 3D BATTALIONS, 24–25 NOVEMBER

Lieutenant Colonel Kunzig said the enemy mortar fire made Road W "a living hell."[19] The day after Thanksgiving opened in the 2d Battalion zone with a 30-minute-long mortar barrage that delayed the attack and killed or wounded all but one noncommissioned officer in a Company G platoon.[20] That afternoon, engineers cleared nine roadblocks protected by antitank and antipersonnel mines from the branch of Road W leading to Hürtgen.[21]

During the afternoon, Lieutenant Boesch warned a messenger not to take a shortcut on his way back to the battalion CP. The messenger ignored the warning, and a few minutes later, Boesch heard an explosion followed by a scream. Boesch reported that he heard "two more explosions. More screams. I knew instinctively what had happened. The man had set off one mine and then others as, in agony, he thrashed about."[22]

Boesch and some others tried to follow the still faintly audible moans, but they could see nothing in the approaching darkness. An engineer officer who did not believe the Germans had mined the bed of the Weisser Weh Creek sent a litter party through the cold water. When a medic strayed just a foot or two from the creekbed, part of his leg disappeared in the flash of an exploding mine. The engineer officer had him carried to an aid station. Boesch decided not to risk another soldier in the search. That afternoon, Lieutenant Colonel Kunzig ordered Boesch to take command of the 30 or so surviving riflemen in Company G.[23]

Major Hogan's 3d Battalion meanwhile was still trying to push up the Germeter-Hürtgen road and the adjacent woods. M4s from the 709th Tank Battalion pushed through the jagged, torn remains of the trees until the lead tank struck a mine. When the platoon leader dismounted to check on the damage, he lost both legs to a mine. Seconds later, a German antitank gun firing from the south edge of Hürtgen scored three hits on the disabled tank. The remaining tanks withdrew, and the infantry advance stalled once again.[24]

Major Hogan then ordered Company K to attack without tank support. Antipersonnel mines buried in the ditches along the road caused a dozen engineer casualties and 30 more losses in the rifle platoons. Hogan ordered the company commander to make another try. The attack failed, and Hogan relieved the commander.[25]

A platoon of engineers went out at dusk to clear the remaining antipersonnel mines from the shoulders of the Germeter-Hürtgen road a few yards north of Wittscheidt. More engineers went out after dark to clear antitank mines from the surface of the road. The Germans had no need to bury the mines because tree branches and other debris covered the road. Less than an hour after engineers had reported the road clear (about 10:00 P.M.), however, a mine blew a track off the recovery vehicle trying to reach the tank disabled earlier in the day. Evidently, the Germans had infiltrated the American positions and placed more mines on the road after the last platoon of engineers had completed its work. More engineers went out a few minutes before 11:00 P.M. to try once more to remove the tank, but they discovered two large craters on or near the road. The engineers worked until about 1:00 A.M. on 25 November, when they again declared the highway clear of mines. The Germans heard the Americans and opened fire. Some of the engineers sought cover—in a crater filled with antipersonnel mines.[26]

TASK FORCE BOYER

The 121st Infantry Regiment paid dearly for its gains between 21 and 24 November. At least 50 men had been killed, and nearly 600 more had been wounded. This represented nearly 20 percent of the assigned strength of the regiment and its attachments. The procession of replacements did little to help; they needed training, but many of them did not last long enough to get any. Three days after the 8th Division entered the battle, it was still over three miles from the Roer. Hürtgen, Kleinhau, Brandenberg, and Bergstein remained in German hands, and reports of enemy reinforcements made it imperative for the 8th Division and CCR to capture Hürtgen as soon as possible. When the 4th Division on 24 November reached positions from where it could help cover the flank of the 121st Infantry, Hodges approved Collins's and Gerow's plans for a coordinated attack to seize Hürtgen.[27]

Stroh and others met the same day at division headquarters, where they discussed having CCR strike Hürtgen the next morning, even though the 121st Infantry had failed to secure an adequate LD either west of Hürtgen or along the Germeter-Hürtgen road. Stroh ruled out the Weisser Weh Valley approach because of the lack of progress by his 2d Battalion. Given the requirement to move on 25 November, the only feasible route was a drive up the Germeter-Hürtgen road, through the positions of the 3d Battalion, 121st. The CCR commander, Col. Glen H. Anderson, had several concerns. He did not believe Hogan's battalion could move rapidly enough to support his tanks and armored infantry. Hundreds of mines remained on or near the road. The engineers still had to either bridge or fill craters in the area, including one on the road itself. Anderson warned Stroh that the attack would not succeed, but "the only response [from Stroh] was an order to attack" at 7:30 A.M. on 25 November.[28]

Company B, 47th Armored Infantry Battalion, part of CCR's Task Force Boyer (Lt. Col. Howard E. Boyer), reached the vicinity of Wittscheidt before daylight on 25 November. Another element of the task force, Company B, 10th Tank Battalion, had departed Roetgen at midnight. The company commander, Capt. Frank M. Pool, was originally led to believe that the road as far as the LD (near the bend in the Germeter-Hürtgen road) was clear of obstacles, though he was subsequently informed that it was not. Pool also contacted the 8th Division engineer at the 121st Infantry Regiment CP shortly after 4:00 A.M. on 25 November to determine if the crater had been spanned. The engineer reassured Pool that the crater would be spanned before the attack began.[29]

German indirect fire slammed into the American formations as soon as the first tank reached the Germeter-Hürtgen road. Lieutenant Jack A. McAuley, leader of the 2d Platoon, Company B, 10th Tank Battalion, found that the crater still had no bridge. He thought the rim of the crater might support a tank, and he radioed Pool that he was "going to try to jump the damned thing." The driver gunned the engine, but the tank hit the opposite side of the crater and rolled on its side. McAuley and his crew remained in the tank and took the Germans under fire using the tank's traversing mechanism to elevate the 75mm gun. The woods exploded with German fire. The attack stalled.[30]

Company B, 47th Armored Infantry Battalion (1st Lt. Richard S. Lewis), was also in position in the woods near the road. When Lewis arrived at Wittscheidt, he contacted Major Hogan, who gave him the locations of the 3d Battalion troops and provided a guide to get Company B through the minefields. The guide probably thought he would be able to follow cloth engineer tape through a cleared path, but a combination of rain and fire had torn the tape away. The men began to step on mines. The explosions alerted the Germans, who immediately brought down mortar and artillery fire. Lewis's men could not remain in the minefield, and they had no choice but to run toward the tanks (and the fire). Company B's 2d Platoon managed to reach the tanks, but the platoon leader was wounded twice, and the platoon lost all but one of its squad leaders. Fewer than ten men in the platoon were able to fight at the end of the day.

Captain Pool reached the scene soon after McAuley's attempt to jump the crater. Pool found that the engineers who had arrived to put a bridge across the crater were under fire and reluctant to continue work. They resumed work only after a crane operator moved forward alone to begin work, and it was noon before they completed the span. Unfortunately, the first tank to cross the crater hit a mine, and antitank fire from Hürtgen hit the tank before all five of the crew could evacuate it. Two other tanks then began to fire at the suspected location of the enemy gun to cover a third tank, which moved up to tow the tank disabled by the mine. The Germans spotted the vehicles, fired, but missed the recovery tank. The crew of the tank reacted quickly and put an enemy gun out of action. A split second later an antitank round knocked out this tank. It was nearly 2:00 P.M. before another tank reached the bend in the road. The weather had cleared enough to allow P-47s to bomb and strafe German positions around Hürtgen, but CCR's next attack failed to get past the artillery and mines.[31]

The premature commitment of CCR cost over 150 casualties and served no useful purpose other than to alert the Germans to American intentions along the Germeter-Hürtgen road. At least 50 men from Company C had been wounded or killed. Company B, 10th Tank Battalion, had also suffered high losses. Company B, 47th Armored Infantry Battalion, had only 80 of about 225 assigned riflemen able to fight. Anderson moved his units to Roetgen for rest and reorganization.[32]

THE CAPTURE OF HÜRTGEN

General Stroh no doubt wondered whether his division would ever reach Hürtgen and Kleinhau. Hoping to breathe new life into the lead 121st Infantry, he relieved Jeter and replaced him with the division chief of staff, Col. Thomas J. Cross. Jeter, a very capable graduate of the Citadel, was a victim of circumstances. He took command of a regiment in another division, survived the war, and ultimately retired to South Carolina.[33]

CCR's failure forced Colonel Cross to have the 1st and 2d Battalions move again about daylight on 26 November, and by noon, a few riflemen were at the edge of the woods opposite Hürtgen. The same day, in anticipation of what he planned to be the final assault on the town, General Stroh attached the 1st Battalion, 13th Infantry, to the 121st Infantry.[34]

About 3:00 P.M., news from Company F patrols confirmed a previous report that the Germans had evacuated Hürtgen. At the direction of General Canham (the assistant division commander), Colonel Cross ordered Lieutenant Colonel Kunzig to move his battalion to Hürtgen and put out an outpost line on the south part of town. Cross ordered the commander of the 1st Battalion, 13th Infantry, to be in Hürtgen "by dark."[35]

The remainder of the 2d Battalion, 121st, got underway about 4 P.M., and when Company F reached positions in an open field just 300 yards west of Hürtgen, the GIs found that the earlier patrol reports were wrong. The infantrymen drew fire from Hürtgen. Some of the men dug in, and others returned to the woods. Other patrols from the 2d Battalion reached the southern outskirts of Hürtgen that evening, but they also withdrew under fire.[36]

It was now Stroh's turn to join the ranks of those who failed to demonstrate progress in the forest. On Monday, 27 November, he forwarded through General Gerow to General Hodges a request for 20 days' leave. Stroh was physically and mentally tired, and he was still recovering from the recent death of his 24-year-old son, a pilot. Hodges used the request as grounds to recommend 60 days' leave in the United States. Eisenhower wrote General Marshall, "I am sending him home to see whether he can recover his spirits and again feel equal to the task of leading a division."[37]

Stroh did not return to the 8th Division, though he did return to the ETO in February 1945 to command the 106th Infantry Division. He was the highest ranking American officer to lose his command as a result of the events in the Hürtgen Forest. Brig. Gen. Walter Weaver was his replacement. Ironically, had Stroh hung on for just a few more hours, he would have witnessed success at Hürtgen.

The final attack on Hürtgen began on the morning of 27 November. The 1st Battalion, 13th Infantry, tried to cut the Hürtgen-Kleinhau road, but enemy fire forced it to withdraw. The 2d Battalion, 121st Infantry, had more success, and by 10:00 A.M., Companies E and F had troops in the western part of Hürtgen. TDs arrived later, and both the 2d Battalion, 121st Infantry, and the 1st Battalion, 13th Infantry, reported that German reinforcements were en route from Kleinhau. Darkness once again caught up with the Americans, and the fighting on 27 November ended with both sides holding a share of the town.[38]

The 1st Battalion, 13th Infantry, seized Hill 401, north of Hürtgen, on the morning of 28 November and had men in the Hürtgen church a short time later. A few men from the 2d Battalion, 121st Infantry, were by then in the shattered buildings in the south part of town. Tanks from Company A, 709th Tank Battalion, burst from the woods line west of Hürtgen, followed by troops from Companies E and F, 121st Infantry.[39] This group included Paul Boesch and about 60 of his Company G infantrymen who had spent 27 November pinned down in a drainage ditch about a hundred yards from town. Boesch ordered a lieutenant to lead half of the men on the south side of the road to their front; he took the north side. He ran from man to man explaining what the company was about to do. When the tanks and infantry passed, the men in the ditch made their move. "It was sheer pandemonium," recalled Boesch.[40]

A soldier told Boesch that a colonel wanted to see him immediately. Boesch arrived at a damaged house, where he found Col. Phillip DeWitt Ginder, whose own 2d Infantry Division was overstrength in colonels. General Gerow, perhaps not fully trusting the chain of command in the 8th Division, had ordered Ginder to take charge of the final assault on the town. Ginder told Boesch to keep his men moving and not to stop. Ginder later said, "No movie script could equal the actual action in the taking of this town. Men didn't work in any formation, they worked in teams like clockwork.

Ginder would later greet interviewers with the statement, "Boys, I'm the one that took this town of Hürtgen."[41]

Boesch described the fight as "a wild, terrible, awe-inspiring thing. . . . We dashed, struggled from one building to another shooting, bayoneting, clubbing. Hand grenades roared, fires cracked, buildings to the left and right burned with acrid smoke. Dust, smoke, and powder filled our lungs, making us cough, spit. Automatic weapons chattered while heavier throats of mortars and artillery disgorged deafening explosions. The wounded and dead—men in the uniforms of both sides—lay in grotesque positions at every turn. From many the blood still flowed."

Boesch remembered that the tanks would first spray the buildings with machine gun fire, and use their cannon to blow holes for use by the

M4 "Sherman" Tanks of the 8th Infantry Division's attached 709th Tank Battalion near the Hürtgen District Forest Office about 30 November. This is near where Hubert Gees (275th Infantry Division) was taken prisoner. The tank in the foreground has burned. (Courtesy National Archives, #111–SC–197426)

infantry. "We hurled our bodies through the holes or through windows or splintered doors. Then it became a battle from floor to floor—from room to room."[42]

The Americans took nearly 300 prisoners. One of them was Hubert Gees of the 275th Fusilier Battalion. The previous night, Gees and a companion had sought shelter in a building next to the town church. They started a fire and slept. Gees later wrote, "At dawn I woke up. At once my comrade whispered, 'Pssst, Amis in the house!' I heard plenty of English sounds. After a while the door was opened but closed immediately after. More time went by before a GI opened the door a second time, moved about in the darkness, and then called out something, of which I only understood 'light.' Flashlights lit up, and we were ordered, 'Hands up!' It could not be misunderstood. I was a POW." The Americans took their weapons and personal items and threw letters from

Gees's family into a corner. (In 1962, the German government returned the letters to Gees.) "More than two years of captivity lay before me; however, I left the hell of the Hürtgen Forest alive," said Gees.[43]

As the sounds of battle subsided, Boesch "started to shake, and it wasn't the cold. I realized that I had not been afraid during that whole day. Not once did I feel afraid. I was busy as hell, and that occupied my mind. But when I shook, visibly, on that floor with a roof at least two feet thick over my head, I was hoping that I would not forget to be afraid because that was the best way to stay alive, to not make careless moves." A few hours later, the concussion from a German shell knocked Boesch down a flight of stairs. He injured his back and did not return to combat.[44]

Colonel Cross said the battle for Hürtgen was "the most bitter fight I have seen since I have been overseas. The Nazis we met were fanatics. It was a matter of digging them out. One of our men went after a Jerry. He killed our man and then surrendered. Naturally we didn't accept his surrender." He told an interviewer the artillery was perhaps as heavy as any he had seen during World War I.[45]

Lt. Paul Stevenson of Company C, 644th Tank Destroyer Battalion, said, "I shall not soon forget watching some Graves Registration guys loading dead GIs, most of them frozen stiff, on the back of a 2½-ton truck. Working in pairs, they'd each grab one end and toss the rigid bodies like so many logs into the truck bed. More than one truck was filled to its capacity before they cleaned up. All were members of the 121st Infantry or the 12th Combat Engineers. I cannot tell you how many I saw collected that day, but it was certainly more than 100 and may have been many more."[46]

During November 1944, the 8th Infantry Division suffered 1,092 battle casualties, including 154 officers and men killed, and another 1,051 nonbattle casualties. The division received 1,317 officer and enlisted replacements.[47] Though personnel officers reported casualties by month, it is safe to say that most of the losses occurred after 20 November.

The V Corps was now ready to move on the Roer River—nearly three months after the first attack on Hürtgen. Since mid-September, the 9th Division had tried twice to penetrate the center of the forest. The 28th Division had failed miserably in its attack on Schmidt. The 1st Division was nearing the edge of the forest, but the Germans were waiting at Merode. The 4th Division's 22d Infantry Regiment was close to Grosshau, but progress had been slow and difficult.

The next action in the Hürtgen area was an armored sweep conducted between 1 and 7 December by CCR, 5th Armored Division. The tankers and armored infantrymen, supported by the 8th Division, drove on Kleinhau and the Brandenberg-Bergstein Ridge—ground that had been so decisive in the 28th Division's fight. CCR was nearly destroyed in the process. The Germans were playing a high-stakes game. The Ardennes attack was just a few days away, and it was imperative that they hold the Americans at the Roer.

11

The Capture of Grosshau, Kleinhau, and Bergstein

The 22d Infantry Regiment gained only about 3,000 yards in the center of the Hürtgen Forest between 16 and 26 November. The regiment was less then 500 yards from Grosshau, but those remaining yards might well have been miles. Still, on the afternoon of 25 November, the division G-3 told Colonel Lanham, the commander of the 22d Infantry, to prepare the regiment for another attack on Grosshau the next day. Lanham knew that, given the condition of the regiment, this would be impossible. He told the G-3 that he would not attack unless General Barton, the commander of the 4th Division, gave him a direct order to do so. Barton knew better—he told Lanham to reorganize the regiment, but not to attack Grosshau.[1] The regiment would instead conduct only "limited" operations. But during the next two days, it would have been hard to convince any of "Buck" Lanham's riflemen that he was involved in limited attacks to straighten the regiment's line. One example will suffice to describe the nature of these actions.

Company B attacked on the morning of 27 November to clear the woods west of Grosshau. Enemy fire wounded several officers, including the company commander, and killed or wounded 16 of 17 men in the 1st Platoon. Pfc. Marcario Garcia assaulted a machine-gun position by himself and killed three Germans with rifle fire. Sustaining a wound in the arm, he took advantage of covering smoke to return across open ground to his platoon and announced, "Goddamn, I killed three Germans and knocked out the machine gun!" When another machine gun took the platoon under fire a short time later, Garcia rushed this position also, killed the crew, and took four prisoners. He returned to his platoon and

S.Sgt. Marcario Garcia, 22d Infantry, received the Medal of Honor for his actions near Grosshau. (Courtesy National Archives, #111–SC–210283–S)

proclaimed, "That's all of the bastards here." He received the Medal of Honor and ended the war as a staff sergeant.[2] The survivors eventually reached what was left of the woods just west of Grosshau. (The constant shell fire had literally mowed down the trees.) The executive officer of the 1st Battalion said the men were "having an awful hard time" and were "being cut up by machine gun fire. . . ." Lanham ordered the 2d

Battalion to assist. General Collins asked Lanham how many more days the regiment could remain in action. Lanham told him about three days if they were "very rough."[3]

Capt. Donald Faulkner, the commander of Company E, recalled his company's effort to help the 1st Battalion: "We moved out at the double and down into a stream draw. I thought, 'This is a natural spot for a mortar concentration,' and either the Krauts had mental telepathy or good observation, for immediately a heavy mortar concentration swished in through the trees, smack dab on top of the command group. . . . We kept going and came in on the run to a picture of real carnage—arms, equipment, dead and wounded Jerrys and GIs strewn all through the woods. Blasted trees, gaping shell holes, and the acrid smell of small-arms and mortar fire completed the terrible scene. It looked just like Hell."[4]

Faulkner's men relieved the 30 men remaining in the rifle platoons of Company B. The artillery fire continued, and according to Faulkner, "The rest of the woods fell down over our heads. We had several casualties. We dug deeper and deeper."[5]

The Germans were in temporary control of the situation. For example, the commander of the 3d Battalion reported that when a patrol tried to exit its foxholes, the Germans responded with a sustained barrage of mortar fire. The commander of the 1st Battalion, Major Goforth, reported that there were "lots of KIA's. Half of the replacements were wounded just digging in."[6]

The riflemen needed armor support, but the crewmen of the supporting tanks and TDs, located on a narrow, muddy road leading into Grosshau, refused to assist. The soldiers believed the road was mined and that nearby antitank weapons would destroy their vehicles. They did not move until a lieutenant who was assigned to the regimental antitank company drove a half-track by himself down the road to prove it was not as dangerous as the others thought.[7]

A patrol finally managed to enter Grosshau that night. Lanham's S-2 had told the patrol leader that the town was deserted, but no sooner had the GIs entered Grosshau's rubble-filled streets than the lieutenant in charge spotted several Germans. They opened fire, and the patrol withdrew. The patrol leader estimated that at least 50 Germans remained in the rubble.[8] "They came out of cellars and shot at the patrol from all directions," Lanham told Barton. Division artillery fired throughout the night to prevent the Germans from forming for a counterattack.[9]

Lanham told the commander of the 1st Battalion: "We are still being shelled. One of their aid men turned over our wounded to us, and the aid man [German] came back with them. Believe the Krauts in town [Grosshau] have orders to stay till the last man. . . . Every time they [riflemen] move mortars open. . . . Watch out for counterattack."[10]

Lanham decided to envelop Grosshau. He intended to have the 1st Battalion support a 3d Battalion attack on the 29th to seize high ground north of Grosshau in preparation for a final attack on the town. The 2d Battalion would remain in place. The regiment jumped off according to plan, about 11:00 A.M., three hours and forty-five minutes after CCR, 5th Armored Division, attacked Kleinhau. About 11:15 A.M, however, General Barton had his chief of staff, Col. Richard S. Marr, tell Lanham to have the regiment move on Grosshau immediately. Because the 1st and 3d Battalions were already underway, Lanham ordered the 2d Battalion to make the attack. Just minutes before, Lanham's S-3 had told the battalion commander, Lieutenant Colonel Kenan, that his battalion would likely not move at all.

Only Captain Faulkner's battered Company E plus a platoon of Company F (the remainder of the company attacked later) were available. The company got underway within an hour after Marr's phone call, under orders to "fight house-to-house if necessary." Armor support was at first limited to a single TD. Lanham told the battalion commander not "to take too many PWs. If they want to fight to the death, then see that it is their death."[11]

It was far easier said than done. There was a wide stretch of open ground between Company E and Grosshau, and German fire stopped the company before it was a hundred yards from its LD. American dead and wounded, lying alone and in grotesque heaps, soon littered the open area west of Grosshau. Faulkner lost radio contact with the artillery and had to rely on runners to transmit orders.[12] The tank support was slow in coming as antitank guns knocked out the first two M4s from Company C, 70th Tank Battalion, to join the attack. Two others mired in the mud, and mines accounted for two more. The remaining tanks reached the infantry by running to the rear of the damaged tanks and using them as shields.

Faulkner recalled that the tanks were blasting "a house at a time with HE and tracer. Their MGs went like a bat out of hell. Regular movie stuff—noise, fire, smoke, movement, confusion."[13]

One officer recalled that "the craters . . . in the ground served as excellent holes for our men, and they pressed their attack forward by running from crater to crater."[14]

Grosshau was in Americans hands that night. The commander of the 2d Battalion told Lanham, "The entire town is ours. We have a TD on the eastern end. E Co. suffered heavy casualties. F Co. is in fair shape. G Co. is also in good shape."

Barton told Lanham, "We are whipping those Krauts—we are paying for it, but we are whipping them."[15]

The regiment was now ready to move on Gey. Barton attached the 5th

Armored Division's 46th Armored Infantry Battalion (Lt. Col. William H. Burton, Jr.) to the 22d Infantry effective at 6:30 P.M., 29 November. The next day, Burton's men were to occupy Hill 401.3, supposed to be under control of CCR, 5th Armored Division, and then move on the woods to the east.[16] However, unexpected fire from Hill 401.3 stopped the dismounted leading companies cold. The 4th Division headquarters insisted that Burton's men faced friendly fire. Burton disagreed, and he ordered his battalion to assault the hill. Events proved Burton's assessment correct. His men spotted an enemy machine gun and later took 50 prisoners at a complex of log bunkers on the hill. By midnight, the battalion held positions well inside the woods south of Gey. Litter parties worked all night under artillery fire to evacuate the casualties. The battalion remained in the area for a few more days and withdrew on 5 December after suffering about 40 percent casualties in its brief but costly encounter with the Hürtgen Forest. The German defenses in the area remained unbroken.[17]

THE 22D INFANTRY REGIMENT TO 3 DECEMBER

Meanwhile, on 30 November, the 2d Battalion had renewed its attack east under unmerciful mortar and artillery fire. Only about a hundred men reached the woods.

Lanham told the commander of the 1st Battalion "not to take more PWs from Grosshau."[18]

The next day, the 1st Battalion's Company C, followed by Company A (now under the command of Capt. Don Warner), drove to the woods opposite Grosshau. A smoke screen concealed Company C, but the wind picked up and exposed Company A. A soldier who began the November attack as a rifleman and ended the month as a platoon leader said, "Every step you'd take, there'd be a shell to help you along."

Warner believed the effort to conceal Company C as it spearheaded the attack made things more difficult for his own company, which had only 35 men still able to fight at the end of the day.[19] Major Goforth, the battalion commander, reported that the smoke screen "surprised the hell out of the Krauts. They cut up the next two outfits [Companies A and B], but they got through."[20]

The next day, German fire nearly destroyed Company A's 2d Platoon. An officer later said, "The enemy captured two of our men, and they must have talked or something, for soon afterward mortar fire started coming down on our positions. It wasn't just the ordinary type of mortar fire . . . but the shells walked our lines and dropped with uncanny accuracy every ten yards precisely into the holes of the men of the 2d Platoon."[21]

Hürtgen, 30 November 1944. (Courtesy National Archives, #111–SC–197428)

Warner combined the survivors of that platoon with those of the 3d. Only 21 men (nearly all replacements) remained in the rifle platoons of Company A; only six of them had been assigned to the company on 16 November. Eight platoon leaders had been killed or wounded; privates now led two of the platoons.[22]

The same day, several of the riflemen of Company F (in reality, now little more than a platoon),[23] under the leadership of an inexperienced lieutenant, reached the woods southeast of Grosshau but became disoriented and dug in on the wrong objective. A German counterattack routed them. Colonel Kenan, the battalion commander, once more sent Captain Faulkner's Company E into action. Faulkner sent a platoon across the open ground east of Grosshau, but German artillery fire pinned it down, and only 9 men reached the woods. At dusk, Faulkner led his 60 remaining riflemen to the Company F positions, where he found the company commander, Lt. George F. Wilson, and about 15 survivors of his company. Company G had 50 men and one officer.[24]

Lanham reported the situation to General Barton, who replied that he understood the problems but could not end the attack at that time.

Jeeps of the 22d Infantry in Grosshau, 1 December 1944. (Courtesy National Archives, #111–SC–197536)

Lanham had to order the regiment's Antitank Company, Service Company, and headquarters units combed for men to fight as infantry.[25]

American artillery fire interdicted the area between the 3d Battalion and Gey during the night of 1–2 December. At 6:50 A.M. on the 2d, a German counterattack (probably from the 943d Infantry Regiment) hit Company I and threatened the battalion CP. The Germans captured the Company I commander, a forward observer, and a dozen other men. The 2d Battalion sent a platoon to help, and Lanham ordered forward the few dozen reserve rifleman he had to spare. The 12th Infantry sent a battalion to Grosshau to help contain the penetration.

"Send all available men to forward CP," radioed the battalion commander to his rear CP. He later asked Lanham, "Send some tanks up here right away, as we need them badly." Only after Lanham committed the makeshift reserve of antitank, service, and headquarters troops did the regiment halt the German attack.[26]

The 22d Infantry's encounter with the Hürtgen Forest was mercifully drawing to a close. It was not the same regiment that had entered the

Hürtgen Forest three weeks earlier. Between 16 November and 3 December the regiment paid 103 officer and 2,575 enlisted casualties for a mere 7,500 yards of muddy forest. Even at that price, it still failed to reach its assigned objectives.[27]

The Hürtgen Forest cost the 4th Division 4,053 battle casualties, including 432 known dead and 255 missing. Over 3,300 men were wounded or injured. Casualties for the 22d Infantry alone were at least 1,730 soldiers wounded and 233 killed. This does not count casualties from disease and other nonbattle causes. The authorized strength of the regiment was 3,257 officers and men.

Collins ordered the 4th Division to halt its operations. The reliefs began with the arrival on 3 December of the 83d Infantry Division's 330th Infantry Regiment. The 83d Division assumed responsibility for the 4th Division sector on the afternoon of 7 December.[28] The division had reached a line running roughly from Grosshau to northwest of Hof Hardt.

Colonel Lanham left the 4th Division early in 1945 to assume duties as assistant commander of the 104th Division. He commanded the 1st Infantry Division during the early 1950s and retired as a major general in 1954. Lanham later took an executive position with the Xerox Corporation. He died in 1978. His daughter recalled an incident in the 1950s during a return visit to the Hürtgen Forest. "All shells and ammunition had been cleared out, we were told, so it was safe to walk around. The workers were just starting on the trees, which looked like brown match sticks. As Dad said, you could just as easily get killed by a tree sliver as a bullet."[29]

THE CAPTURE OF KLEINHAU

During the 22d Infantry's push to Grosshau and beyond, the V Corps continued its battle for Kleinhau, Brandenberg, and Bergstein. The capture of Hürtgen and progress by the 22d Infantry toward Grosshau enabled CCR, 5th Armored Division, to move on Kleinhau, which was defended by about 200 men in three companies of infantry (353d Infantry Division) and elements of a machine-gun battalion.[30] The 8th Division/CCR plan called for Task Force Hamberg, built around Lt. Col. William A. Hamberg's 10th Tank Battalion, to take Kleinhau on the morning of 29 November and then move on Hill 401.3. Elements of the 1st Battalion, 13th Infantry, would follow.

Three days of preparatory artillery fire blasted Kleinhau from end to end. An 18-battalion TOT, followed on the afternoon of 28 November by fighter-bombers dropping napalm, completed the destruction of the village.[31] The CCR S-3 reported that the road from Hürtgen to Kleinhau was clear of mines and that engineers would work throughout the night of the 28th to clear the LD of damaged equipment.[32]

The ferocity of the preliminary shelling and air strikes did nothing, however, to clear the road from Hürtgen to Kleinhau. The tankers and armored infantrymen of Company C, 10th Tank Battalion, and Company C, 47th Armored Infantry Battalion, had trouble getting through Hürtgen and reaching the LD. Reports of a minefield on the southern outskirts of Kleinhau then prompted Hamberg to order the infantry to dismount from the half-tracks, and German artillery fire caught the unprotected infantrymen in the open. They quickly fell behind the tanks.[33]

The results of POW interrogations, reports from American sources, and his own experience had led Hamberg to order the infantry to dismount. Also, an aerial photograph of the area appeared to show the pattern of a minefield where the sun had melted the snow on each mine. Hamberg walked over the area the next day and saw that what he and others thought were mines were actually piles of cow manure.[34]

A few tanks were in Kleinhau before 10:00 A.M., but the infantry did not reach Kleinhau for another hour. Antitank gunfire from Grosshau was a surprise because the tankers had been told the town was under assault by the 22d Infantry. As noted above, the 22d Infantry was not scheduled to attack until over three hours after CCR had moved.[35]

Some time after the attack began, General Weaver radioed his congratulations to Anderson. "What on?" asked Anderson in reply.

"Armor throughout the town," replied Weaver.

"Town is not yet ours," stated Anderson,[36] as the congratulations were premature. In fact, it took until the afternoon to clear out the enemy.

Company A, 10th Tank Battalion, later established a roadblock north of Kleinhau, and elements of the 13th Infantry reached the area late on 29 November. Yet, these soldiers did not occupy the roadblock or Hill 401.3 as planned. They told CCR they did not have the strength to hold that area as well as Kleinhau. The infantry thought the tanks would draw enemy fire and requested that the tankers not occupy the hill either. (As noted above, this decision caused problems for the 46th Armored Infantry Battalion.)

What was left of Kleinhau offered little cover for TF Hamberg. Though the original CCR plan called for the TF to withdraw to a covered assembly area some distance away, V Corps headquarters overruled the plan. No doubt staff officers thought the tanks would comfort the frayed nerves of the infantrymen. There also was the possibility that some might interpret the CCR move as a retreat. In view of recent events, any hint of withdrawal would have been out of the question.

This decision forced TF Hamberg to spend much of 30 November needlessly exposed on the open ground west of Kleinhau. The Germans brought up several self-propelled assault guns and placed fire on the task force assembly area. Hamberg requested an air strike, but V Corps refused the request on the grounds that troops of the 4th Division were operating nearby. He later moved the task force a few hundred yards west to a covered area, and higher headquarters approved the decision. Kleinhau cost Task Force Hamberg eight tanks, 13 half-tracks, a tank destroyer, and about 60 men, but the Americans had taken another step toward securing the Brandenberg-Bergstein Ridge.[37]

PREPARATIONS TO CONTINUE THE ATTACK

On 29 November General Hodges issued new instructions to his corps commanders. The 5th Armored Division, less CCR, was now attached to VII Corps in preparation for the final push to Düren and the Roer.[38] Hodges ordered the V Corps to move as soon as possible to take both the Brandenberg-Bergstein Ridge and Hill 400, located outside Bergstein. This would provide a secure flank for continued operations and would put V Corps at the Roer; however, the new orders forced Gerow on 29 November to cancel a planned CCB, 5th Armored Division, attack on Brandenberg.[39] There would be no rest for CCR; it had to go back into action.

Gerow also ordered the 8th Division to reconnoiter toward the east and southeast of Vossenack in an effort to protect the flank of CCR by clearing the southern slope of the ridge. Colonel Hogan's 3d Battalion, 121st Infantry, found that the defenses in the area were "nearly impossible to take." By 3 December the battalion had reached the ridge, but according to an officer on the staff of the 121st Infantry:

> The men of this battalion [are] physically exhausted. The spirit and will to fight are there; the ability to continue is gone. These men have been fighting without rest or sleep for four days and last night were forced to lie unprotected from the weather in an open field. In some instances men were forced to discard their overcoats because they lacked the strength to wear them. These men are shivering with cold, and their hands are so numb that they have to help one another on with their equipment. I firmly believe that every man up there should be evacuated through medical channels.[40]

By the end of the first week in December the 8th Division held the Brandenberg-Bergstein Ridge and the line from Hill 400 southwest along the Kall to the division boundary with elements of the 28th Infantry Regiment and 102d Cavalry Group. The Pathfinders would remain in position after transfer to the VII Corps on 18 December. The division finally crossed the Roer in late February 1945.

THE CAPTURE OF BRANDENBERG AND BERGSTEIN

Brandenberg was CCR's next target, and Colonel Anderson's men made good progress on 2 December—until the tanks ran into a minefield stretching across the road between Kleinhau and Brandenberg. When one tank hit a mine, a lieutenant dismounted to reorganize his platoon. Artillery fire hit nearby, and he and his men fell to the ground for cover. While trying to maneuver out of the fire, the tanks ran over some of the men. The attack stalled, and General Weaver ordered the task force to move to better positions.

A platoon from Company C, 22d Engineer Combat Battalion, worked throughout the night of 2–3 December to clear the road. The Germans had booby-trapped many of the mines with antilifting devices, but by morning the engineers were able to remove about 250 mines. This allowed the tanks and half-tracks of Company C, 10th Tank Battalion, and Company C, 47th Armored Infantry Battalion, to speed into Brandenberg under the covering fire from Companies A and D, 10th Tank Battalion, and Company A, 47th Armored Infantry Battalion.[41]

But there were still losses. An artillery shell hit one tank, tore off the cover on the open commander's hatch, killed the tank commander, blew open two closed hatches, and threw two crewmen from the tank.[42] One NCO "watched as this and that vehicle was hit. It was a terrible feeling as I had a bird's-eye view, knowing that I was going through that fire in minutes. Just then, I saw a shell hit Sergeant Helm's half-track. [He] staggered out to fall against his vehicle. I told my driver to pull out, and I jumped out to see how bad Helms was hit. He said, 'Get the hell back in and get going!'"[43] An aggressive platoon leader even took three tanks to Bergstein, where they knocked out two German antitank guns. Hamberg recalled the platoon because higher headquarters believed the 10th Tank Battalion did not have the strength to hold both towns.[44]

In preparation for the attack on Bergstein, Anderson requested air support and the return of Task Force Boyer from Vossenack, where it had reduced the last enemy resistance in the easternmost parts of that shattered village. Anderson planned for Hamberg's task force to take the area north and northeast of Bergstein. One tank company would keep the road between Kleinhau and Brandenberg open and maintain contact with the 121st Infantry, then operating in the woods north and east of Brandenberg. Elements of TF Boyer would secure the area to the south and east of Bergstein.[45] TF Hamberg had 16 medium tanks remaining operational and the attached Company C, 628th Tank Destroyer Battalion, had only 6 of its 12 tank destroyers available. There were an estimated 400 defenders from the 2d Battalion, 980th Infantry Regiment, and the 189th Antitank Battalion.

Bad weather delayed the attack, but CCR finally jumped off at 2:00 P.M. Company C, 10th Tank Battalion, and Company C, 47th Armored Infantry Battalion, attacked the eastern part of Bergstein. Company A, 10th Tank Battalion, and Company A, 47th Armored Infantry Battalion, followed the leading elements sweeping in from Brandenberg, and some of the tanks ran into either an unreported minefield or mines missed by engineers the night before. One tank hit a mine and blocked the route of withdrawal for the rest, and artillery fire killed the platoon leader when he dismounted to direct the other tanks out of the minefield. The tanks remained in place to support the attack by fire.

Lt. Roy M. Hanf took charge of Company C, 47th, when the commander was hit. "I saw two other officers hit along with several noncommissioned officers and had to make numerous squad and platoon leaders on the spot. This was done on the basis of their rising to the occasion, assuming leadership, rather than protocol; there was no time for any proper chain of command. Hürtgen was a maturing, growing up experience in double time," he later recalled.[46]

Pockets of resistance held out for hours, though Colonel Anderson declared the town secure at 5:00 P.M. The Americans found themselves occupied during the cold night with a tense house-to-house search for German snipers. CCR at the time was little more than a reinforced company defending a pencil-like penetration with only the road to Brandenberg available for supply and withdrawal.

The Germans believed the Americans would reinforce the units at Brandenberg and attempt a crossing of the Roer, which would disrupt preparations for the Ardennes offensive. Though it was scheduled to participate in that attack, the 272d Volksgrenadier Division was the only reserve available to throw against the Americans. Model reluctantly released the division to General Brandenberger. Supported by about ten tanks and at least one assault gun, the 1st Battalion, 980th Grenadier Regiment, hit CCR just before daylight on 6 December.[47]

Hamberg's weary men reacted quickly and fired "everything [they] had," but the rounds from the short-barreled 75mm guns that were on most of the M4s ricocheted off the German tanks that had accompanied the enemy infantry. Frantic calls for fire support brought round after round of corps and 8th Division artillery on the Germans.

The close-quarters battle raged among the burned-out buildings and in the adjacent farmland. Tanks lumbered through the rubble-filled streets. Infantrymen of both sides were intermixed in the debris. Tracer rounds ricocheted off the brick and stone and into the sky. Earl Lutz of the 47th Armored Infantry said, "My eye could see the shells hit the German tanks and glance off into the air. My heart sank."[48]

Only the three or four M4s mounting the new 76mm high-velocity

Pfc. Joseph Sorobowski *(left)* and Pvt. Roy E. James, survivors of the 47th Armored Infantry Battalion's (CCR, 5th Armored Division) fight from the Wilde Sau minefield to Bergstein, on 7 December 1944. (Courtesy National Archives, #111–SC–326605)

gun proved effective against the German armor. The Company B command tank, for example, had a 76mm gun, and it accounted for five German tanks and another vehicle.

An American light tank hit a mine that "blew [the] hell out of the tank." An M10 knocked out a Panther at a range of only 75 yards, but another German tank then knocked it out. However, two new M36 TDs mounting 90mm guns remained silent. The crew refused to leave the cellar in which they sought shelter because they feared the Panthers would pick up the muzzle flashes of their guns and destroy their thinly armored vehicles.

American artillery finally broke up the attack. But according to the executive officer of the 10th Tank Battalion, Maj. William M. Daniel, "If the Germans had come back they could have overrun the battalion." Two more attacks came later in the day, but CCR held the town.

The 5th Armored Division headquarters directed 60 men who had just returned from hospitals to enter the line at Bergstein. Not only were the men too physically weak to be effective, but they had no blankets and had to pick up weapons from the dead. Company A, 10th Tank Battalion, lost 12 of 17 tanks and finished this phase of the battle with only 3 officers and 23 men. Company B lost 8 of its tanks and had fewer than 50 men remaining; all the armored infantry companies were at platoon strength, and only 1 of 12 TDs was serviceable.[49]

What was left of CCR was unable to carry the attack to Hill 400. The only unit available to take the hill was the 2d Ranger Battalion, under V Corps control but attached to the 8th Division since 19 November. And this battalion's attack would be another example of a relatively fresh unit thrown into the battle long enough for it to take a single objective and then pull back decimated.

12
Operations to 16 December

On the afternoon of 6 December, General Weaver asked General Gerow to release the 2d Ranger Battalion for employment at Hill 400, known to the Americans as Castle Hill and to the Germans as Burgberg. It was situated at the eastern end of the Brandenberg-Bergstein Ridge and dominated the approaches to the Roer in the northern third of the V Corps sector. From the hill on a clear day, one could see as far as Düren, nearly six miles away.

The executive officer of the 2d Ranger Battalion, Capt. George S. Williams, Jr., received the attack order that evening at the 8th Division forward CP. General Weaver wanted the Rangers to attack the hill at 3:00 A.M. on 7 December, but Williams convinced him to delay the attack until daylight. This would both allow the Rangers to reconnoiter the hill before the attack and ease the difficulties of command and control with which units always had to contend in the forest.

Later that night, the Ranger battalion commander, Lt. Col. James E. Rudder, returned from a meeting at First Army headquarters. He met the Rangers while they were en route to Brandenberg and announced Williams's promotion to major. Rudder also reported that he would depart that night to take command of the 28th Division's 109th Infantry Regiment. Rudder, Williams, and the S-2 then went on to Brandenberg, where they met with Colonel Anderson to discuss the details of the operation. The remainder of the battalion followed later.[1]

About midnight, T5 Earl Lutz, one of three guides from CCR, went to meet the Rangers and bring them to Bergstein. "I was told to go to a certain road [and] . . . meet the 2d Ranger Battalion. I got to the road [but] there was nothing to be seen, no sound, not even a cricket. I guess I swore a little, and the [Rangers] raised up all around me," he recalled.[2]

Word of the Rangers' arrival spread quickly and sent the morale of TF Hamberg "up in a hurry."[3]

CCR officers directed the Rangers to the perimeter around Bergstein. The Rangers had only a few hours in which to prepare for the attack, for they did not begin arriving in Bergstein until after 2:30 A.M. Three companies (A, B, C) set up roadblocks on the south, southwest, and southeast sides of Bergstein; Companies D and F would make the assault. Company E remained in Bergstein as reserve. According to Major Williams, CCR provided no guides, nor did it have enough troops to man a credible defense.[4] It was fortunate for the Americans that the Germans did not then have the ability to mount a credible attack.

Not long afterward, a Company F patrol slipped through the task force's outer defenses to reconnoiter the enemy dispositions. The patrol made no contact and returned to Bergstein shortly before the attack began. Unfortunately, in the darkness, the patrol could not see a large concrete bunker built into the side of the hill and sited to fire across the approach the Rangers would use later in the morning.

The company commanders met with Major Williams to discuss a plan of attack. They had two choices. One was a flanking attack that would take the Rangers through known minefields; the other was a frontal assault across open ground not protected by mines. They chose a frontal attack. About 6:45 A.M., Companies D and F formed an assault line facing the hill. The companies were about 100 yards from the Bergstein church, along a 200-yard-long terrace about three feet high. The Rangers fixed bayonets and waited for the preparatory artillery fires to lift. Capt. Otto Masny, commander of Company F, found that most of his men were calm and ready to go.

A German sentry spotted the Rangers and fired a flare as they prepared to attack. Seconds later, mortar shells began to explode about 75 yards behind the Rangers. Subsequent rounds fell even closer. Some of the Rangers grumbled that they needed to move before the mortar rounds found their mark.

"I think that every man on the line was convinced that the mortars would reach us before our artillery lifted. I know I was. Caught in a space of less than 150 yards between two barrages, tension was building up to the exploding point," said Bill Petty, a platoon sergeant.

A platoon leader told Petty to "send out a scout." Petty refused to send a man out to face two barrages, but the officer repeated the command to another NCO. He also refused. The officer shouted to a private who was nearby and ordered him to get out in front. The soldier stood and walked across the field, and German small-arms fire cut him down within seconds. A section leader yelled, "Let's go get the bastards!" The Rangers charged.

Company C, 2d Ranger Battalion, near Bergstein. (Courtesy National Archives, #111–SC–341763)

Their line began to waver. Some men ran faster than others, and some fell to the ground to avoid shell fragments. When the Rangers reached the woods at the base of the hill, they ran into the American artillery fire. Several men lay wounded or dead. When Bill Petty reached the hill, he "found a situation of turmoil. There were people trying to help the wounded, others hesitant to move forward. . . . No organization, platoon personnel becoming intermixed, each man on his own. . . . I should have tried to get them organized. I didn't. I guess my adrenaline was pumping to the extent that I reacted as an individual."

Petty and a soldier named Anderson approached the bunker and heard Germans inside. Petty pointed the muzzle of his BAR into a flap in the door. They opened the door, and Anderson threw two grenades inside. Just when they were ready to clear the bunker, a shell exploded a few feet away and blew Anderson into Petty's arms. Anderson was killed instantly by a shell fragment in the heart. About this time, two more Rangers reached the summit and started digging in. Seconds later, Captain Masny arrived with the remainder of Company F. Masny decided to return through the artillery fire and bring back some desperately needed reinforcements. When a platoon leader sought refuge in the bunker, Petty found himself in command of the remainder of Company F. By this time, the bulk of Company D was also on the hill and a few men were already digging foxholes that overlooked the Roer. It was about 8:00 A.M.

The continual shelling tore away much of the heavy tree growth on the hill, and the surviving Rangers exhausted themselves pulling wounded men from the tangle of fallen limbs. Petty recovered Anderson's dying brother and "had the dubious distinction of having hold of both brothers while they were in the process of dying within an hour's time."

The Germans used the cover of the woods to approach close to the American positions. They counterattacked in company strength about 9:30 A.M. Using machine pistols, rifles, machine guns, and hand grenades, they rushed the Americans. The wounded who were still able to fight left the safety of the bunker and manned the line. The platoon leader who had ordered a scout to advance earlier in the morning was himself wounded in the chest. A Ranger picked him up and carried him back to the bunker, but a German bullet hit the wounded officer in the head. Apparently, a few of the Germans had reached positions on ground slightly above the Rangers and were firing as snipers. Petty was wounded a few minutes later. He returned the fire and killed the German.[5]

As the day wore on, the precise direction of artillery fire broke up one German attack after another. The forward observer, 1st Lt. Howard K. Kettlehut, did much to save the surviving Rangers. On one occasion, he coordinated the fire of 18 battalions of artillery on enemy targets near Hill 400. It is possible, however, that the artillery that would do so much to break up five enemy counterattacks during the next two days also added to the Ranger casualties. By the afternoon of 7 December, Company F had only 17 men remaining in condition to fight. At dusk, the commander of Company D reported, "Counterattacks on hill all afternoon; very heavy artillery; only 25 able-bodied men left; help needed badly; are surrounded." The reserve platoon of Company C rushed to the hill. Kettlehut continued to call for the artillery, which placed a ring of fire around Hill 400.

The coming of night helped the Rangers hang on, yet before daylight on 8 December the combined strength of Companies D, E, and F was just 5 officers and 86 men. Just after daylight, a German artillery concentration hit Bergstein. The concentration "was so heavy that it seemed to have a 'drumming' sound while that which fell on the Hill was of such intensity that one explosion would cover the sound of the next approaching shell." American artillery broke up two more counterattacks that morning.

That afternoon, between 100 and 150 German infantrymen supported by artillery, mortars, and self-propelled guns moved on Bergstein. The Germans hit the town from three sides. The Americans wavered, gave some ground, and then finally held with the help of artillery. The Germans nevertheless managed to slip to within 100 yards of the town church, then used by the Americans as an aid station, before artillery forced them to withdraw.

Bergstein and Hill 400 remained in American hands largely because of responsive artillery support. Had the Germans been able to field another battalion, they might have retaken both.

Elements of the 8th Division's 13th Infantry completed relief of the Rangers early on 9 December. The Ranger casualties totaled about 133, with 23 killed, 86 wounded, 20 injured, and another 4 men listed as missing.[6]

On 8 December, elements of the 121st Infantry and 644th Tank Destroyer Battalion relieved the remnants of TFs Hamberg and Boyer. CCR relocated to Walhorn, Belgium, for rest and refit. The command had 70 fit infantrymen out of an original 750. CCR's losses, added to those of the 2d Ranger Battalion and the 8th Division, brought the casualties for this part of V Corps operations in the Hürtgen Forest to nearly 4,000—out of about 16,000 in the 8th Division, CCR, and the 2d Ranger Battalion.[7]

The high ground that had served the Germans so well during the 28th Division's abortive attempt to take Schmidt was now in American hands. To the north, the VII Corps was edging closer to the river, and the Ninth Army was nearly ready to cross it. Yet no unit could safely do so because the Roer dams remained in German hands.

THE DRIVE TO GEY AND STRASS

At the end of the first week in December, Hodges had only one (V Corps) of his two attacking corps at the Roer. The main effort, Collins's VII Corps, had failed to break through the Hürtgen Forest and Stolberg Corridor. It was still three miles away from the Roer on 6 December, the day Hodges ordered Collins to continue the attack on the Düren-Cologne axis. Both attacking divisions, the 1st and 4th, were too weak to complete the drive to the Roer. The newly arrived 83d Infantry Division (Maj. Gen. Robert C. Macon), which had been assigned to the VIII Corps in Luxembourg, had replaced the 4th Division and would spearhead the VII Corps' final attack through the northern reaches of the forest. (The veteran 9th Division began its relief of the 1st Division on the 5th of December.) Hodges wanted the VII Corps along the river when the V Corps launched the unavoidable ground attack against the two largest Roer dams.[8]

General Macon, a 1912 graduate of Virginia Polytechnic, knew that speed was essential to success. The 83d Division had to take Gey and Strass before the Germans could pour in reinforcements and prevent the

Pfc. Thomas W. Gilmore, Company A, 121st Infantry, near Hürtgen, 7 December 1944. (Courtesy National Archives, #111–SC–196969–S)

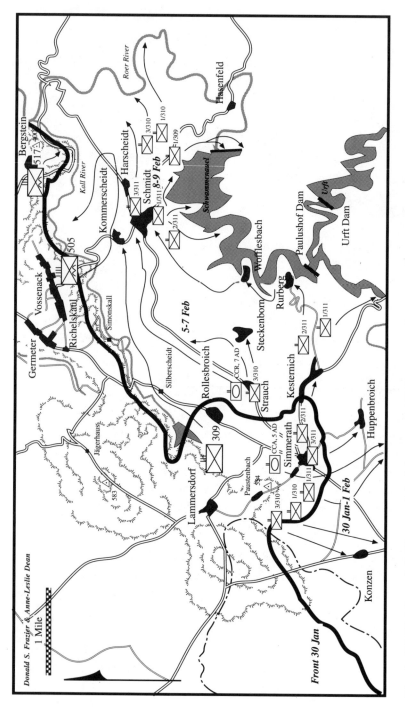

Map 6. 78th Division and the Capture of the Schwammenauel Dam, December 1944–February 1945

follow-on attack by the 5th Armored Division. Macon assigned a regiment to each town (Gey—the 331st Infantry, commanded by Col. Robert T. Foster; Strass—the 330th Infantry, commanded by Col. Robert H. York).

After Gey and Strass were in American hands, CCA (Brig. Gen. Eugene A. Regnier) and CCB (Col. John T. Cole), 5th Armored Division, would clear the south portion of the corps zone as far as the Roer. CCA would move through Gey and take Hill 211, which overlooked Kreuzau. CCB would push through Strass and take the Hemgenberg (Hill 253), high ground between Hill 211 and Hill 400. On the division's north flank, the 329th Infantry Regiment (Col. Edwin B. Crabhill) in the former 8th Infantry Regiment zone, would take Hof Hardt, Gürzenich, and Roer crossings west of Düren.[9]

The 2d Battalion, 331st Infantry, set out in the chilling early morning darkness of 10 December and had troops in Gey by daylight. The Germans made the Americans fight for every house, and the GIs had no tank support. Three of the supporting tanks lost tracks to mines and blocked the muddy trail that led to Gey from the west. The Germans took advantage of the delay to reinforce their troops in Gey. The Americans did the same on 11 December, and neither side made any progress.

The S-3 of the 331st Infantry thought the heavily mined, high-banked trail was the major factor that delayed the progress of his regiment. There were so many shell fragments buried in the trail that the soldiers had to probe for the mines by hand. Metallic mine detectors were useless. The S-3 of the 2d Battalion, 331st Infantry added that the mine belts extended for 20 to 30 yards on either side of the road as well. The Germans had buried the mines so deeply that a tank might pass over them unharmed. However, the next tank in line, following the ruts of the first, would detonate the mines.

The Germans also felled trees on top of rows of antipersonnel mines laid on the road or alongside it. The trees themselves were booby-trapped with plainly visible charges of explosives. A trench some 1500 yards long ran west of Gey.

An estimated 20% of the German prisoners reported living in or near Gey before the war and knew the area well. The defenders had reinforced selected basements with concrete, and one had steel reinforcing beams. "When artillery is falling," stated the S-3, "Jerry always goes to these basements."[10]

Companies K and L of the 330th Infantry meanwhile bypassed Schafberg and entered Strass about midmorning of 10 December. The Germans counterattacked an hour later. The attached tank battalion got a company on the road to support, but one platoon took a wrong turn and ended up in the sights of German antitank guns. This error cost the company all five tanks in the platoon. The remaining tanks (Co. C,

774th Tank Battalion) later entered Schafberg but damaged the unpaved access road to such an extent that it was nearly impassable for even jeep traffic.[11] The Germans then took advantage of the oncoming darkness to infiltrate the tree-cloaked road between Schafberg and Strass and isolate the 3d Battalion, 330th Infantry, even though the Americans had achieved a measure of concentration in the area.

General Macon was anxious to get General Oliver's tanks into action. Macon told Oliver that it was only a matter of time before Gey would be clear of the enemy. Oliver nevertheless voiced his concerns to Collins, but Macon instead convinced the corps commander to have Oliver begin the attack as scheduled. Presumably, Collins heard from Macon what he wanted to hear—positive news. As events happened, German resistance would stop CCB 200 yards east of Schafberg.

Day two of the 83d Division's attack brought little progress. A counterattack at Schafberg caused problems for the Americans, and it took them several hours to regain control of the situation. Things continued to go slowly at Gey. Colonel York reported to Macon, "This down here [Gey] isn't going as well as expected. We will be late."

Collins asked Macon, "What is the situation in Schafberg?"

"The situation is not clear; Foster's outfit is a bit disorganized," replied Macon.

"Tell Foster to get organized. Is the south flank buttoned up?" Collins was asking about the woods south of Schafberg.

"Yes."

"Have Foster and everybody else police those woods west of Schafberg and keep on going now. How do they stand in Gey now?"

Macon replied that Gey would be clear "shortly."

"You mean there is still some enemy in there?"

"Yes, sir," stated Macon.

Collins's reply was characteristic: "Surround them and cut them off. The whole situation west and southwest of Gey has got to be cleared up fast." Foster committed his 2d Battalion to the battle.[12]

Meanwhile, at 7:45 A.M., troops of CCB's 15th Armored Infantry Battalion and 81st Tank Battalion had headed through Kleinhau toward an LD south of Schafberg. Contact with elements of the 330th Infantry led Lt. Col. Glenn G. Dickinson, the commander of the 15th Armored Infantry Battalion, to believe the road to Schafberg was secure and prompted his decision to have the men dismount from their half-tracks. This was a mistake. The unprotected infantrymen suffered heavy casualties. German fire killed the commander of Company A, wounded the commanders of Companies B and C, and killed several platoon leaders and platoon sergeants. Artillery and mortar fire made it impossible to resupply the forward platoons and to evacuate casualties, which now littered the countryside. It took the battalion two more days of hard fighting to clear the enemy from a wooded area less than a square mile in size. On the night of 13 December, the rifle companies had 4 officers and 170 men out of an assigned strength of 18 officers and 735 men.[13]

THE PUSH TO BIRGEL

The 329th Infantry Regiment (Col. Edwin B. Crabhill) entered the battle on the 12th and by night was at the edge of the woods overlooking Gürzenich. "I want to warn you," Macon told Crabhill, "it isn't the enemy personnel that will hold you up, it is the artillery fire that they put in front of them. Tell your people not to bunch up and use all the overhead cover because those tree bursts cause a lot of wounds."[14]

Soon after the regiment set out for Gürzenich on 13 December, Macon grew impatient with the progress. He told Crabhill, "Your dispositions show no main effort. A & B Cos. are spread out on a wide front just like the others. . . . Is that correct?"

"Yes," replied Crabhill. He went on to tell Macon that up to this point he did not have the resources to make a strong main attack.

"You must get to Gürzenich," he ordered Crabhill. "What do you propose to do?" Macon suggested that Crabhill send two companies from the 1st Battalion into Gürzenich, followed by two companies from the 3d Battalion.

"I don't think they are moving fast enough," Macon noted. "You must push out with a point and bypass that stuff [resistance outside the town] and come back after it later. . . . we must get into Gürzenich."

The exasperated Crabhill, still concerned about the threat of bypassed German troops, retorted, "If you want the town, I will go right down the road."

The exchange continued for a few more minutes, Macon demanding progress and Crabhill searching for a way to achieve it. The 2d Battalion appeared to be making the fastest progress. Macon's final comment to Crabhill was, "You are about 1000 yds fr[om] the first house of the town right now. Get into that town." The 2d battalion entered Gürzenich that afternoon.[15]

The regiment moved on the village of Birgel the next day, where the surrender of a battalion of the 47th Volksgrenadier Division caused a crisis in the German 15th Army. The American positions at Birgel amounted to a salient along the boundary of between the LXXXI and LXXIV Corps. This was a frightening prospect at the last stages of the buildup for the Ardennes offensive. The commander of the 15th Army, General von

Zangen, ordered counterattacks at both Birgel and Gürzenich to restore the situation.[16]

At least six assault guns or tanks broke through the 3d Battalion, 329th Infantry, line and entered Birgel that afternoon. The Americans ran out of bazooka ammunition, and the situation soon became critical. General Macon contacted Colonel Crabhill: "I understand you have a ticklish situation in that town [Birgel]?"

"Apparently they are holding part of the town, and we the other. . . . We ran out of bazooka ammunition and had to get back for more," replied Crabhill.

"We are keeping artillery fire on the approaches of the town," he continued. "I don't think they can get infantry in there."

A few minutes Macon told Crabhill, "I am sending you three more medium tanks right away and will try to get three more later."

Macon had asked the commander of the 774th Tank Battalion for assistance, and the commander had replied that he had four Shermans that had just been returned from maintenance, ready for combat.

"There is an emergency in 329 area & we want to hold what we have," explained Macon.

The tank battalion commander was ready to help. He promised Macon his headquarters tanks. "I will scrape up the personnel and have [the tanks] go to the 329th CP."

Sgt. Ralph G. Neppell, a machine-gun squad leader in Company M, meanwhile, single-handedly accounted for 20 enemy infantry and drove off an assault gun before a round from another vehicle wounded most of his squad and severed one of his legs below the knee. He dragged himself back to the position and continued to fire the machine gun, wounding several more enemy infantry. The fire forced another armored vehicle to withdraw. Neppell later received the Medal of Honor.

Birgel remained in the hands of the 329th Infantry.[17]

12–16 DECEMBER

On 13 December the 331st Infantry Regiment was finally making progress at Gey. Macon told the regiment's commander, Colonel York, to "push it as hard as we possibly can." York reminded Macon that it would be tough work,[18] but with tank support on hand, its capture was only a matter of time.

The situation at Strass, however, remained in doubt. The Germans had turned back every attempt to break through to the trapped 3d Battalion, 330th Infantry, which faced annihilation. The battalion had lost four commanders in two days (10–11 December). It was out of food and water and dangerously short of ammunition. The casualties desperately needed

medical attention. They probably owed their survival to German preoc-
cupation with the Ardennes buildup. The Germans were unable to shift
enough troops into the area to influence the outcome of the battle. Yet
their grip on the town did not end until the Americans swept the road
from Grosshau to Gey and took the woods west of Schafberg. Only then
could they get ambulances as far as the clearing outside town. They had
already managed to get medical supplies to the trapped men before
daylight on the 12th. A liaison plane dropped emergency rations that
afternoon. The 2d Battalion, 330th, finally relieved the men in Strass
that night, after darkness had prevented the crews of enemy assault guns
from spotting targets.[19]

CCA's 34th Tank Battalion (Lt. Col. William L. Cabaniss) had meanwhile tried but failed to take Kufferath on 14 December. A company
each of tanks and armored infantry could not get past the German
antitank guns. CCA had better luck the next day, taking both the town
and Hill 211, but the German artillery continued to pound the Americans. On the night of 17–18 December, battalion headquarters personnel
counted over 800 shells hitting the area.

Companies B and C, 15th Armored Infantry Battalion, attacked on the
morning of 14 December to seize Hills 253 and 266 and the towns of
Bergheim and Bilstein. The first objective was a quarry, surrounded by
woods, southeast of Strass. The poor road between Schafberg and Strass
delayed the arrival of supporting tanks, and German mortar and artillery shells began to fall as soon as the infantry emerged from the woods.
Company C lost several men; the loss of a squad leader in Company A
caused problems until a private took charge and reorganized the men.
Such personal acts of heroism were noteworthy, but the German defenders were too well dug in for the infantry to dislodge. An artillery
TOT and an air strike also failed to help, and the Americans withdrew
to the woods.

They tried again soon after daylight on the 15th. The infantrymen
climbed aboard the idling tanks and waited for the word to move. About
900 yards away, the crewmen of six German antitank guns, supported by
infantry, waited for the artillery fire that always preceded an American attack. It was different this time. The tanks broke from the woods,
entered the open field, and picked up speed. Most of the Germans fled
when the tanks opened fire with cannon and machine guns; those who
remained fired hardly a shot when the GIs dismounted and swarmed
into the quarry. CCB took Hill 253 the next morning and outposted the
high banks overlooking the Roer River towns of Winden, Untermaubach,
and Üdingen.[20]

The northeastern reaches of the Hürtgen Forest were now in American hands, though it took a few more days of bitter fighting to clear

pockets of resistance on the west bank of the Roer near Gürzenich. The cost to the 83d Division was 1,951 battle casualties, including 589 dead, and another 790 nonbattle casualties. For the 5th Armored Division (-CCR) the toll was 70 dead, 505 wounded, and 223 nonbattle casualties.[21]

It had taken the VII Corps four weeks of very hard fighting to get to the Roer River. Now that it was there, it still could not safely cross it.

THE V CORPS ATTACK

In late October, Ninth Army engineers had calculated that if the Germans opened the floodgates on the Schwammenauel and Urft Dams, "artificial flooding, to an extent sufficient to render the river unfordable below Linnich, is possible. . . . It is estimated that such a flood would extend itself within a few days, but it might render cross-country movement through the area difficult for a considerable period of time." The Roer would rise 25 to 30 feet at Düren. The width of the river would reach a mile and a half.[22]

As noted earlier, it is not clear exactly when the Americans began to notice the importance of the Roer Dams. It is clear, however (contrary to what the First Army Report of Operations states), that it was well after September. To reiterate, there were no operations orders or plans before December which list the Roer Dams as objectives of a ground attack. But by late November, it was apparent to most that the First Army must finally come to terms with the Roer Dams. The issue had come full circle—until November no one appears to have been concerned with the dams. Now, in late November and early December, everyone was.

Aerial reconnaissance missions over the dams occurred as often as the weather permitted. After General Hodges realized the November attack would not produce quick success, he asked Bradley to support his request for air attacks to damage or destroy the dams. This tactic would save his troops from making a costly ground attack. Air staff officers at first turned down Hodges's request but relented during the final week of November. Bad weather forced cancellation of RAF attacks planned for 30 November and the first two days of December. The next day, 190 planes dropped markers, but no bombs, on the Urft Dam. On 4 December, 200 planes set out for the dam, but only 28 attacked. A few bombs hit the base of the dam and the road leading across it, but the results were disappointing; poor weather forced cancellation of another attack planned for the next day. Though RAF Bomber Command protested wasting more time and resources on the effort, Eisenhower ordered the attacks to continue. On 8 December, 205 planes dropped 797 tons of bombs on the Urft, Schwammenauel, and Paulushof Dams. Attacks scheduled for 11, 13, and 14 December either failed or were canceled because of bad weather.[23] Hodges ordered that no unit in First Army would cross the Roer without prior instructions.

"There can be no question of the value of our present operations. . . . our problem is to continue our attacks as long as the results achieved are so much in our favor, while at the same time preparing for a full-out, heavy offensive when weather conditions become favorable," wrote General Eisenhower to Gen. George C. Marshall on 5 December. Eisenhower noted that the Germans had "the capability . . . of producing a sudden rush of water by blowing the dams near Schmidt. Bradley has about come to the conclusion that we must take that area by a very difficult attack from the west and southwest."[24]

The outcome of the air attacks reinforced Hodges's opinion that his belated decision to order a ground attack against the Schwammenauel and Urft Dams was correct. Already on 7 December General Gerow had issued Field Order 33, directing that an attack on the dams begin not later than 13 December. This order was in accordance with earlier instructions from Hodges. The V Corps would envelop the dams with a simultaneous attack by the 78th Infantry Division (part of the corps as of 7 December) and the 2d Infantry Division.[25]

The corps faced difficult terrain that restricted most cross-country movement. The roads in the zone of attack were narrow and winding. The main terrain features were the hill mass outside Monschau, the Dreiborn Ridge running southeast from the Urft reservoir, and the Roer and Olef Rivers. The plan was as follows. The 78th Division's 309th and 310th Infantry Regiments would take the Monschau Corridor villages of Simmerath, Kesternich, Rollesbroich, Konzen, Eicherscheid, and Imgenbroich. The division would then capture Steckenborn and Strauch, followed by the high ground south of Schmidt and then the Schwammenauel Dam.[26] The 2d Division would attack through the Krinkelter Forest in Belgium and take a customs station at Wahlerscheid. The division would then enter the Monschau Forest and attack the Dreiborn Ridge. The objectives were the village of Rohren, a hill 3,000 yards to the east, a road junction near Morsbach, and the Urft Dam. Gerow recognized the difficulty of the terrain and attached the 99th Division's 395th Regiment to the 2d Division to protect the division's right flank as it passed through the Monschau Forest.

Intelligence officers estimated German strength at about 21,750 men opposite the V Corps, emplaced mainly against the 8th Division. In the north, these were the remnants of the 85th and 89th Infantry Divisions, both part of LXXIV Corps. (Remnants of the 275th Infantry Division were in the area but posed no real threat.) General der Infanterie Otto Hitzfeld's LXVII Corps (6th Panzer Army) controlled the Kommerscheidt-Wahlerscheid sector, its 272d Volksgrenadier Division defended the

Monschau Corridor, and the 277th Volksgrenadier Division defended the Hollerath area.[27]

THE NORTHERN WING

The day before the attack (12 December), General Hodges told the commander of the new 78th Division, Maj. Gen. E. P. Parker, that the division had "nothing to be nervous about" as it entered combat, "that it had been proven time and time again, that our training methods in the United States were not only correct but completely adequate to defeat the Boche, and that he had the utmost confidence that the 78th would tomorrow begin its battle history with a fine showing."[28]

Hodges was correct—the training methods were physically demanding and effective. Soldiers progressed through a series of steps from individual training through large-scale unit problems at the division level. In the periods of instruction, army schools included training in lessons learned from combat, with emphasis on close-combat weapons firing. The training centers emphasized realism, but actual combat was really the only way to determine just how well the men were prepared.[29] The 78th Division paid a high price in men killed, wounded, and missing during its indoctrination to combat, but it learned its lessons very well indeed.

Wednesday, 13 December, dawned very cold with a dense fog when the 310th Infantry's (Col. Earl M. Miner) 3d Battalion began its attack across the rolling, snow-covered farmland to take Rollesbroich. About 5:00 A.M., the squad and platoon leaders ordered the men to leave their foxholes and begin an exhausting climb up the 200-foot-high hill marking the LD.

Company K remained undetected by the Germans until a soldier stepped on a mine. Not long afterward, as the faint gray light of early morning began to silhouette the GIs moving across the fields, the Germans began to pick out their targets. One squad rushed through the fire, took a few prisoners, and reached a hill near Rollesbroich. Company L, meanwhile, came under fire from enemy troops in a Westwall bunker camouflaged to look like a farmhouse. A few men bypassed the bunker and ran through mortar fire to reach Rollesbroich, where a house-to-house firefight raged until late afternoon.[30] General Parker told Colonel Miner, "Make sure you button up tonight because you can expect something in the morning."[31]

Another unit in action that day was the 1st Battalion, 309th Infantry. Assisted by the 3d Battalion, it took Simmerath, which looked like "a jumbled mess, buildings leaning crazily as if after a hurricane."[32] Automatic weapons fire from concrete bunkers meanwhile delayed the attack of the 3d Battalion, 309th Infantry, on Bickerath, and the regiment's 2d Battalion ran into serious trouble at Kesternich, which became the 78th Division's own small piece of hell. Capture of Kesternich would give the division complete control of the southern approaches to Schmidt, and once and for all, give the Americans free use of the Simmerath-Duren Road.

The commander of the 2d Battalion, 309th Infantry, Lt. Col. Wilson L. Burley, Jr., designated Company E to make the main effort. Company F would protect its flank; Company G would support.

The Germans knew full well the importance of Kesternich to the Americans. Despite the pressure throughout the Monschau Corridor on 13 December, the 980th Infantry Regiment (272d Volksgrenadier Division), with strong artillery support, was ready for Colonel Burley's battalion.

The lead elements of Company F, 309th, hit a dense belt of antipersonnel mines a few hundred yards past the LD west of Kesternich. Mortar and artillery fire then trapped several men in the snow-covered ground. This eliminated flank protection for Company E.

The tanks (Companies A and C, 709th Tank Battalion) carrying about 160 Company E soldiers, meanwhile, were silhouetted dark against the snow, perfect targets for the German artillery and antitank guns. German mortar fire hit the tanks and infantry soon after they had moved from Lammersdorf. This caused a 25-minute delay, and it was already past 2:00 P.M. Darkness would arrive within three hours.

More fire hit the column at Witzerath. The Germans had blocked the road leading from there to Kesternich and probably had it under observation by antitank gun crews. This led the Americans to decide to leave the road and set out cross-country. The tanks had moved only a few yards off the road just northwest of Kesternich when they hit a section of soft ground covered by deep snow. Antitank rounds began to slam into the tanks. The infantry had to dismount, and plans for a combined-arms attack ended with failure. With the exception of a few men from Company F, those of Company E were alone and desperate to get to the relative safety of the buildings in the town. It was about 4:00 P.M. The commander of Company E thought his men had surprised the German infantry; however, he added, "the mortar fire . . . was intense."

The commander, Capt. Richey V. Graham, talked with Colonel Burley. The elements of the rifle company were in danger of becoming separated as they dismounted and pushed toward Kesternich. Graham "stood out on the road and directed them like a traffic cop."

The tanks, or rather, targets, withdrew into an assembly area.

Kesternich was far too strongly defended to fall to the few riflemen, who quickly came to think that the war was now "a fight between Company E and the German Army." The shelling had so disrupted communications that Colonel Burley was not certain of the location of Company E; he hoped there might be a few men in Kesternich. Burley, who had ridden on a tank, was himself in a foxhole near the road leading into Kesternich.[33]

Burley halted the attack after dark. The first attack on Kesternich was over.

It was nearly impossible that night for V Corps headquarters to get reliable information from the 78th Division about the situation at Kesternich. The only report to reach Hodges was from a liaison officer to the division. Hodges did not like the report, which indicated that there was a "confused situation and lack of knowledge" at the 78th Division CP. The army commander feared that General Parker's new division would "get itself smacked by the Boche as was the 28th Div. at Schmidt, and he told the corps commander in very definite language to get the thing straightened out."[34]

THE PUSH FROM THE SOUTH

The 2d Infantry Division confronted a major problem from the outset of the December attack. For a main supply route and axis of attack, the division had to use a single unpaved, narrow road leading north from the Belgian villages of Krinkelt and Rocherath to the Wahlerscheid customs post and the Westwall, where it joined a road leading to Monschau. The division commander, 56-year-old Maj. Gen. Walter Roberston, directed Col. Chester J. Hirschfelder's 9th Infantry Regiment to make the division's main effort astride the road. Robertson wanted "only *minimum essential* vehicles" (emphasis in original) to use the road, and he assigned the division's engineer battalion the task of maintaining it. The dangers were obvious should a German counterattack against the sides or base of the penetration succeed. The enemy could easily cut off any unit on the forest-cloaked road.

After taking Wahlerscheid, the 9th Infantry would move northeast to hit the German positions behind Höfen and Alzen. Col. Francis H. Boos's 38th Infantry would follow in column one hour behind the 9th Infantry as far as Wahlerscheid, where it would turn northeast and move against the Urft Dam. The 23rd Infantry (Col. Jay B. Loveless) would be in reserve at Camp Elsenborn. As an added measure of security, the 99th Infantry Division's 395th Infantry Regiment (Col. Alexander J. Mackenzie) and a battalion of its 393d Infantry would make a supporting attack through the forest on the flank of the 9th Infantry.[35]

To maintain secrecy, the division conducted no patrols before the attack. Once on the road to Wahlerscheid, the infantry had to contend with mines buried under several inches of wet snow. The ground was generally flat, but the men tired quickly from wading through the snow while carrying full packs, extra rations, and ammunition. To compound the discomfort, a midmorning thaw caused the frost and snow to fall from the trees like a rain shower. Nevertheless, by early afternoon, the cold and wet troops faced only sporadic German fire and had reached the vicinity of the customs station.

Scouts saw that the defenses consisted of interlocked, felled trees, protected by booby traps and mines and concertina and barbed-wire obstacles that were up to 30 yards deep. At least six concrete bunkers and four log bunkers dotted the area. Heavy mortar, small-arms, and artillery fire crashed down as soon as the enemy realized the Americans were in the area. The GIs could not withdraw or advance. They dug in and endured a cold night during which their clothing froze to their skin.[36]

KESTERNICH, 14–16 DECEMBER

Lt. Col. Byron W. Ladd's 2d Battalion, 310th Infantry, received orders late on 13 December to assist the 2d Battalion, 309th Infantry, at Kesternich. Ladd's inexperienced battalion had received word only that a battalion of the 309th needed help. He received no details about enemy dispositions or defenses. Kesternich would have been a tough place to take even for an experienced unit—it was impossible for a new outfit.

Ladd's battalion failed to conduct proper reconnaissance. A concrete troop shelter that covered the western approaches to Kesternich remained undiscovered, as did the extent of a system of trenches protected by automatic weapons and snipers.[37]

The attack began about 6:00 A.M. Automatic weapons fire from the troop shelter hit the Company E and F riflemen soon after they had left Simmerath. Because of reports that a platoon's worth of troops from the 2d Battalion, 309th, were in Kesternich, division would not give permission to fire artillery into the town ahead of the 2d Battalion, 310th. While trying to escape the fire, Company F riflemen touched off antipersonnel mines buried throughout the area. The reserve, Company G, was so close behind the attacking companies that it suffered several casualties from the same fire that hit Company F. Thus, Colonel Ladd was unable to use Company G to properly assist the remainder of the battalion.

Company commanders estimated the casualties in the 2d Battalion, 310th Infantry, at 25 percent. This attack stalled just outside Kesternich. The Americans used the darkness as cover to evacuate the wounded and dead and for resupply.[38]

Lt. Colonel Burley, the commander of the 2d Battalion, 309th Infantry, went into Kesternich to assess the situation for himself. His body was later found in the town. The executive officer also disappeared and was presumed dead, though his body was never recovered. The commander of Company H, Capt. Douglas P. Frazier, took command.[39]

Company E, 309th, meanwhile was still without tank support. The tankers told the infantrymen that the German fire was too intense, and they wanted a bulldozer to clear the road of snow and debris. The commander of Company E and the commander of the 774th Tank Battalion were arguing about the issue when a shell hit and wounded several men. (The tank battalion commander, who was standing only a few feet from the others, was not hit.) Nothing improved when the bulldozer finally arrived. It "would not advance in front of the tanks, and the tanks would not advance without a bulldozer in front. . . . Therefore nobody advanced—except the infantry."[40] Troops dubbed the battalion CP "88 Junction" because of the enemy fire.[41]

That night, patrols maintained contact between the separated elements of the 2d Battalion, 309th Infantry, and 2d Battalion, 310th Infantry. Companies F and G of the 309th were north of town. Companies E, F, and G of the 310th were along the road leading from Simmerath. The patrols would silently leave their foxholes and enter the no-man's-land around Kesternich. These night patrols resembled hunting—or to use a more accurate description, stalking an enemy. Some patrols disappeared without a trace; others brought back prisoners, who were useful sources of combat intelligence.

About 1:00 A.M. on the 15th, the executive officer of the 309th Infantry, Lt. Col. Creighton E. Likes, took control of the two battalions. He would direct a coordinated tank, artillery, infantry attack, scheduled to begin at dawn.

Some ten minutes of artillery fire hammered the rubble of Kesternich. The Americans neutralized the troop shelter, and some medium tanks and elements of Company E, 310th, reportedly entered Kesternich before noon. Company F swept along the southern fringe of the town and secured its objective, as well. Despite the artillery and the rather well executed tank-infantry attack, the Germans still forced the Americans to fight house to house. The reserve, Company B, meanwhile assaulted the troop shelter.

Problems arose, however, as soon as the process of consolidating the objective began. Every step along the single main road running the length of Kesternich caused problems with command and control of the separated squads and platoons. Soldiers returned to the rear with prisoners and were therefore unavailable for the preparations to defend the town. Other men acted on their own and took shelter in the houses that still stood. This caused disorganization because the squad and platoon leaders no longer knew where their troops were. German artillery fire continued, and the troops were tired from fighting their way through the snow as well as the enemy fire. Losses among junior leaders had been high as well.

Colonel Ladd and his S-2 went to the town about 2:00 P.M., but they left the artillery observer behind. Ladd met with Colonel Likes, who instructed him to begin defensive preparations immediately. The radios were not working, and Likes then left Kesternich to report to the commander of the 309th at the regimental CP. Likes returned to Kesternich a few hours later.

About 4:00 P.M., just after the battalion communications section finished laying wire to Ladd's CP, German artillery fire began to fall with renewed intensity. At the time, Ladd was meeting with his company commanders. Then, a breathless messenger arrived and reported a counterattack. Ladd told the commanders to hold the town "at all costs."

The phone lines went out almost immediately, but the artillery observers were not in position to call for fire support anyway. Ladd told his S-2 to get back to Colonel Likes and get tank support. But darkness was approaching, and by the time the observers had word of the events in Kesternich, it was too dark for them to see, and they had made no plans for prearranged defensive fires.

The S-3 of the 2d Battalion, 310th, reported that Company E withdrew into the houses and that Company F temporarily stopped the counterattack in its sector. This gave the company enough time to organize a line in the western part of the town. Fifty-six of the estimated 70 men in this group remained alive and surrendered on the 16th.

Company G, meanwhile, became scattered as its men tried to plug gaps throughout the town. The Germans fired an estimated 800 rounds of artillery and mortar fire on the 2d Battalion, 310th. Ladd led several men from Company G in a futile stand near the battalion CP. The Germans took most of this group prisoner.

To this day, no one is really sure what happened in Kesternich during the night of 15–16 December. Isolated fighting continued throughout the night. Captain Frazier, the commander of the 2d Battalion, 309th, accompanied a patrol from his battalion that reached the edge of Kesternich. Though Frazier believed there were still some Americans holding out, the patrol heard only German voices in the town. Another patrol actually entered a house, which they found full of Germans. The GIs used grenades to cover their hasty withdrawal.

On the afternoon of the 16th the 3d Battalion, 309th, together with the remainder of the 2d Battalion, 310th (a makeshift force of clerks, cooks, and heavy weapons men), managed to reenter the western part of Kesternich. The S-3 of the 2d Battalion, 310th, said later that "very few men from the battalion were found in any of the houses, none [of them] were alive."

When Colonel Ondrick, the commander of the 309th, decided there were no survivors, he withdrew the attackers. Later estimates of losses in the 2d Battalion, 310th Infantry, were 6 officers and 63 enlisted men killed; 5 officers and nearly 100 enlisted men wounded; and nearly 300 officers and men missing. Some 75 men sustained nonbattle injuries, mostly trench foot.[42] The authorized strength of the battalion, less attachments, was 871.[43]

Kesternich would remain in German hands for weeks. In three days the 78th Division lost nearly a thousand men and failed to clear the Monschau Corridor. The division was unable to meet General Parker's directive that "ground once gained will not be given up."[44]

HEARTBREAK CROSSROADS

The enemy resistance at Wahlerscheid meanwhile remained too strong for the 9th Infantry to break on 14 December. A map taken from a captured German lieutenant revealed that there were only two narrow strips of safe ground along the regiment's front. The commander of the 2d Battalion, Lt. Col. Walter M. Higgins, decided on the 15th to push through a narrow gap cut in the wire on the first day of the attack by a patrol from Company G. For a variety of reasons, including the wounding and evacuation of the company commander, Higgins had not learned of the first penetration of the German defenses until the 15th.

After dark, a squad leader led his men to the gap in the wire. About 9:30 P.M., he spoke quietly into the phone and reported that his men had surrounded a concrete bunker. The Germans inside were apparently too tired or too comfortable to notice the Americans. Before dawn on 16 December, Higgins sent first Company F and then Company E through the gap, and the Americans took 71 prisoners. Robertson ordered the commander of the 38th Infantry to push his 1st and 2d Battalions through the lines of the 9th Infantry.

The renewed attack was short-lived. German artillery fire was unusually heavy on 16 December. The 99th Division reported strong attacks along its front. In view of the uncertain situation, General Robertson and the new deputy V Corps commander, Major General Hubner (who had been transferred to V Corps and replaced at the 1st Infantry Division by Brig. Gen. Clift Andrus), agreed to have the units at Wahlerscheid halt their attack. The danger was apparent. If the 99th Division failed to protect the 2d Division's right flank, the Germans might cut off the 9th and 38th Infantry Regiments. The Americans withdrew from Wahlerscheid. They called that miserable, snow-covered piece of ground Heartbreak Crossroads.[45]

Between 16 November and 16 December, over 100,000 First Army soldiers fought in and immediately around the Hürtgen Forest. The losses in VII Corps (less the 104th Division) amounted to 11,699 battle casualties, including 1,722 killed. There were another 6,481 nonbattle casualties. Losses in V Corps were well over 7,000 battle casualties and nonbattle casualties. This was over 24 percent of the troops actively engaged.[46]

The straight-line distance from Roetgen to the Roer at Düren is less than ten miles, but it took three months for the First Army to cover that distance. And even after the Americans had reached the Roer, they still could not cross the river because the dams remained in enemy hands.

The start of the Battle of the Bulge signaled the end of the first phase of the battle of the Hürtgen Forest. The Germans had managed to fight the First Army to a stalemate. They bought the time they needed for buildup of the forces for the Ardennes attack. Had they not wasted valuable resources on the ill-fated drive through the Ardennes, the Germans probably could have conducted a fighting withdrawal to the Rhine behind a flooded Roer plain. This might have delayed until well into 1945 the Allied crossing of the Rhine.

The Germans were able to capitalize on American weakness, while the Americans were for the most part unable to do the same with the German weaknesses. The supply situation in First Army throughout the fall of 1944, coupled with the effects of the terrain and attrition on its ability to apply the combined-arms doctrine of air, artillery, and mobile firepower were important reasons for this failure. Still, the Germans, for all their manpower and logistic problems, fought a well-executed delaying battle. Had the Americans won the race for the Westwall in September and reached Germany fully supplied, they might have gained the Roer weeks if not months earlier than they did. Yet this meant little without early recognition of the importance of the Roer dams.

Some combat in the Hürtgen Forest was almost inevitable, given the axis of the First Army's attack into Germany. Thus, the principal failure of the First Army's approach to the obstacle of the Roer River was not the fact that it entered the forest. The failure was in not seeing the importance of the Roer dams and at least attempting to take them before December. As a result, the struggle in the Ardennes meant not so much a delay in reaching the Rhine as it did another obstacle along the way to the Roer.

13
Final Battles and Capture of the Dams

The outcome of the battle of the Ardennes was clear by the first week of 1945, and the Allies could at last turn their attention to the battle for Germany's interior. The combined chiefs of staff accepted Eisenhower's plan, which called for first bringing the armies to the easily defensible Rhine before launching the main attack into Germany north of the Ruhr industrial area. A secondary attack would pass through the terrain corridor in the Mainz-Frankfurt area and then to Kassel. The 21 Army Group (with the Ninth U.S. Army) would make the main effort, beginning with an attack by the Canadian First Army to close to the Rhine. The Ninth U.S. Army would attack on 10 February to cross the Roer, reach the Rhine, and then link up with the Canadians.[1] But nothing could happen unless the First Army had control of the Roer dams, and they had to be in American hands by the start of the Ninth Army attack. The dams were so important, in fact, that Eisenhower would cancel a 12th Army Group attack in the Eifel. He ordered First Army to go over to the defensive, pending capture of the dams.[2]

SETTING THE STAGE: 30 JANUARY–2 FEBRUARY 1945

The 78th Division (then assigned to Ninth Army) participated in the canceled 12th Army Group operation with a limited objective attack to secure the north flank of the First Army. This also set the stage for the final drive on the dams. Two regiments of the division, plus CCA, 5th Armored Division, fought in the frozen hill country of the Monschau Corridor to take the north bank of the Roer River between Monschau and Einruhr.[3]

The 3d Battalion, 310th Infantry, supported by armor, took Konzen against weak opposition on 30 January. Meanwhile the 2d Battalion, supported by British-manned Crocodile flame-thrower tanks, took 32 Westwall bunkers near Bickerath and Am Gericht in less than two hours. The 1st Battalion entered Imgenbroich on the morning of 31 January and contacted elements of the neighboring 9th Division.

The 1st Battalion, 311th Infantry, attached to CCA, 5th Armored Division, also fought on the 30th, and it ran into trouble at Eicherscheid. Minefields, snowdrifts, and narrow roads slowed the tanks and separated them from the riflemen. The snow also stopped the half-tracks and forced the armored infantry to dismount. The Americans took 230 prisoners in the town, including three women. A lieutenant who entered a German aid station found the medics were armed with pistols. A medical officer said the weapons were for the fatally wounded—since the medics lacked enough supplies to treat every soldier, they planned to kill the mortally wounded to end their misery.[4]

The 3d Battalion, 311th Infantry Regiment (Lt. Col. Andy A. Lipscomb), attacked Huppenbroich. There were problems here with command, control, and combined-arms cooperation. Company K was in the town before noon, but it took until the next morning to clear all the buildings, and the battalion lost about 125 men killed and wounded, a high number for such a brief action. Lipscomb later said, "We were fighting the elements. The men were tired when they moved up the hill. The snow was very deep. The wind was very high, sweeping the snow in their eyes so that they could barely see or hear. They were so very numb and tired that they couldn't hit the ground when the artillery and mortar fire fell beside them. . . . Every house contained enemy." He added, "My men were evacuated by German sleds and horses. Some of my men died from exposure after being wounded. A reasonable amount of casualties could have been saved if we had the winter equipment to evacuate the wounded."[5]

The division also renewed its attack on Kesternich. Nearly all of the town had remained in German hands after the 15 December counterattack that had virtually destroyed the 2d Battalion, 310th Infantry. "You couldn't approach the damned place," said the division G-3.[6]

The bitter lessons of the December battle were still fresh in the minds of the soldiers of the Lightning Division, and Parker's staff prepared very detailed plans. Each rifle squad in the attacking battalion (2d of the 311th) was assigned a specific building to take. Special maps had each building designated by number. The 736th Tank Battalion and the 893d Tank Destroyer Battalion were in support.

This attack also began on 30 January, but the detailed plans quickly began to fall apart. The snow covered landmarks. The tanks tried to plow through the snow but lost traction and fell behind. Mines knocked out four tanks. Radio communication between the infantry and tanks failed, and about 10:30 A.M., Lt. Col. Richard W. Keyes, the commander of the 2d Battalion, committed his reserve company.[7] He said, "The situation became confusing. The battle had lost its coordination, and the fighting had become piecemeal. . . . It was very difficult to pick out specific buildings indicated on the sketch. Most of them had either been demolished completely or had lost their form. . . . Many elements of the companies were scattered and difficult to control."

Keyes left his CP and entered Kesternich for a first-hand look at the situation. The commander of Company E told him that he had committed all three of his rifle platoons but had not gained the company objective. Why not hold in place and reorganize, he asked Keyes. The battalion commander replied that "our objective was the other end of town and that that was where we were going."

Keyes then ordered both companies E and F to make a coordinated attack at 2:30 P.M. Keyes arranged for artillery. He told the company commanders their men would "open up with maximum small arms fire including automatic weapons and advance by marching fire."

The battalion succeeded in gaining a few hundred yards, though not all of the town. Keyes later stated, "The tank-infantry coordination was not favorable. The tanks seemed to expect the infantry to lead them and the infantry was prone to wait on the tanks. The telephones on the rear of the tanks were out in every instance and the radio net was [an] on and off proposition, sometimes operating and sometimes not."

The battalion dug in for the night. The tanks withdrew for maintenance and resupply.[8]

A squad leader in Company F, S.Sgt. Jonah E. Kelley, was wounded in the back and left hand, but he refused evacuation, permitting medics only to bandage the wounds. He was unable to hold his rifle with both hands, and he rested it on rubble or on his left forearm. Despite his wounds, he rushed a house alone and killed three of the enemy. The next day, he ordered his men to remain under cover while he charged an enemy-held building. He was hit several times as he ran across open ground and fell mortally wounded 25 yards from the enemy. Before he died, he silenced the enemy with rifle fire. He was awarded a posthumous Medal of Honor.[9]

The attack continued on the morning of the 31st, and radio communications with the tanks failed again that afternoon. Colonel Willingham, the commander of the 311th Infantry, later said that problems with the armor caused the attack to take an extra day. "Hesitation and lack of aggression on the part of this tank unit, in my opinion, resulted in over

50 unnecessary casualties. A tank unit that is not aggressive is a detriment to the infantry."[10]

The division secured Kesternich the next day; the cost was another 224 men. The Americans soon understood why the Germans held to the town with such determination. From Kesternich, American artillery observers could direct fire on all German positions in the area immediately west of the Schwammenauel reservoir.

BACKGROUND TO THE CAPTURE OF THE SCHWAMMENAUEL DAM

The final chapter in the battle for the Hürtgen Forest and Roer dams began on 2 February 1945, when the 78th Division returned to First Army control. General Parker, the division commander, and his G-3, Lt. Col. Charles A. McKinney, met that evening with General Hubner at V Corps headquarters. Hubner told Parker and McKinney that it was vital to capture the dams before 10 February. He was prepared to give Parker whatever support he needed.[11]

Parker had the division concentrate against successive objectives. He intended to avoid the Kall River gorge and approach Schmidt from the south. This would allow the division to approach the Schwammenauel Dam from the north. The 3d Battalion, 309th Infantry, would move from Rollesbroich and seize both an enemy troop barracks complex on the south edge of the forest and a nearby settlement called Silberscheidt. The 311th Infantry would make a simultaneous attack to secure the approaches to the Schwammenauel reservoir at Rurberg, Wofflesbach, and Hechelscheidt. The 3d Battalion, 310th Infantry, with CCR, 7th Armored Division, would take Strauch and Steckenborn, two objectives in the Monschau Corridor the division did not take in December. In the next phase, the 310th Infantry would pass through the positions of the 309th Infantry at the barracks and drive on Schmidt and Harscheidt. The 311th would then pass through the 310th Infantry to secure the northeastern approaches to the dam. The 309th Infantry would take the dam. General Hubner, the new V Corps commander (he had replaced Gerow in mid-January), reinforced the 78th Division with CCR, 7th Armored Division, a battalion of combat engineers, and the fires of several battalions of artillery. The attack was scheduled to begin at 3:00 A.M., 5 February.[12]

Lieutenant Colonel McKinney remembered: "It was decided to spare nothing to make the attack go. Troops were to be committed in sufficient strength to overcome any opposition. There was pressure from SHAEF all the way down. Generals Eisenhower, Bradley, and Hodges

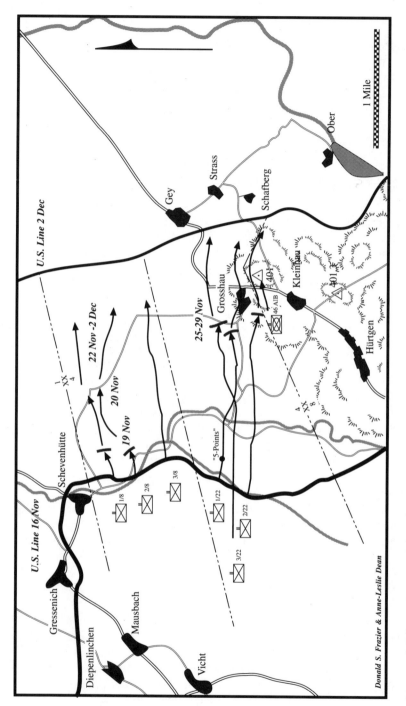

U.S. Line 16 Nov

U.S. Line 2 Dec

Gressenich

Diepenlinchen

Schevenhütte

Mausbach

Vicht

1/8

2/8

3/8

3/22

1/22

2/22

"5-Points"

19 Nov

20 Nov

22 Nov - 2 Dec

25-29 Nov

XX
4

Grosshau

Gey

Strass

Schafberg

401
46 AIB

401

Kleinhau

Hürtgen

XX
4
8

Ober

1 Mile

Donald S. Frazier & Anne-Leslie Dean

Map 7. 4th Infantry Division, November–December 1944

stayed in close contact with the situation. General Hubner of V Corps was frequently at the division CP. . . . the 78th was a new [division], and Corps did not want anything to go wrong."[13] This statement goes a long way in explaining the pressure on Parker and the division.

Parker ordered the 311th Infantry to make a preliminary attack to clear the division's sector as far as the Roer south of the Schwammenauel reservoir. One of the targets was Dedenborn, a village perched on high ground on the east bank of the river.

Early on 3 February, two platoons each of Companies A and C, 1st Battalion, 311th Infantry, moved slowly through a draw outside Huppenbroich into the Roer Valley. The Germans reacted quickly. Grazing fire ripped through the underbrush. The Roer here was narrow, normally slow running, and only chest deep, but melting snows had turned it into a torrent. Attempts to bridge the river with logs failed. Company A managed to establish a base of fire to cover Company C when it tried to cross the river. One officer reported, "No one who got across knows how he did it."

The riflemen hit the water firing their weapons, but of two platoons sent across, only 2 officers and 31 enlisted men reached the east bank. At least a dozen men drowned or were killed by enemy fire. The current pushed some men back against the western bank and swept others away. The commander of Company A nearly drowned before a soldier rescued him. "One would get across and crawl painfully up from the water," reported a company commander. Few of those who survived the crossing able to fight still had their weapons. The surviving platoon leaders organized an assault and secured Dedenborn that afternoon. Fortunately, there was no resistance.[14]

The 311th Infantry's 3d Battalion (Lieutenant Colonel Lipscomb) meanwhile cleared the road between Kesternich and Einruhr, a village nestled along the Roer and Schwammenauel reservoir, opposite the ridge upon which Kesternich was located. The draws on either side of Company I were full of Germans. The company commander was "damned glad the Germans are not good shots. We would get one Jerry, he would squeal like hell and roll down the hill, then another would come up just like a duck in a shooting gallery. The sons of bitches didn't know any better."[15]

THE FINAL ATTACK, 5–10 FEBRUARY

Monday, 5 February 1945, brought a cold, driving rain. The 3d Battalion, 309th Infantry, with Company E attached, attacked before daylight. The men slowly worked their way through the forest, stumbling into trees and falling over debris and bushes. By daylight, the leading elements were nearing the barracks. The 2d Battalion, 309th Infantry, meanwhile closed in on several concrete bunkers. More than 100 Germans surrendered without firing a shot.[16]

About 9:00 A.M., General Parker ordered the 310th Infantry (Col. Earl M. Miner) to move through the positions of the 309th. However, before the 310th Infantry could move, engineers had to check the roads for mines. While the 310th Infantry waited in the rain for the engineers to complete their work, Parker for a time considered ordering the 309th Infantry to continue the attack. Hubner, however, moved first. He was under pressure from Hodges, and he ordered the 9th Division to cross the Roer near the Urft Dam and set up blocking positions to deny the Germans access from the east. He ordered Parker to move a regiment across the Roer at Rurberg to take the Paulushof Dam and secure wooded high ground to the east. From there, the regiment would move on the Schwammenauel Dam. Parker selected the 311th Infantry. McKinney attributed the change in orders to an "excited" staff officer at corps headquarters.[17]

The result was a hastily organized and ultimately needless attack by the 311th Infantry. The operations officer of the regiment's 1st Battalion said that at Rurberg "it was raining like a son of a bitch. Isolated fighting was going on the right side of us. We laid around in the rain all day. Then after a while, the Jerries began to throw mortar fire in on us. Just at the first house going into Rurberg six mortar shells came in, and every shell hit somebody." The fire wounded the battalion commander, his communications officer, and the Company A commander. The S-1, artillery liaison officer, and four other men were killed, including two war correspondents.[18] Officers on reconnaissance later found that the crossing site was under enemy observation and the river current in the area was too strong to bridge anyway. Hubner canceled the operation.[19]

Meanwhile, in the vicinity of the barracks, the engineers determined that the roads were not clear enough for the employment of tanks. Then, about 11:00 A.M. (5 February) Parker, acting under instructions from Hubner, also ordered the 309th Infantry to continue as far as possible before digging in. He also ordered the 310th Infantry (with the attached 1st Battalion, 309th) to continue moving when it reached the forward positions of the 309th, wherever they may be.

Hubner next told Parker to push the 309th Infantry all the way to Schmidt, whether or not the 310th caught up. This was a more difficult proposition than Hubner realized. The 3d Battalion, 309th Infantry, had already begun to dig in and was waiting for the 310th Infantry. The 2d Battalion was still some distance away, and it would be difficult for it to break contact with the enemy.

The 1st Battalion, 309th Infantry, was rested and had not been engaged. Yet for the battalion to enter the attack, it had to work through the two battalions of the 310th already on the move. Parker ordered the 310th Infantry to allow the 1st Battalion, 309th Infantry, to pass. By this time, however, it was growing dark, and the battalion was still nearly 1,000 yards from the front line. When it became clear that there were too many generals issuing too many conflicting orders, Parker and Hubner agreed to halt the attack and have the 310th Infantry take the lead on 6 February. The confusion caused by the changing orders affected morale. Staff officers wrote in the 310th Infantry operations journal: "Corps unhappy about progress. Stopped when it hit resistance. Must attack Schmidt at daylight."[20]

At 3:00 A.M. on 6 February, the 1st and 2d Battalions, 310th Infantry, attacked through the lines of the 309th Infantry at the barracks. The soldiers were unable to determine their exact locations in the pitch-black darkness. The 1st Battalion lost several men, and some were pinned down until daylight. The 2d Battalion also suffered several casualties. Some of them were due to soldiers falling into old German foxholes. By 10:00 A.M., the attacking battalions had advanced less than 500 yards, the men were lost, and they repelled a German counterattack only after a hard fight.[21] Unfortunately for Parker, General Hubner visited the division the same day. He told Parker that he was displeased with the division and that "with all the strength we had in that area, greater gains should have been made."[22]

This led Parker on 7 February to commit all three of the division's regiments. Things went a little better. The 309th Infantry took Kommerscheidt. The 3d Battalion, 310th Infantry, attacked along the Strauch-Schmidt road to take Hill 493, located on the southern outskirts of Schmidt. The 311th Infantry drew the mission of taking Schmidt itself. To add weight to the attack, Hubner issued an order early the same day that directed the 82d Airborne Division to assist Parker's division. Hubner was anxious to ensure no recurrence of the confusion of the first day, and he personally directed the operation from Parker's CP.[23]

At midmorning, Lieutenant Colonel Lipscomb, commander of the 3d Battalion, 311th Infantry, received orders to have his battalion "keep fighting right thru; go as far as you can; our objective is the dam." The night before, Lipscomb had received a warning order to this effect and had coordinated the attack with the commander of the attached Company A, 774th Tank Battalion. Antitank fire hit the lead tank soon after the battalion jumped off, and the others lost no time in returning to the LD. They were still carrying the infantry.[24]

The commander of the tank company refused to move his vehicles forward. Neither Lieutenant Colonel Lipscomb nor Lt. Col. Harry Lutz, whose battalion was by then on Hill 493 and who begged the company commander to move the tanks, got him to do so. Two infantry lieutenants offered to lead the tanks personally from their covered positions to the riflemen. The tanks did not budge.[25] One company commander said, "The tanks would not go with the infantry, nor without the infantry."[26] Despite the fire, Company I, now greatly understrength, managed to reach Schmidt.

On the night of 7 February, Parker directed the 309th Infantry to take the Schwammenauel Dam. The 310th Infantry would pass through Schmidt early the next day and secure the LD. The 311th Infantry was the division reserve. When he issued the order, Parker believed Schmidt was securely in the hands of the 311th Infantry. Early on the 8th, the 3d Battalion, 310th Infantry, learned this was not the case.[27]

The 1st Battalion, 311th Infantry, held positions only as far as 100 yards into the town. Two officers from the 3d Battalion reported several firefights. The commander of Company I sent a rifle platoon supported by two tanks through the town. German fire pinned the men down before they had moved 200 yards, but by night they had reached positions about a mile east of the town. By this time, the streets in Schmidt were covered by debris, mud, and water-filled shell craters. Here and there, the dead animals were beginning to thaw. So were dead American and German soldiers from the November battle.

The slow pace of the fight to clear Schmidt led General Hodges to telephone General Hubner to state his disappointment with the 78th Division. According to Lieutenant Colonel McKinney, "By this time some of the units were getting groggy. The corps commander decided that the division was getting tired."[28] The 3d Battalion, 309th Infantry, for example, reported high morale but indicated that the troops were in poor physical condition "due to fatigue and exposure."[29]

Coincidentally, General Craig, the commander of the 9th Division, entered Hubner's CP a few minutes after the phone conversation. The 9th Division had captured the Urft Dam on 5 February and was still near Simmerath. Hubner lost no time in putting Craig in charge of the attack on the Schwammenauel Dam. He asked Craig how long it would take to reinforce the 78th Division with a regiment from the 9th Division. Craig said a regiment could move immediately. Hubner then decided to attach the 309th and 311th Regiments to the 9th Division, effective at 9:00 P.M. That afternoon, Hubner issued a letter of instructions directing the 78th Division to "continue aggressive attack" until the 9th Division (less the 39th Infantry) moved to the Strauch area and took responsibility for the attack on the dam.[30]

At a meeting that night of the battalion commanders, a regimental staff officer recorded the following in the 310th Infantry's journal: "Operations must be completed regardless of casualties. Large operations depending on this dam. . . . Time limit Feb. 10. Fan out and maneuver

The final objective: the Schwammenauel Dam. Lieutenant Colonel Schellman's 1st Battalion, 309th Infantry, made its attack from the high ground in the top center of the photograph. (Courtesy U.S. Army)

around obstacles. This is a maximum command order. Key factor on Western Front. This will shorten the war."[31]

As a precaution, First Army Headquarters had already issued a "Roer River Flood" warning memorandum to the subordinate corps commanders on 6 February "to advise all concerned in the event of a flood on the Roer River." The army headquarters established an alert system using the communications network of the antiaircraft air warning service. Ground observers would transmit an in-the-clear radio or telephone message to their operations officers. The S-3 or G-3 would then relay the message to army headquarters. "Warning of a break in the dams and resultant floods will take precedence over any other [communications] traffic," stated the memorandum. The 82d Airborne Division Situation Summary of 8 February contained a warning that "the greatest damage would be caused by the flood wave, which would destroy everything in its path." The summary went on to say that the Germans would not blow the dams until they could "bring about as many casualties as possible."[32]

In accordance with earlier instructions, the 82d Airborne Division began combat operations in the Hürtgen Forest on 7 February. The 505th Parachute Infantry Regiment replaced the 309th Infantry in Kommerscheidt and elements of the 311th Infantry in Schmidt. The 517th Parachute Infantry Regiment attacked across the Kall River Valley southeast of Bergstein to cut off the German escape route from Schmidt to the northeast.

The history of the 505th noted that "throughout Sicily, Italy, Normandy and Holland this unit has seen the devastation of war, but never anything to compare with this. Had the houses [in Schmidt] not had cellars, the troops would have found absolutely no cover at all." There were "tanks, tank destroyers, jeeps, 2½-ton trucks, weazels [sic] and all sorts of GI equipment as well as countless American dead. . . . It was no wonder the men referred to this as death valley." The regiment closed into Kommerscheidt during the late afternoon of 8 February.[33]

THE CAPTURE OF THE SCHWAMMENAUEL DAM

The savage fight for an assembly area for the battalion designated to make the final attack against the Schwammenauel Dam began on 9 February. The 9th Division's 60th Infantry left Schmidt before daylight to take Hasenfeld, a village that had been the site of General Bruns's 89th Infantry Division CP. The Germans fought hard for the village, and as late as that evening still held a few houses. The 311th Infantry's fight to drive the Germans from the nearby high ground was equally difficult.

The original plan had been for the 309th Infantry's 1st Battalion to occupy its assembly area once Hasenfeld was secure. This was why the 30-year-old commander, Lt. Col. R. H. Schellman, had expected to move against the dam on 10 February. But the fight for Hasenfeld was taking longer than expected, and not long after dark on the 9th, Schellman learned there had been a change in plans. His battalion had to take the dam as soon as possible.[34] The Germans might blow the dam at the first sign of an American attack, and there already were reports of rising water levels downstream (XIX Corps would report within minutes after the attack began that the river level was up about three feet). One report stated, "Water passing over dam at present rate will raise water level 2 feet over flood stage for 4 days. Will take 6 days to drain lake. Water also being released from [Urft] Dam."[35]

It was nearly dark and a light rain was falling when Schellman gathered his company commanders to brief them on the change in plans. So loud and frequent were the bursts of German artillery and mortar shells that Schellman had to shout the orders in the ear of each officer in turn.

The terrain was difficult to negotiate in daylight; in the darkness, it would be nearly impossible.

Companies A and B departed the assembly area about 7:00 P.M. With Company A was a team of five engineers led by Maj. Harry E. Gerleman of the division's 303d Engineer Combat Battalion. The engineers were to inspect the dam for damage.

The steep ground was so covered by debris from fallen trees that each attacking company moved in a column of platoons with the men in file. Even this precaution failed to keep the men together, but the deafening artillery bursts and the roar of water being released from the reservoir masked the approach of the infantry. The men used the noise of the rushing water to guide them. The company commanders stopped every few minutes to read their maps and aerial photos by using a flashlight under the cover of a poncho. Still, it took an hour for the GIs to stumble and grope the first 800 yards, which brought them half way to the dam. In these circumstances, luck, more than skill enabled Company B, for example, to reach its exact attack position.

It was about 9:00 P.M. Schellman had set up his CP in a dugout on the side of the hill overlooking the dam.

No one was prepared for what happened soon afterwards. The leader of Company B's 2d Platoon stepped by accident into an occupied German foxhole. This disturbance alerted other nearby Germans, who responded immediately to the threat. Flares lit up the sky and revealed to the shocked GIs that they were in the middle of a line of German positions. Machine-gun and small-arms fire from the vicinity of the powerhouse (about 50 yards away) began to hit the Americans. It was hard to tell friend from foe in the eerie light of flares. Several Germans who had been taken prisoners were killed during the first minutes of close combat.

The Americans then heard the ominous rumble of explosions coming from the valvehouse. The Germans had demolished the control valves, and water was now pouring uncontrolled through the dam. The valve-house was destroyed as well.

Soldiers in Company A also stumbled into the German positions, but they managed to deploy and take the gatehouse as well as the buildings near the top of the dam. They also gained control of the road leading across the dam. The company commander gave the signal for the engineers to move up.

About 11:00 P.M., a rifle platoon and the engineers set out to make the 400-yard run along the road to the site of the spillway, which they planned to use to get to the base of the dam. German fire drove the Americans back. Schellman called for artillery. A 30-battalion TOT hit the German-held south side of the reservoir with such force that flashes from the explosions illuminated the area as if daylight were approaching. The battalion S-3 recalled, "It was truly impressive to watch it hit along the German side of the river."

Both Companies A and B now sent patrols across the road. When the riflemen and engineers finally reached the spillway, they found that the bridge across the spillway was out and that the spillway was 50 feet wide and 40 feet deep with vertical concrete walls. There was no way to reach the tunnel from this direction. But there was one other approach: they slid 200 feet down the face of the dam.[36]

The riflemen protected the engineers while they searched in the darkness for explosives. Surprisingly, the Germans had not prepared the dam for demolition. Only the outlet valves appeared to be damaged, and by 2:00 A.M. the Americans were in control of the dam. The engineers reported a normal flow of water, and an inspection after daylight revealed no evidence of attempts to damage the spillway, though the upper inlet was damaged enough to prevent the opening of the floodgates.[37]

The Americans consolidated their gains as best they could in the darkness. Daylight would bring German fire. Colonel Ondrick, the commander of the 309th told Schellman's executive officer, "You don't want to get caught around there in daylight. We have to hold. Dig in nicely and hold. . . . Disperse, dig in, and protect."[38]

The German fire, in fact, picked up on schedule. By midday "it was impossible for the men to move out of their foxholes, due to the steady rain of enemy mortar shell[s]. . . . It was not until nightfall [10 February] that all of the wounded could be evacuated to the rear by vehicles and rations and ammunition brought forward to the dam." Tragically, once during the day, American counter-battery fire fell on the 1st Battalion's positions.

The 1st Battalion, 309th Infantry, sustained an estimated 50 casualties on 9 and 10 February 1945. The hastily planned and successful night attack was noteworthy because the battalion was inexperienced in night operations. Its success rested upon several factors, such as sound and simple planning, a secure LD, and the flexibility of the chain of command when presented with a last-minute change in orders. For a change, communications was not a significant problem, as Schellman depended on radios and plenty of spare batteries, instead of vulnerable phone lines. The artillery observer was always close at hand, and he was able to successfully coordinate the TOT.[39]

The 78th Division's eight-week campaign in the Monschau Corridor and Hürtgen Forest ended successfully on 10 February 1945. Though the February battle began with confusion and frayed nerves, it ended with the elimination of a significant threat to the renewed Allied offensive. The 9th Infantry and 82d Airborne Divisions contributed immeasurably to the success of this last operation in the Hürtgen Forest, but in the end, the First Army owed its success to the untried "Lightning" Division.

14
Analysis

Generalmajor von Gersdorff, chief of staff of the German 7th Army,
said after the war: "I have engaged in the long campaigns in Russia
as well as other fronts, . . . and I believe the fighting west of the Roer, and
especially in the Hürtgen, was the heaviest I have ever witnessed."
He added, "The fighting in the Hürtgen was as costly to the defending
troops as it was to those engaged in the offensive."[1]

General Collins believed the fighting in the forest was the "deadliest . . . of the war."[2]

In 1983 he told an interviewer that he "would never pick it [the forest]
as the place to be. It was assigned as part of my corps sector, and reluctantly we had to fight in it. . . . "[3] In his autobiography, he said, "The
Aachen-Stolberg-Hürtgen campaign [was] the toughest, most costly of
VII Corps' operations in Europe."[4]

The tragedy of the battle for the Hürtgen Forest and Roer dams was
the Americans' insistence on trading their tactical advantages in firepower and mobility for the wrong objectives—from the early operations
of the 9th Division in September until the debacles at Merode and Kesternich in December. It took weeks for the senior leaders in the 12th
Army Group (including subordinate headquarters) to come to grips with
the importance of the Roer dams.

All or part of the following U.S. divisions fought in the forest: 1st, 4th,
8th, 9th, 28th, 78th, and 83d Infantry Divisions and the 82d Airborne
Division. The 2d Infantry Division played a major role in the December
attack, and the 5th Armored Division and several separate units such as
the 2d Ranger Battalion also sustained high losses in the forest. On the
German side, the larger units were the 12th, 47th, 272d, and 277th Volksgrenadier Divisions; the 85th, 89th, 275th, 344th, and 353d Infantry Divisions, plus the 3d Parachute and 116th Panzer Divisions.

Who won the battle for the forest and Roer dams? Each side, in a way, can claim victory. The Germans succeeded in preventing the Americans from crossing the Roer before the beginning of the Ardennes offensive. The Americans, in turn, inflicted very high casualties on their enemy, including trained NCOs and officers, whom the Germans could not replace that late in the war. Yet I believe the real answer to the question of winner and loser lies in determining which side accomplished its stated objective, and the importance to the campaign as a whole. The U.S. Army often placed the concept of objective first among the nine principles of war that it recognized. Army doctrine stipulated—and still does—that all levels of command have a clear, defined objective toward which it directs its forces.

Because the ultimate strategic objective in the ETO was the destruction of the enemy's capability to wage war, the stated American aim was to take the Ruhr and Saar industrial areas while trying to destroy the German Army in the field. Along these lines, a stated interim objective was the capture of crossing sites over the Rhine. But before the Americans could cross the Rhine, they had to cross the Roer—and take the nearby dams. Thus, the Ruhr, Rhine, and Roer were stated goals of the 12th Army Group, but the dams were not. Why did the Americans fail to target them also?

One possibility involves what the late historian Charles B. MacDonald called a torpor that "enveloped American commanders and staffs" exhausted by the strain of three months of constant operations during the summer and fall of 1944. The added prospects of a winter campaign exacerbated this mental exhaustion and lethargy and might in fact have prevented key leaders from seeing beyond the immediate problem of getting through the Westwall.[5] These officers might have found it difficult to focus their attention on objectives such as the dams and to understand fully their importance.

Historian Martin Blumenson suggests another explanation of American conduct of the campaign during the late summer of 1944. As discussed in chapter 1, the unexpected success of the campaign in France after the breakout from Normandy led American commanders such as Eisenhower and Bradley to anticipate "reality and set about laying future plans." The generals dismissed too easily the fighting strength of the Germans during the battles in Normandy.

Perhaps this contributed to the Germans' apparently high estimate of their ability to bring the Allies to a halt along the German border. Rather than concentrating on the destruction of the German armies in the field, notes Blumenson, Bradley had his eyes set on breaking through the Westwall and reaching the Rhine, and Eisenhower "was gazing beyond [it]."[6] The Germans, meanwhile, were rebuilding their shattered, though not destroyed, armies and gearing up for a defensive battle against

The Hürtgen Forest in 1946. (Courtesy U.S. Army)

an enemy critically short on supplies. In any case, the fact remains that the Americans probably did not take full advantage of their opportunities in France. They paid the bill, however, for this failure at places like Dead Man's Moor.

As for First Army, in mid-September certainly no senior officer intended to become locked in a battle that would last for months and result in so little. Hodges no doubt hoped that once the First Army was through the Westwall, it might reach the Rhine before it had to pause and rest. This consideration forced Hodges to make his plans around the possibility of a strongly defended Westwall. He also had to ensure the safety of the flank of the VII Corps that in September came to rest in the forest. Collins believed strongly that this was the correct estimate of the situation facing his corps in September 1944. In 1983 he said: "The Germans didn't counterattack against my flank, because we had some troops there [the Hürtgen] that would have prevented them from doing so, but if we would have turned loose of the Hürtgen and let the Germans roam there, they could have hit my flank. It's easy to go back to second-guess and say, 'Well, you shouldn't have done that.' Then what would you have done? Who would have cleared it? How much time would it have taken?"[7]

Collins was right, of course—it is easy to second guess the decisions made under the pressures of battle, and one should be careful in doing so. But there is no excuse for the failure to notice in September or October just what a threat to long-term operations the dams in fact were.

As the pursuit transitioned to a battle of attrition, Hodges and his generals made plans to take nearly every key objective except the one most important to safely crossing the Roer. The result was that the First Army spent weeks in pursuit of towns, hills, and road centers—important objectives, to be sure, but ones that meant little unless they led to operations aimed at the dams.

One can ask whether the Americans saw the importance of the dams early on and stubbornly fed divisions into the forest, hoping the Germans would eventually surrender them. My research turned up nothing in the records of 12th Army Group, First Army, VII Corps, or V Corps that notes any discussion during the period from September to early November of attacking the dams. In other words, there is nothing to indicate that Hodges sent divisions into the forest for any reason other than those reflected in operations plans and orders—seizure of key terrain, roads, and towns in order to maintain an attack to the Roer and the Rhine.

Historian Russell Weigley calls this failure to designate the dams as an objective early in the campaign a part of a "pattern of uninquisitive headquarters planning" among the Allies during the late autumn.[8] A possible explanation for this might be the events described by Blumenson. Thus it should come as no surprise that the Americans failed until the period from late November through December to designate the dams as targets, despite reports like Major Houston's of October, and travel guides which described the dams in detail. As long as the war seemed to be won, it was easier to dismiss the dams as a problem than to make a detailed plan for their capture.

The best avenue of approach for the American attack to the Roer was the relatively flat ground north of Aachen. But Hodges delayed the advance of the XIX Corps, best situated to use this ground, in order to divert supplies to the VII and V Corps. In fairness to both Hodges and Collins, the location of the dams meant that the Americans would have to fight in at least the southern part of the forest. Collins, whose VII Corps faced the Hürtgen and the dams, like Hodges, failed to consider the dams. The stated objective of the September reconnaissance in force was only to continue the momentum of the pursuit, and as noted elsewhere in this book, this was a sound decision. As long as he held the initiative, Collins was justified in trying to get through the Westwall.

He then sent the 9th Division into the forest to take the roads necessary to support the drive to the Roer. His approach to the problem of the German border defenses was sound; however, once in Germany, he failed to go after the dams—or urge that Hodges do so.

The sound initial approach to the battle for Germany did not, however, last long, and the First Army by autumn found itself locked in a battle from which it could not withdraw. To compound the difficulties of the fighting, few commanders above the battalion level appreciated the advantages the forest gave the defender. This, coupled with false reports to the division and corps headquarters concerning the effectiveness of the decimated units, led to the assignment of missions that were impossible for them to carry out. Thus, even had the Americans sought to take the dams, by late autumn they would have had a very hard time doing so.

Mental exhaustion, failure to see the importance of objectives, and inexcusable deception on the part of some commanders were not the only reasons for American failure. Other causes relate to the organization and training of the army itself. They deserve more research but are described briefly below.

Committed units often were unable to withstand the attrition of battle. The army in World War II fielded a light, agile infantry division free of unnecessary overhead and reinforced by "pools" of attached tanks, TDs, and artillery. Yet the shortage of manpower noted elsewhere in this book forced the army to keep divisions in the line long after their effectiveness had disappeared. Units so hard hit took weeks to reconstitute. Only the fact that the Germans were even weaker than the Americans made it possible for units to get even a short rest and refit.

Another topic that deserves additional research is the performance of American weapons and equipment. The onset of bad weather revealed problems with the trafficability of the otherwise mechanically reliable medium and light tanks in the inhospitable forest terrain. The tanks were no match for their German counterparts in firepower and armor protection. This no doubt led to the reluctance of the tankers to stay forward when confronted by the superior German tanks. However, the infantry, protected only by their field jackets, were understandably reluctant to move forward without tank support. Only the thinly armored tank destroyers had a gun that was a match for some of the German tanks, but the open-turreted TD was certainly not suited to a world of tree bursts.

There can be no success on the battlefield without dependable communications. There were problems for the Americans here as well. Tactical radios were subject to problems caused by the wet weather, and resupply of batteries was as difficult as anything else. Phone lines were constantly subject to breaks caused by artillery and infiltrating Germans.

The life expectancy of runners could be measured in minutes. It is easy to see why higher headquarters often had no precise knowledge of unit locations and thus could not plan effectively.

The GIs also thought their automatic weapons were inferior to those of the Germans. The light .30-cal. machine gun had a much slower rate of fire compared with its German counterpart. The M1 rifle was a superior weapon, but for close-in fighting, the Americans could have used more submachine guns than their organizational tables allowed. The effectiveness of the American's observed artillery fire has been recounted in several instances in this book.

Logistic problems also contributed to the outcome of the battle. As noted in earlier chapters, the weather and terrain adversely affected the distribution of rations, fuel, and ammunition. It was indeed a world where a pair of dry socks was a luxury. Also, though not discussed at length here, many GIs were poorly clothed. Certain critical items of the uniform such as overshoes, overcoats, and the early-model field jackets were poorly designed and failed to fully meet field requirements. The rubber-soled canvas overshoes did not provide adequate protection from the elements, and there were never enough for all the front-line troops. The excellent model 1943 field jacket was wind and water resistant, but it also was in short supply, and far too many troops had to wear the older model 1941 windbreaker-style jacket. The wool overcoat became very heavy after a few days in the mud; for troops exhausted by the rigors of combat, it literally became too heavy to wear.

The subject of the GIs' reluctance to move under fire unless very well supported by artillery, tanks, and airplanes has for years been the topic of heated debate, and though discussion of the subject is not the purpose of this book, some comment is necessary. The army was not so much an organization of warriors as it was a group of civilians under arms trained to expect overwhelming fire support. When it failed to appear, soldiers were often reluctant to close with the enemy. But as Ray Fleig said, "A wool shirt and a field jacket are no defense against tank cannon and machine guns or 15.0-cm. mortars and no sane man will confront those fearsome weapons with his M1 rifle [alone]."[9] The preparation of replacements also played a significant role in the battle. By late 1944, few veterans of the campaign in France were still serving in the line units. Those who were still around were understandably tired, both mentally and physically, and there was little time in which to train the new men.

An obvious question concerns lessons learned. Since so many units passed through the forest and endured the same hardships as others, one must ask to what extent they shared their experiences and perhaps made things a bit easier for other units. In addition, what training, if any, did units receive prior to entering the Hürtgen Forest? The answer to both questions is, unfortunately, "very little"—in terms either of sharing information or of receiving specialized training. The reasons included the expectation that one unit or another would eventually break through the enemy defenses. Another is that attrition drained experienced men from the ranks so quickly that new soldiers had no time to learn, nor did they have any teachers.

William Pena, of the 3d Battalion, 109th Infantry, recalled that tactical problems conducted in woods usually took place during daylight hours—when it was easier to maintain control. Pena's former company commander, Bruce Paul, remembers that while some soldiers received training in woods fighting while in the States, "nothing prepared us for the Hürtgen Forest."[10]

The 28th Division's 112th Infantry Regiment, in contrast, held "conferences" a few days before the disastrous attack on Schmidt.[11] Elements of the 22d Infantry Regiment conducted "schools" in the techniques of woods fighting.[12] The 12th Infantry, however, had no time for such preparation because it was rushed into the line too fast for any special training.

Shortly before he entered the battle, Paul Boesch met a veteran of the 28th Division who said that the forest was "pure, unadulterated hell."[13] This was the extent of Boesch's special training in forest fighting.

What, if anything, did the fight through 16 December accomplish? The Americans decimated several German divisions that might have been put to use in the Ardennes, but that was all. The First Army gained only one major city (Aachen) but no industrial areas or terrain that would have enabled it to take the dams or influence operations once the army was across the Roer.

Would it have been dangerous for the Americans to bypass all or part of the forest? It might very well have been in September. There was little doubt that the Allies would eventually win the war, but it was not worth the risk of a counterattack to neglect the forest altogether. This does not mean Hodges and Collins were correct in allowing continued operations there unless they were aimed at the dams. It simply means that after securing the VII Corps flank and testing the ability of the Germans to use the Hürtgen Forest as a base from which to launch an attack, First Army should have secured only the approaches to the forest and then moved on the dams.

Could the V Corps have succeeded instead? An attack against the dams by V Corps might have succeeded had it taken place in September or October. Intelligence reports confirmed that the front opposite Gerow's corps was not heavily defended. The weather was turning bad, but it was not nearly as bad as that which delayed the start of the November attack. Had Hodges and Bradley been willing to take the risk on another part of the front in order to reinforce V Corps with even one or two regiments of infantry, V Corps would likely have taken the Urft and Schwammenauel Dams in November.

Yet there was great urgency to launch the November attack. One would think that with what was riding on its outcome, someone would have noticed the relation of the dams to its success. No one apparently did, and they were never a stated objective of the attack.

What about the German conduct of the battle? Their original objective was simply to prevent the Americans from overrunning the Westwall. They did not have the combat power to turn their attention to the Ardennes attack. They could use the American interest in the forest to their advantage and prevent the Americans from disrupting the preparations for the December attack. The German soldiers were not the only ones to contribute to success; forestry officials familiar with the woods, civilians, and agents alike provided valuable intelligence to staff planners. The main German advantage early on was their ability to reorganize units around staff cadres and get them to the front before the American logistic situation could improve. They won the race against time.

The Germans knew from the start that the forest was easy to defend and would be extremely hard to take. They were surprised when the Americans failed to drive on the dams and also could not comprehend why they traded away so freely their matériel advantages with continued attacks in the forest. According to Gersdorff, "There was no use in the Americans going through the Hürtgen Forest. . . . Had you gone around it on both sides, you would have had almost no opposition."[14]

Field Marshal Model was able to take advantage of the piecemeal American attacks of September because he recognized before the Americans themselves just what they had sacrificed by fighting in the forest. Brandenberger's 7th Army managed to buy valuable time, which allowed the 12th Infantry (later Volksgrenadier) Division to go into action where the American advance seemed most promising—the Stolberg Corridor. Meanwhile, the units in the forest were able to reinforce their defenses. In short, a few German infantrymen made all the difference in the world, and by October, they were ready to meet the American attacks that followed.

Did chance play a role in German successes? To an extent, it did. One example is the logistic situation of the Americans in September. The Germans were unable to influence this, and the Americans' original plans never anticipated logistic difficulties of such magnitude. Another example is the Germans' quick reaction to the 2 November attack of the 28th Division. The Army Group B command post exercise saved countless hours of time in planning a counterattack against the penetration near Schmidt. The weather and terrain were also on the side of the Germans. Bad weather hampered American air power and made it easier for the Germans to concentrate their forces at times and places of their own choosing. The terrain stripped the Americans of their numerical advantage in armor and qualitative advantage of artillery.

Was German success due to American weakness? Not to a great extent. The Americans chose to neglect the dams and rush headlong into some of the worst ground in the Rhineland; they accepted at face value too many false reports from the front-line units; they committed several inexcusable tactical mistakes (such as putting a battalion of troops on the exposed ground at Vossenack). It is true that the Americans entered the battle overextended and tired from the pursuit; however, the Germans were no better off. In the final analysis, German success in the forest was due to advantages in weather and terrain, skills in organization, excellent generalship, and a clear idea of what they needed to do to delay the Americans.

The American insistence during the first phase of the battle on taking roads, towns, and hills with no thought to taking the dams cost weeks and thousands of lives. The fact that the Germans could launch the Ardennes attack with a secure north flank is testimony to their success and American failure.

The place of the battle of the Hürtgen Forest is secure in history because of what it teaches about the need to identify the critical objectives and the need to focus energy toward gaining them. It is extremely important to conduct a wide-ranging analysis of the mission at hand. Staffs and commanders must see beyond the immediate challenges and take a look at all facets of a problem. In the case of the Hürtgen Forest, this did not happen for nearly three months—between September and mid-December, 1944—until the 2d and 78th Divisions finally launched a drive aimed specifically at taking the Schwammenauel and Urft Dams.

Staffs and subordinate leaders must analyze events and then get the right story to their commanders, who in turn must be willing to take risks (including changing their plans) as soon as there is a clear need to do so. The senior leaders must translate their vision to attainable goals and have enough self-confidence to let their subordinates execute a mission with as little interference as possible.

Lack of imagination and vision within the leadership of the First Army and its corps in late 1944 proved costly. By the time of the attack on the Roer dams, the Allied armies had come to a halt all along the front. The Germans had done their job well and would soon redirect the attention of their enemies to the Ardennes. Between mid-December and early February 1945, an uneasy calm settled over the snow-covered fields of the Monschau Corridor and the blasted woods to the north. But it would be only a matter of time until the Americans would be across the cold, rushing Roer, on their way to the Rhine.

Hubert Gees, of the 275th Infantry Division, related the following to the author in 1990, which can serve as a fitting epitaph for the soldiers who fought on both sides. "While carrying a dead soldier to the forester's lodge at Hürtgen, we were attacked by American artillery. We jumped into the nearest shell hole for cover, and it took me several seconds to realize I was next to the body of an American soldier. His open mouth seemed to cry out with condemnation, imploring God's mercy and hoping in anticipation. I was filled with sincere compassion. Is there a place in America where a mother will mourn for him?"[15]

APPENDIX
Major Units and Commanders Mentioned in the Text

U.S. 12th Army Group: Lt. Gen. Omar N. Bradley

First U.S. Army: Lt. Gen. Courtney H. Hodges

V Corps: Maj. Gen. L. T. Gerow (to 15 January 1945)
Maj. Gen. Clarence R. Huebner

2d Infantry Division: Maj. Gen. Walter M. Robertson
9th Infantry: Col. Chester J. Hirschfelder
23d Infantry: Col. Jay B. Loveless
38th Infantry: Col. Francis H. Boos

8th Infantry Division: Maj. Gen. Donald A Stroh (to 27 November)
Brig. Gen. Walter Weaver
13th Infantry: Col. Numa A. Watson
28th Infantry: Col. Merritt E. Olmstead
121st Infantry: Col. John R. Jeter (to 25 November)
Col. Thomas J. Cross

28th Infantry Division: Maj. Gen. Norman D. Cota
Brig. Gen. George A. Davis (Assistant Commander)
109th Infantry: Lt. Col. Daniel B. Strickler (to 8 November)
Col. Jesse L. Gibney (to 8 December)
Lt. Col. James. E. Rudder
110th Infantry: Col. Theodore A. Seeley
112th Infantry: Lt. Col. Carl L. Peterson (to 7 November)
Col. Gustin M. Nelson
707th Tank Battalion (Attd.): Lt. Col. Richard W. Ripple

78th Infantry Division: Maj. Gen. Edwin P. Parker, Jr.
309th Infantry: Col. John G. Ondrick
310th Infantry: Col. Earl M. Miner
311th Infantry: Col. Chester M. Willingham

2d Ranger Battalion: Lt. Col. James E. Rudder (to 8 December 1944)
Maj. George S. Williams, Jr.

5th Armored Division: Maj. Gen. Lunsford E. Oliver
CCA: Brig. Gen. Eugene A. Reginer
CCB: Col. John T. Cole
CCR: Col. Glenn H. Anderson

VII Corps: Maj. Gen. J. Lawton Collins

1st Infantry Division: Maj. Gen. Clarence R. Huebner
16th Infantry: Col. Frederick W. Gibb
18th Infantry: Col. George A. Smith, Jr.
26th Infantry: Col. John F. R. Seitz

4th Infantry Division: Maj. Gen. Raymond O. Barton
8th Infantry: Col. Richard G. McKee
12th Infantry: Col. James S. Luckett (to 21 November)
Col. Robert H. Chance
22d Infantry: Col. Charles T. Lanham

9th Infantry Division: Maj. Gen. Louis A. Craig
39th Infantry: Lt. Col. Van H. Bond
47th Infantry: Col. George W. Smythe
60th Infantry: Col. Jesse L. Gibney (to October)
Col. John G. Van Houten

83d Infantry Division: Maj. Gen. Robert C. Macon
329th Infantry: Col. Edwin B. Crabhill
330th Infantry: Col. Robert H. York
331st Infantry: Col. Robert T. Foster

3d Armored Division: Brig. Gen. (later Maj. Gen.) Maurice Rose
CCA: Brig. Gen. Doyle O. Hickey
CCB: Brig. Gen. Truman E. Boudinot
TF Lovelady (2d Bn., 33d Armor): Lt. Col. William B. Lovelady

German Army Group B: Generalfeldmarschall Walter Model

7th Army: General der Panzertruppen Erich Brandenberger
Chief of Staff: Generalmajor Rudolf-Christoph Freiherr von Gersdorff

15th Army: General der Infanterie Gustav von Zangen
5th Panzer Army: General der Panzertruppen Hasso von Manteuffel

Corps Subordinate to Army Group B:

LXXIV Corps: General der Infanterie Erich Straube
General der Infanterie Karl Püchler

    272d Infantry Division: Oberst Georg Kosmala

    275th Infantry Division: Generalleutnant Hans Schmidt

    344th Infantry Division: Generalleutnant Eugen König

    347th Infantry Division: Generalleutnant Wolf Trierenberg

    353d Infantry Division: Generalleutnant Paul Mahlmann

    89th Infantry Division: Oberst Eberhard Rösler (to October)
    Generalleutnant Walter Bruns

LXXXI Corps: Generalleutnant Friederich-August Schack (to late September)
General der Infanterie Friederich J. M. Köchling

    12th Volksgrenadier Division: Generalmajor Gerhard Engel
    48th Grenadier Regiment: Oberst Wilhelm Osterhold

    47th Volksgrenadier Division: Generalleutnant Max Bork

    9th Panzer Division: Generalmajor Harald von Elverfeldt

    116th Panzer Division: Generalleutnant Graf Gerhard von Schwerin (to late September)
    Generalmajor Siegfried von Waldenburg

    3d Parachute Division: Generalmajor Wadehn

Notes

Unless otherwise stated, official documents and combat interviews cited below can be found in Records Group 407, Washington National Records Center, Suitland, Maryland. The Combined Arms Research Library (CARL), Fort Leavenworth, Kansas, also maintains copies of many of the records. Manuscripts cited below were prepared from interviews with senior German officers after the war under the direction of historians on the staff of the United States Forces, European Theater. Those cited are on file at CARL and the U.S. Army War College Library. The combat interviews cited below were conducted by teams of soldier-historians working under the direction of the Historical Section, ETO. The interviews vary in quality but overall provide a good supplement to official records. Most divisional associations published histories after the war. The majority are of little value to scholars, but those cited below are some of the better ones.

Terrain details are based on visits to the area and on topographical maps (scale 1:25,000) both from the wartime period and those published in 1990 by Landesvermessungsamt Nordrhein-Westfalen, Bonn. Sheet numbers (1990 ed.) that apply are L 5102, L 5103, L 5104, L 5202, L 5203, L 5204, L 5303, L 5304, L 5403, and L 5404.

The following abbreviations are used throughout the notes:

CI	Combat Interview
FO	Field Order
LOI	Letter of Instructions
MS	Historical Section manuscript
OCMH	Office of the Chief of Military History
OM	Operations Memorandum
PR	Periodic Report
RO	Report of Operations
SITREP	Situation Report
UJ	Unit Journal
UR	Unit Report

CHAPTER I

1. The horror was described in the chapter epigraph by Capt. Kenneth W. Hechler, Combat Interview with Capt. Jennings Frye, Lt. George Kosmetsky, T3g. Harry I. Fingerroth, 20 Dec 44 (hereafter cited as Frye CI). Although Morgan held the position of armorer-artificer in his company, the CI notes that he spent most of his time "collecting bodies."

2. Charles B. MacDonald, *The Mighty Endeavor* (Oxford: Oxford University Press, 1969), pp. 312–13.

3. Ibid.; Martin Blumenson, *The Battle of the Generals* (New York: William Morrow & Co., 1993), p. 262.

4. Russell F. Weigley, *Eisenhower's Lieutenants: The Campaign of France and Germany, 1944–1945,* Book Club edition (Bloomington: Indiana University Press, 1981), pp. 314–15; MacDonald, *The Mighty Endeavor,* p. 318.

5. MacDonald, *The Mighty Endeavor,* pp. 317–18.

6. Ibid., p. 318.

7. Richard Lamb, "Kluge," in *Hitler's Generals,* ed. Corelli Barnett (New York: William Morrow, 1989), pp. 407–408; Capt. James F. Scoggin, ed., MS B-308, "OB West (Atlantic Wall to Siegfried Line), A Study in Command" (Oct 46), pp. 152–55, 176–80.

8. Carlo D'Este, "Model," in *Hitler's Generals,* ed. Barnett, pp. 323–26.

9. Ibid., p. 326; Earl F. Ziemke, "Rundstedt," in *Hitler's Generals,* ed. Barnett, p. 201.

10. Generalmajor Rudolf-Cristoph Freiherr von Gersdorff, MS A-892, "Questions for Consideration and Reply by General Frhr., von Gersdorff" (Nov 45); Wolfgang Trees and Adolf Hohenstein, *Hölle im Hürtgenwald: Die Kämpfe vom Hohen Venn bis zur Rur, September 1944 bis Februar 1945* (Aachen, Germany: Triangle Verlag, 1981), p. 42; MS B-308, pp. 176–80.

11. Manfred Gross, *Der Westwall zwischen Niederrhein und Schnee Eifel* (Cologne: Rheinland Verlag, 1982; 2d printing, 1989), chap. 2 and pp. 150–62, 222–29. A very detailed technical study.

12. MacDonald, *The Mighty Endeavor,* pp. 335–36.

13. Ibid., p. 336.

14. Unless otherwise noted, all biographical information on German officers was supplied by Günter von der Weiden, Stolberg, Germany.

15. General der Panzertruppen Erich Brandenberger, MS B-730, "Seventh Army 1–20 September 1944" (1947); Lucian Heichler, *The Germans Opposite VII Corps in September 1944* (Washington, D.C.: OCMH, 1952), pp. 1–7; SS-Obergruppenführer und General der Waffen-SS Georg Keppler, MS B-155, "I. SS Pz. Korps 16 Aug.–8 Oct. 1944" (30 June 46).

16. Weigley, *Eisenhower's Lieutenants,* p. 374.

17. Robert N. Laurent, undated letter to author, received Jun 90.

18. Forrest C. Pogue, *The Supreme Command,* U.S. Army in World War II (Washington, D.C.: GPO, 1954), pp. 249–54; Charles B. MacDonald, *The Siegfried Line Campaign,* U.S. Army in World War II (Washington, D.C.: GPO, 1963), p. 7.

19. Pogue, *The Supreme Command,* pp. 251–52.

20. HQ, VII Corps, "The Battle of Belgium: Participation of VII Corps, 2–12 Sept. 1944," typed report, VII Corps Opns. Files.

21. HQ, 3d Armored Division, *Spearhead in the West* (Frankfurt, Germany, 1946), p. 89. This is one of the better postwar unit histories.

22. HQ, First U.S. Army, Report of Operations, 1 Aug 44–22 Feb 45 (n.p., n.d.), pp. 40–42 (hereafter cited as First Army RO).

23. Martin Blumenson, *Breakout and Pursuit*, U.S. Army in World War II (Washington, D.C.: GPO, 1961), p. 701.

24. First Army RO, p. 45; MacDonald, *The Siegfried Line Campaign*, pp. 37–38; Charles B. MacDonald, *The Operations of VII Corps in September 1944* (Washington, D.C.: OCMH, 1956), p. 1.

25. MacDonald, *The Siegfried Line Campaign*, pp. 37–38.

26. Ibid., pp. 37–38, 66.

27. War Department, *Field Service Regulations, Operations*, FM 100–5 (Washington, D.C.: GPO, 1944), p. 55 (hereafter cited as FM 100–5).

28. VII Corps OM 91, 12 Sep 44; Lt. Col. Charles C. Sperrow, typed transcript of interview with Gen. J. L. Collins, 1973, copy at OCMH (hereafter cited as Sperrow interview).

29. Information on Collins is from an official army biography.

30. Omar N. Bradley and Clay Blair, *A General's Life* (New York: Simon and Schuster, 1983), p. 472.

31. Maj. Gary Wade, *Conversations with General J. Lawton Collins*, Combat Studies Institute Report no. 5 (Fort Leavenworth, KS: U.S. Army Command and General Staff College, 1983), p. 6 (hereafter cited as Wade interview).

32. Weigley, *Eisenhower's Lieutenants*, p. 124; Charles B. MacDonald, *The Battle of the Huertgen Forest* (New York: Jove Books, 1963), p. 7.

33. Bradley and Blair, *A General's Life*, p. 463.

34. Ibid., pp. 218, 463.

35. Dempsey Allphin, letter to author, 1 Oct 93.

36. 3d Armd. Div. G-3 PR 79, 12 Sep 44; 2d Lt. Fred L. Hadsel, Combat Interview with Lt. Col. William B. Lovelady, Germany, 1944, VII Corps CI File (hereafter cited as Lovelady CI).

37. Lovelady CI.

38. A. Eaton Roberts, *Five Stars to Victory: A True Story of Men and Tanks* (n.p., 1949), p. 48.

39. Ibid.

40. Robert Laurent, letter to author, 1 Oct 90.

41. Lovelady CI.

42. Ibid.

43. MacDonald, *The Operations of VII Corps*, pp. 4–6; VII Corps, OM 92, 13 Sep 44; VII Corps FO 11, 13 Sep 44; Heichler, *The Germans Opposite VII Corps*, pp. 16–22. Collins and the commander of the 1st Infantry Division, Maj. Gen. Clarence Huebner, discussed the prospects of taking Aachen. Huebner wanted first to take the surrounding high ground (Aachen lies in a "bowl" surrounded by higher ground), but not the city itself. Collins agreed that the resources of the corps could better be used elsewhere, especially if Aachen was heavily defended. (See Sperrow interview.)

44. Generalleutnant Gerhard Graf von Schwerin, "116th Panzer Division from the Seine to Aachen," European Theater Historical Interview (ETHINT) 18, Oct–

Nov 45. The German side of the Story of Aachen is found in this document and in Heichler, *The Germans Opposite VII Corps.*

45. Von Schwerin, ETHINT 18, and Heichler, *The Germans Opposite VII Corps,* provide details on the German situation in Aachen.

46. Brandenberger, MS B-730; Heichler, *The Germans Opposite VII Corps,* pp. 12, 20–23.

47. Generalmajor Gerhard Engel, MS A-971, "The First Battle of Aachen [16–22 Sep 44]" (Mar 46); Wilhelm Osterhold, letter to author, 7 May 89.

48. Engel, MS A-971.

49. Heichler, *The Germans Opposite VII Corps,* p. 47.

50. Lovelady CI; information on the German dispositions provided by Günter von der Weiden during an interview on 14 Aug 92.

51. Roberts, *Five Stars to Victory,* p. 57.

52. MacDonald, *The Siegfried Line Campaign,* p. 95.

53. FM 100–5, p. 6.

CHAPTER 2

1. Von Gersdorff, ETHINT 53.

2. FM 100–5, p. 117.

3. 1st Lt. Harry D. Condon, "Penetration of the Siegfried Line by the 47th Inf. Regt.," revised draft of a CI with Col. George A. Smythe and others.

4. Capt. Joseph B. Mittelman, *Eight Stars to Victory* (Columbus, OH: F. J. Heer, 1948), p. 243.

5. Condon, "Penetration of the Siegfried Line."

6. Chester H. Jordan, letter to author, 14 Mar 91.

7. Heichler, *The Germans Opposite VII Corps,* pp. 41–47, 89–91.

8. MacDonald, *The Siegfried Line Campaign,* p. 89.

9. Wilhelm Osterhold, letter to author, 2 Mar 91.

10. Ibid.

11. 9th Div. G-3 PR 93, 22 Sep 44; Generalmajor Gerhard Engel, MS B-415, "12th Infantry Division 22 Sep–22 Oct 1944" (1946); author's interview with Günter von der Weiden, Stolberg, Germany, Aug 92.

12. Oberst (a.D.) Hasso Neitzel, MS B-793, "89th Infantry Division, 13 Sep–1 Oct 1944" (1948). Another occurrence during the early battles near Monschau involved passive resistance by German civilians. Some of them assisted German reconnaissance patrols to slip behind American lines to "observe the movements of the enemy and, if possible, to harass them and interfere with their attack preparations. . . . [soldiers assigned to the 89th Div.] would bring back one or two Germans who as proof that they had actually been prisoners of the Americans would show us rations they had received [from the Americans]."

13. 2d Lt. Fred Hadsel, Combat Interview with Lt. Col. Lee W. Chatfield, Capt. John W. McIndoe, and S.Sgt. L. F. Cuifo, Nov 44, 9th Div. CI Files (hereafter cited as Chatfield CI).

14. 2d Lt. Fred L. Hadsel, Combat Interview with Lt. Col. Oscar H. Thompson and others, 1st Bn., 39th Inf., Nov 44 (hereafter cited as Thompson CI); MacDonald, *The Siegfried Line Campaign.*

15. Thompson CI.

16. Neitzel, MS B-793.

17. 2d Lt. Fred L. Hadsel, Combat Interview with Lt. Col. Frank L. Gunn and Capt. Frank E. Bryant, 2d Bn., 39th Inf., n.d. (hereafter cited as Gunn CI).

18. Billy F. Allsbrook, letter to author, 30 Aug 89.

19. Gunn CI.

20. MacDonald, *The Siegfried Line Campaign*, pp. 85–86.

21. FM 100–5, pp. 138–44; 9th Inf. Div. RO, Sep 44, Annex 3, Lessons Learned; Committee 7, "Armor in the Hürtgen Forest," pp. 22–24.

22. 9th Inf. Div. RO, Sep 44, Annex 3, Lessons Learned.

23. MacDonald, *The Operations of VII Corps*, pp. 44, 50–51; VII Corps OM #94, 18 Sep 44. This written order confirmed Collins's oral order of 17 Sep.

24. MacDonald, *The Siegfried Line Campaign*, pp. 92–93.

25. 9th Inf. Div. RO, Oct 44.

26. Oberstleutnant Klaus Hammel, "Vor 40 Jahren, die Schlacht im Hürtgenwald, September 1944–Februar 1945," *Truppenpraxis*, October 1984, p. 757.

27. Thompson CI.

28. Generalleutnant (a.D.) Paul Mahlmann, MS B-411, "353d Infantry Division, 19 Sep–1 Oct 44" (1947).

29. Mahlmann, MS B-502, "353d Infantry Division, Rhineland" (1947).

30. Ibid.

31. Chatfield CI.

32. Von Gersdorff, "Defense of the Siegfried Line," ETHINT 53, 24 Nov 45.

33. Pogue, *The Supreme Command*, pp. 294–95.

34. Alfred D. Chandler, ed., *The Papers of Dwight David Eisenhower*, vol. 4, *The War Years* (Baltimore: Johns Hopkins University Press, 1970), pp. 2175, 2185–86.

35. Bradley and Blair, *A General's Life*, p. 334.

36. 12th AG, LOI 9, 25 Sep 44, reproduced in 12th AG, Report of Operations, vol. 5, pp. 93–95 (hereafter cited as 12th AG RO); First Army RO, p. 54; MacDonald, *The Siegfried Line Campaign*, p. 326.

37. In the 1983 interview with Wade, Collins said that his G-2 and corps engineer failed to provide him with an analysis of the impact of the dams.

38. Annex 1, 9th Inf. Div. G-2 PR 78, 2 Oct 44.

39. MacDonald, *The Siegfried Line Campaign*, pp. 326–27.

40. Generalleutnant Hans Schmidt, MS B-810, "Kämpfe im Rheinland, 275. Infanterie Division, 3 Oct–21 Nov 1944" (1947), and MS B-373, 275 Inf. Div., 31 Jul–10 Oct 44 (1946). Schmidt's division also became responsible for the combat troops of the 353d Division after the LXXIV Corps transferred that division's headquarters and noncombatant troops to another sector. To consolidate responsibility for the Hürtgen Forest, on 26 September the 7th Army transferred the 275th Division to the LXXIV Corps, giving it four divisions: the 89th, 275th, 347th, and 353d.

41. Ibid.

CHAPTER 3

1. The basic source for American operations is the 9th Inf. Div. RO, Oct 44, dtd 1 Nov 44 (hereafter cited as 9th Inf. Div. RO), the division G-3 Jnl and file for

1–16 Oct 44, and 9th Inf. Div. FOs 38 (1 Oct 44) and 39 (3 Oct 44). Estimating unit locations is difficult because the soldiers themselves did not always know their exact locations. The author made reasonable estimates of the positions based on contemporary maps and visits to the Hürtgen Forest in 1987, 1990, and 1992.

2. Thompson CI; Gunn CI; Combat Interview with Capt. Jack A. Dunlap, Co. B, 39th Inf.; 39th Inf. RO, Oct 44; 9th Inf. Div. RO.

3. 9th Inf. Div. RO.

4. Ibid.; 9th Inf. Div. G-3 Jnl entries, 1140 and 1430 hrs, 6 Oct 44.

5. William M. Cowan, letter to author, 20 Aug 90.

6. William M. Cowan, letter to author, 8 May 92.

7. 9th Inf. Div. RO.

8. Ibid.

9. Thompson CI; Gunn CI.

10. General der Infanterie Karl Püchler, MS B-118, "The Rhineland—74 Armeekorps—The Period from 2 to 27 October 1944 and 16 Dec. 1944 to 23 Mar. 1945 (1946)."

11. Schmidt, MS B-308.

12. Schmidt, MS B-810.

13. Hubert Gees, undated letter to author, received Jun 90; Schmidt, MS B-810.

14. Gees letter to author.

15. Schmidt, MS B-810.

16. 39th Inf. Regt. S-3 Jnl entries, 8 Oct 44, CARL microfilm collection, reel 137, item 949.

17. Schmidt, MS B-810.

18. Ibid.

19. Chatfield CI.

20. 9th Inf. Div. RO.

21. Eugen Welti, letter to author, 22 Apr 89.

22. 9th Inf. Div. RO.

23. Ibid.

24. Michael Harkinish, undated letter to author, received Jun 90.

25. 9th Inf. Div. G-2 PR 89, 13 Oct 44.

26. Gunn CI; Schmidt, MS B-810.

27. Thompson CI; 9th Inf. Div. RO, Oct 44; MacDonald, *The Siegfried Line Campaign*, p. 338.

28. Schmidt, MS B-810.

29. Trees and Hohenstein, *Hölle im Hürtgenwald*, p. 114.

30. Billy Allsbrook, letter to author, 30 Aug 89.

31. 9th Inf. Div. RO, Oct 44, Annex 3, Lessons Learned.

32. Billy Allsbrook, letter to author, 30 Aug 89.

33. 9th Inf. Div. RO, Oct 44, Annex 3, Lessons Learned.

34. MacDonald, *The Siegfried Line Campaign*, p. 340.

35. 9th Inf. Div. RO, Oct 44, Annex 3, Lessons Learned.

CHAPTER 4

1. Bradley and Blair, *A General's Life*, p. 337.

2. See MacDonald, *The Siegfried Line Campaign*, pp. 382–89; and Pogue, *The Supreme Command*, p. 306, for information on the First Army logistic situation.

3. Pogue, *The Supreme Command*, p. 306.

4. Ibid., pp. 307–10; MacDonald, *The Siegfried Line Campaign*, pp. 390–91; Amendment 3 (4 Nov 44) to 12th AG LOI 10, 12 Oct 44, reproduced in 12th AG RO, pp. 96–98. Officials in Washington and London, meanwhile, discussed plans to conduct a major offensive designed to end the war during 1944. On 23 October U.S. Army Chief of Staff General George C. Marshall solicited Eisenhower's comments on such a plan. An attack with this objective, however, depended for success on the new weapons like the proximity fuse and a change in targets for the strategic air offensive. It would also require use of strategic supply stockpiles, which would be difficult to replace without the use of Antwerp. Eisenhower replied that it might be possible to launch an offensive with the divisions either en route or on hand in the ETO, but the nagging question of supply remained unanswered. In Washington, the War Department General Staff revised the plan to allow transfer to the ETO of Allied forces in the Mediterranean. On 29 October, the British Joint Planning Staff replied to the U.S. plan. The British recommended against launching a major offensive without the use of Antwerp because failure would run the risk of prolonging the war well into 1945. Three days later, Marshall told U.S. planners to take no further action on the issue.

5. First Army RO, p. 67; MacDonald, *The Siegfried Line Campaign*, pp. 399–400.

6. MacDonald, *The Siegfried Line Campaign*, pp. 343–44; HQ V Corps, *V Corps Operations in the ETO, 6 Jan 1942–9 May 1945* (published in Czechoslovakia in 1945), p. 284 (hereafter cited as V Corps RO). This is overall accurate and provides copies of several key orders and operations plans issued by Gerow's HQ. It is indispensable for the detailed study of V Corps operations during the war.

7. V Corps RO. Gerow graduated from Virginia Military Institute in 1911. In 1940 he became the chief of the War Plans Division, War Department General Staff. He took command of the 29th Infantry Division in early 1942 and went from there to V Corps. He was the first corps commander ashore in Normandy. Gerow later became the head of the army's Command and General Staff College. He died in 1972.

8. V Corps RO, pp. 282–88.

9. Bradley and Blair, *A General's Life*, p. 341.

10. MacDonald, *The Siegfried Line Campaign*, p. 406.

11. Ibid., p. 400.

12. Bradley and Blair, *A General's Life*, pp. 108–13.

13. See Robert A. Miller, *Division Commander: A Biography of Major General Norman D. Cota* (Spartanberg, SC: Reprint Press, 1989), chaps. 4–9, for the early career of Cota.

14. 28th Inf. Div. UR 5 (RO for Nov 44, dtd 6 Dec 44).

15. Bruce M. Hostrup, letter to author, 24 Sep 89.

16. 28th Inf. Div. UR 5.

17. Charles B. MacDonald, *Three Battles: Arnaville, Altuzzo, and Schmidt*, U.S. Army in World War II (Washington, D.C.: GPO, 1952), p. 254.

18. Gersdorff, MS A-892.

19. MacDonald, *The Siegfried Line Campaign*, pp. 392–95.

20. Schmidt, MS B-810.

21. Gevert Haslob, letter to author, 19 Oct 89.

22. Discussions with several 28th Division veterans at reunions in Sep 88 and Sep 90 provided a common view of the conditions of the forest near Germeter and Vossenack on 2 Nov 44.

23. Raymond E. Fleig, letters to author, 1 Dec 88 and 23 Aug 89.

CHAPTER 5

1. MacDonald, *Three Battles*, p. 259.

2. Harry M. Kemp, *The Regiment: Let the Citizens Bear Arms!* (Austin, TX: Nortex Press, 1990), p. 161. This history of the 109th Infantry Regiment is based on the author's personal experiences as a company commander. Kemp remained on active duty after the war and retired as a colonel.

3. Kemp, *The Regiment*, p. 162.

4. 1st Lt. Harry G. Jackson, Combat Interview with 1st Lt. Charles E. Potter, S-2, 1st Bn., 109th Inf., 9 Dec 44.

5. Jackson, Combat Interview with 1st Lt. Bruce Paul, 1st Lt. William Pena, and other members of Co. I, 109th Inf., Diekirch, Luxembourg, 8 Dec 44. German engineers began construction of the Wilde Sau minefield in late October. Accounts differ on the size of the minefield. Gevert Haslob, an 89th Division staff officer in 1944, indicates the minefield might have been up to 400 yards long, on either side of the Germeter-Hürtgen road. The eastern part of the former mined area is now occupied by a German military cemetery.

6. Schmidt, MS B-810.

7. Paul Brückner, "Experiences and Lessons from the Battle of the Hürtgen Forest," Lt. Col. Joseph Whitehorne, U.S. Army, trans., copy in author's files.

8. Potter CI.

9. Ibid.

10. Kemp, *The Regiment*, p. 168; Kemp questions whether the person sending the radio message misunderstood an order. Unit Jnl entries are unclear regarding the origins of the order.

11. Pena CI.

12. Kemp, *The Regiment*, p. 168–70.

13. Ibid., pp. 168–70; 376.

14. Ibid.

15. 1st Lt. Harry Jackson, Combat Interview with 1st Lt. Donald D. Clark, Co. E, 109th Inf., 8 Dec 44.

16. Kemp, *The Regiment*, p. 172.

17. Clarence Blakeslee, *A Personal Account of WWII by Draftee #36887149* (Rockford, MI: privately published, 1989), p. 26.

18. MacDonald, *Three Battles*, pp. 259–65; Capt. William J. Fox, Combat Inter-

view with 1st Lt. James A. Condon, Co. E, 112th Inf., 14 Dec 44 (hereafter cited as Condon CI).

19. 28th Inf. Div. UR 5, 6 Dec 44.

20. 28th Inf. Div. FO 25, 29 Oct 44; MacDonald, *Three Battles*, pp. 268–71; Capt. William J. Fox, Combat Interview with Maj. Richard S. Dana, 112th Inf., 1 Dec 44 (hereafter cited as Dana CI).

21. MacDonald, *Three Battles*, pp. 272, 292.

22. Gersdorff, MS A-892.

23. 28th Inf. Div. UR 5, 6 Dec 44, Annex, "89th Infantry Division Review."

24. Capt. John S. Howe, Combat Interview with Capt. Bruce M. Hostrup, 1st Lt. Raymond Fleig, and 2d Lt. Richard H. Payne, 707th Tk. Bn., 14 Nov 44 (hereafter cited as Hostrup CI). Hostrup entered private business after the war and lives in Illinois. Fleig retired as a lieutenant colonel, taught at a university, and lives in Ohio.

25. MacDonald, *Three Battles*, pp. 277–80.

26. Randall Patterson, letter to author, 3 Dec 89; interview with author, Fort Indiantown Gap, PA, 12 Sep 90. Patterson entered banking after the war and now lives in Kentucky.

27. Capt. William J. Fox, Combat Interview with Capt. Jack Walker, Co. L, 112th Inf., 2 Dec 44 (hereafter cited as Walker CI). Walker's view is the only available first-person account from a member of the company leadership to survive the action.

28. Combat Interview with Capt. Guy M. Piercey, Co M, 112th Inf., 2 Dec 44 (hereafter cited as Piercey CI).

29. MacDonald, *Three Battles*, Map IX.

30. Walker CI.

31. Ibid., pp. 286–89.

32. MacDonald, *Three Battles*, p. 291.

33. 2d Lt. Charles Fowler, "3d Battalion, 112th Infantry History," MS compiled at Camp Atterbury, IN, May 51, Co. L entry for 3 Nov 44, copy in author's files.

34. Randall Patterson, letter to author, 3 Dec 89.

35. Capt. William J. Fox, Combat Interview with 1st Lt. Leon Simon, 6 Dec 44 (hereafter cited as Simon CI).

36. MacDonald, *Three Battles*, p. 284.

37. MacDonald, *The Siegfried Line Campaign*, p. 352; Capt. William T. Fox, Combat Interview with Maj. Gen. Norman D. Cota and Brig. Gen. George A. Davis, 13 Dec 44.

38. MacDonald, *Three Battles*, p. 288; Hostrup CI.

39. Bruce M. Hostrup, letter to author, 26 Apr 89.

40. Hostrup CI.

41. Ibid.

42. Raymond E. Fleig, *707th Tank Battalion in World War II* (Springfield, OH: 707th Tank Battalion Assoc., 1991), p. 97; Fleig, letter to author, 25 May 89; Hostrup CI.

43. Generalmajor Alfred Toppe, MS C-089, "Units Opposing Our 28th Div. in the Hürtgen Forest" (n.d.); Generalmajor a.D. Siegfried von Waldenberg, in MS A-905, "116th Panzer Division, 1–9 Nov 1944" (n.d.).

44. MacDonald, *Three Battles*, pp. 290–91.

45. Fowler, "3d Battalion, 112th Infantry History," HQ Co. entry, 4 Nov 44.

46. Ibid., Co. L entry, 4 Nov 44.

47. Walker CI.

48. Fowler, "3d Battalion, 112th Infantry History," Co. L entry, 4 Nov 44.

49. Piercey CI.

50. MacDonald, *The Siegfried Line Campaign*, p. 361.

51. Dana CI; Walker CI.

52. Simon CI.

53. Ibid.

54. MacDonald, *Three Battles*, pp. 307, 324.

55. Hostrup CI.

56. Capt. William J. Fox, Combat Interview with S.Sgt. Frank Ripperdan, Co L., 112th Inf., 2 Dec 44 (hereafter cited as Ripperdan CI).

57. Gevert Haslob, letter to author, 5 Oct 89.

58. MacDonald, *Three Battles*, p. 308.

59. Fowler, "3d Battalion, 112th Infantry History," HQ Co. entry, 4 Nov 44.

60. Cota CI; HQ, V Corps, "Summary of the Operations of 28th Infantry Division for the Period of 2–15 November 1944" (18 Nov 44), typed report, copy in V Corps Opns. files.

61. MacDonald, *Three Battles*, p. 313.

62. Hostrup CI; Fleig, *707th Tank Battalion*, p. 98.

63. Hostrup CI.

64. Gevert Haslob, interview with author, 25 Nov 1993, Ofen, Germany.

65. MacDonald, *Three Battles*, p. 323.

66. Fowler, "3d Battalion, 112th Infantry History," Co. K and L entries, 5 Nov 44.

67. Simon CI.

68. Delmer C. Putney, interview with author, Fort Indiantown Gap, PA, 10 Sep 90; MacDonald, *Three Battles*, pp. 331–32.

69. Capt. John S. Howe, Combat Interview with Lt. Col. Richard W. Ripple, 14 Nov 44 (hereafter cited as Ripple CI); Dana CI; V Corps RO, pp. 294–96; MacDonald, *Three Battles*, p. 332.

70. MacDonald, *Three Battles*, p. 350; Fleig, letter to author, 23 Mar 90.

71. Committee on Veterans Affairs, *Medal of Honor Recipients, 1863–1978*, 96th Cong., 1st Sess. (Washington, D.C.: GPO, 1979), p. 604 (hereafter cited as *Medal of Honor Recipients*), citation for 1st Lt. Turney W. Leonard, 893d Tank Destroyer Battalion.

72. Dana CI; MacDonald, *Three Battles*, p. 374.

73. Ripple CI; Dana CI.

74. Ripperdan CI.

75. Piercey CI.

76. MacDonald, *Three Battles*, pp. 380–81.

77. Ibid., p. 377; Ripple CI.

78. Fleig, letter to author, 20 Feb 89.

CHAPTER 6

1. Condon CI; MacDonald, *Three Battles*, p. 335.

2. Capt. William J. Fox, Combat Interview with Capt. John D. Pruden, 2d Bn., 112th Inf., Dec 44 (hereafter cited as Pruden CI); Capt. William J. Fox, Combat Interview with 1st Lt. Clyde R. Johnson, Co. G, 112th Inf. (hereafter cited as Johnson CI); MacDonald, *Three Battles*, p. 336.

3. Condon CI; Johnson CI.

4. Pruden CI; Fox, Combat Interview with 1st Lt. Melvin Barrilleaux and 1st Lt. Eldeen Kauffman, 2d Bn., 112th Inf. (hereafter cited as Barrilleaux/Kauffman CI).

5. Condon CI; Johnson CI; Barrilleaux/Kauffman CI.

6. MacDonald, *Three Battles*, pp. 345–55; 707th Tk. Bn. S-3 Jnl entries, 2–10 Nov 44; Fleig, *707th Tank Battalion*, pp. 104–107, gives a vivid account of the West-Granger meeting.

7. Pruden CI.

8. Various interviewees, MS C-089, "Units Opposing Our 28th Inf. Div. in the Huertgen Forest," 1951–52.

9. Generalmajor Siegfried von Waldenburg, "116 Pz Div in the Hürtgen Forest," ETHINT 56, Dec 45.

10. Trees and Hohenstein, *Hölle im Hürtgenwald*, pp. 139–40.

11. Pruden CI; MacDonald, *Three Battles*, p. 359.

12. Lt. Col. Carl J. Isley, "Notes on Operations of 146th Engineer (C) Bn. in the Recapture and Defense of Vossenack," typed report in 28th Inf. Div. CI files; MacDonald, *Three Battles*, pp. 363–64.

13. Haslob Interview.

14. Isley, "Notes"; MacDonald, *Three Battles*, pp. 385–86; Committee 7, "Armor in the Hürtgen Forest," p. 46.

15. V Corps RO, pp. 296–98; MacDonald, *Three Battles*, p. 386.

16. Kemp, *The Regiment*, pp. 182–83.

17. Miller, *Division Commander*, pp. 127–28; MacDonald, *Three Battles*, p. 389.

18. Lt. Col. William O. Hickok V, undated letter to author, received Nov 90.

19. MacDonald, *Three Battles*, p. 389.

20. Ibid., pp. 393–94; Ripple CI.

21. Fowler, "3d Battalion, 112th Infantry History," Co. M entry, 7 Nov 44.

22. MacDonald, *Three Battles*, pp. 394–96; Ripple CI.

23. Ray Fleig, letter to author, 23 Mar 90.

24. MacDonald, *Three Battles*, pp. 403–404, 406–11.

25. Gevert Haslob, letter to author, 19 Oct 89.

26. Ibid.

27. "4th Infantry Division in the Battle of the Hürtgen Forest," part 2, "Action of 12th Infantry Regiment Nov. 7 to 21," copy in 4th Inf. Div. Opns. files; Col. James S. Luckett, "Personal Account of the 12th Infantry Regiment in the Hürtgen Forest," typed MS in 4th Inf. Div. CI files; 12th Inf. Regt. RO, Nov 44 (dtd 4 Jan 45).

28. 28th Inf. Div. FO 27, 9 Nov 44; Luckett, "Personal Account."

29. Col. Gerden F. Johnson, *History of the Twelfth Infantry Regiment in World War II* (Washington, D.C., 1947), pp. 205–209.

30. 4th Inf. Div. RO, Nov 44.

31. Kemp, *The Regiment,* pp. 190–91.

32. Ibid., p. 191.

33. Ibid., p. 193. Strickler commanded the 28th Division after its activation during the Korean War. He retired from the army as a lieutenant general and practiced law until shortly before his death in 1992.

34. Ibid., pp. 194–95.

35. Ibid., pp. 195–96.

36. Gersdorff, MS A-891; "The Battle of the Hurtgen Forest," 1945.

37. Fowler, "3d Battalion, 112th Infantry History," entries for all companies, 8–13 Nov 93.

38. Combat Interview with Capt. James H. Burns and other members of 1st Bn., 110th Inf., 12–14 Dec 44.

39. Memorandum, "Message from the Commanding General," enclosure to 28th Inf. Div. UR 5, 6 Dec 44.

40. MacDonald, *Three Battles,* pp. 415–16; 28th Inf. Div. UR 5, 6 Dec 44.

41. HQ, V Corps, "Summary"; Fox, Howe, "Vossenack, Kommerscheidt, Schmidt," synopsis of 28 CIs, filed with CI 74.

42. Committee 7, "Armor in the Hürtgen Forest," p. 85.

43. Harold Denney, "Life on the Western Front," *New York Times Magazine,* 5 November 1944, p. 47.

CHAPTER 7

1. MacDonald, *The Siegfried Line Campaign,* pp. 399, 408–409.

2. First Army RO, pp. 72–73; MacDonald, *The Siegfried Line Campaign,* p. 409; 1st Inf. Div. RO, Nov 44; 1st Inf. Div. FO 53, 6 Nov 44.

3. 4th Inf. Div. FO 53, 7 Nov 44, and 15 Nov revision.

4. First Army RO, p. 71.

5. Gersdorff, MS A-891.

6. Engel, MS B-415.

7. General der Infanterie Friedrich Köchling, MS A-997, "Battles in the Sector of Aachen September/November 1944" (Mar 46).

8. General der Infanterie Friedrich J. M. Köchling, MS A-994, "The Battles of the Aachen Sector" (3 Feb 46).

9. MacDonald, *The Siegfried Line Campaign,* pp. 409–11; Köchling, MS A-993, "Corrections and Supplements [to MS A-997]" (Jan 1946).

10. V Corps RO, p. 306.

11. Schmidt, MS B-810.

12. Gevert Haslob, letter to author, 19 Oct 89.

13. MacDonald, *The Siegfried Line Campaign,* p. 414.

14. Weigley, *Eisenhower's Lieutenants,* pp. 603–604.

15. Maj. Gen. Jacob E. Fickel, Army Air Forces Evaluation Board, ETO, "The Effectiveness of Third Phase Tactical Air Operations in the European Theater, 5 May 1944–8 May 1945" (dtd Aug 45), pp. 168–75, copy in CARL; First Army RO, pp. 72–74.

16. V Corps RO, p. 306.

17. MacDonald, *The Siegfried Line Campaign*, p. 405.

18. Weigley, *Eisenhower's Lieutenants*, p. 604.

19. Fickel, "Air Operations," p. 168; First Army RO, pp. 72–73.

20. 1st Inf. Div. RO, Nov 44.

21. Ibid.

22. 16th Inf. Regt. S-3 Jnl entry, 1340 hrs, 16 Nov 44.

23. First Army RO, p.72; MacDonald, *The Siegfried Line Campaign*, p. 414.

24. PW statements found in XXIX TAC Report on Operation "Q," author's files.

25. Co. E, 16th Inf. Regt., RO, Nov 44.

CHAPTER 8

1. "Captured Communication of 12th Infantry Division," dtd 5 Nov 44, translated and reproduced for inclusion in 1st Inf. Div. CI files (CI 5), 1944.

2. Maj. Kenneth W. Hechler, Combat Interview with Lt. Col. James D. Allgood, 1st Bn., 47th Inf., 1 May 45; 47th Inf. Regt. SITREP, 15–16 Nov 44; 1st Inf. Div. G-3 PR 164, 16 Nov 44.

3. Hechler, Combat Interview with Lt. Col. Edmond F. Driscoll, 1st Bn., 16th Inf., 24 May 45.

4. John B. Beach, letters and other material supplied to author, Oct 93. Beach was wounded and taken prisoner during the fighting outside Hamich and was liberated from a German POW camp in May 1945. He retired from the army as a lieutenant colonel.

5. Beach material.

6. Beach material; *Medal of Honor Recipients*, pp. 605–606, citation for T.Sgt. Jake W. Kelley, 16th Inf. Regt.

7. Committee 7, "Armor in the Hürtgen Forest," p. 70.

8. 16th Inf. S-3 Jnl entry, 0420 hrs, 17 Nov 44.

9. Ibid., entry, 1100 hrs, 17 Nov 44.

10. Ibid., entry, 1405 hrs, 17 Nov 44.

11. Ibid., entry, 1350 hrs, 17 Nov 44.

12. Ibid., entry, 1406 hrs, 17 Nov 44.

13. Ibid., entry, 2049 hrs, 17 Nov 44.

14. Ibid., entry, 2130 hrs, 17 Nov 44.

15. Ibid., entries, 1140 and 1513 hrs, 18 Nov 44.

16. Karl Wolf, material supplied to author, 22 Sep 93.

17. 16th Inf. S-3 Jnl entries, 2124 and 2158 hrs, 18 Nov 44.

18. Wolf to author, 22 Sep 93.

19. 16th Inf. S-3 Jnl entry, 0405 hrs, 19 Nov 44.

20. Ibid., entry, 1210 hrs, 18 Nov 44.

21. Ibid., entry, 0028 hrs, 19 Nov 44.

22. Lt. John W. Baumgartner, *The 16th Infantry Regiment, 1798–1946* (n.p., 1946), pp. 178–81.

23. Co. F, 16th Inf., "Hill 232: A Realistic Account of a Tactical Success," typed report in files of 1st Inf. Div. Museum Library, Wheaton, IL.

24. MacDonald, *The Siegfried Line Campaign*, pp. 418–19.

25. Office of the Assistant Chief of Staff, G-2, 1st Inf. Div., "Selected Intelligence Reports, Volume 1, June 1944–November 1944," p. 105, CARL doc. R-10139.

26. 1st Inf. Div. G-2 PR 153, 19 Nov 44; Co. F, 16th Inf, "Hill 232."

27. 1st Inf. Div. RO, Nov 44; 1st Inf. Div. G-2 PR 153.

28. 1st Inf. Div. G-2 PR 153.

29. Maj. Kenneth W. Hechler, Combat Interview with Lt. Col. Charles T. Horner, 3d Bn., 16th Inf., 24 May 45; The 2d Battalion was at the Aachen-Duren railroad, ready to finish clearing the area south of Wilhelmshohe by 24 November. Before noon on 27 November the 1st Battalion had part of one company in the settlement of Gut Merberich, and Company A was past Langerwehe the next day. During this attack, on 3 December, Pvt. Robert T. Henry was killed in a single-handed attempt to knock out an enemy machine-gun position. He was awarded a posthumous Medal of Honor (*Medal of Honor Recipients*, p. 577, citation for Pvt. Robert T. Henry, 16th Inf. Regt., 3 Dec 44; 1st Lt. James V. Marsh, "D Company's Most Successful Attack, Luchem," typed report to Cdr., 3d Bn., 16th Inf. (n.d.), copy in files of 1st Inf. Div. Museum library).

30. Allgood CI; MacDonald, *The Siegfried Line Campaign*, pp. 479–81.

31. Capt. Henry G. Phillips, "The Operations of the 3d Battalion, 47th Infantry (9th Infantry Division), at Bovenberg Farm, North of Hamich, Germany, 16–24 November 1944" (U.S. Army Infantry School, Fort Benning, GA, 1949), pp. 19–23; MacDonald, *The Siegfried Line Campaign*, pp. 475–76.

32. Chester H. Jordan, letter to author, 27 Jul 91.

33. Maj. Kenneth W. Hechler, Combat Interview with Capt. Gael M. Frazier and Capt. William L. McWaters, 3d Bn., 47th Inf., 15 May 45; Phillips, "Operations of the 3d Battalion, 47th Infantry," pp. 25–29; MacDonald, *The Siegfried Line Campaign*, pp. 481–82.

34. First Army RO, p. 80.

35. Maj. Kenneth W. Hechler, Combat Interview [Hamich Ridge Action] with Lt. Col. Lewis E. Maness, 2d Bn., 47th Inf., 14–15 May 45 (hereafter cited as Maness CI).

36. Ibid; First Army RO, p. 80.

37. Combat Interview with Lt. Col. W. G. Powell and Capt. Henry P. Zech, CCA, 3d Armd. Div., CI 265; MacDonald, *The Siegfried Line Campaign*, p. 482.

38. MacDonald, *The Siegfried Line Campaign*, pp. 482–83.

39. Maness CI.

40. Ibid.

41. Maj. Kenneth W. Hechler, Combat Interview with Lt. Col. Lewis E. Maness and Capt. William L. McWaters (Frenzerburg Castle Action), 14–15 May 45 (hereafter cited as Maness and McWaters CI).

42. Chester H. Jordan, letter to author, 27 Jul 91.

43. Information supplied by Klaus R. Schulz, Meerbusch, Germany, 1993.

44. Maness and McWaters CI.

45. Brig. Gen. Lewis E. Maness (Ret.), undated letter to author, received Oct 91.

46. Chester H. Jordan, letter to author, 27 Jul 91.

47. *Medal of Honor Recipients*, p. 677, citation for Pfc. Carl V. Sheridan, 3d Bn., 47th Inf.

48. Jordan to author, 27 Jul 91.

49. Maness and McWaters CI.

50. Information supplied by Klaus R. Schulz.

51. Jordan to author, 27 Jul 91.

52. Information supplied by Klaus R. Schulz.

53. Maness, letter to author, 12 Apr 92.

54. Information supplied by Klaus R. Schulz; Maness and McWaters CI.

55. First Army RO, p. 78; MacDonald, *The Siegfried Line Campaign*, p. 475.

56. 18th Inf. Regt. S-1 Jnl entries, 1815 and 2043 hrs, 19 Nov 44.

57. 18th Inf. Regt. S-1 Jnl entry, 1135 hrs, 20 Nov 44; MacDonald, *The Siegfried Line Campaign*, p. 477.

58. 18th Inf. Regt. RO, Nov 44.

59. MacDonald, *The Siegfried Line Campaign*, pp. 477–78; 18th Inf. Regt. S-1 Jnl entries, 0445, 0500, and 0605 hrs, 21 Nov 44.

60. 1st Inf. Div. RO, Nov 44; 18th Inf. Regt. S-1 Jnl entries, 0850 and 1328 hrs, 22 Nov 44, and 0330, 0505, and 0630 hrs, 23 Nov 44.

61. Warren B. Eames, "Recollections of War," typed MS (East Templeton, MA: 1990), p. 158, copy in author's files, and interview with author, 19 Feb 90.

62. 2d Lt. George E. Moise, Combat Interview with Capt. Edward W. McGregor, 1st Bn., 18th Inf., 16 Dec 44; 18th Inf. S-1 Jnl entry, 1530 hrs, 22 Nov 44; 1st Inf. Div. RO, Nov 44.

63. 1st Inf. Div. RO, Nov 44; 18th Inf. Regt. S-1 Jnl entry, 1720 hrs, 23 Nov 44; McGregor CI.

64. 1st Inf. Div. G-2, "Interrogation Report of Personnel, 3d Para. Division," 27 Nov 44, in 1st Inf. Div. CI 5.

65. 26th Inf. Regt. S-3 Jnl entries, 1504 and 1729 hrs, 16 Nov 44.

66. Ibid., entry, 1555 hrs, 17 Nov 44.

67. Ibid., entry, 1425 hrs, 18 Nov 44.

68. Ibid., entry, 1325 hrs, 19 Nov 44.

69. Ibid., entries, 1030, 1034, and 1710 hrs, 19 Nov 44.

70. Maj. Kenneth W. Hechler, Combat Interview with Capt. James Libby, Capt. Besor B. Walker, Capt. Gilbert H. Fuller, and Lt. Ray Smith, 2d Bn., 26th Inf., 25 May 45.

71. *Medal of Honor Recipients*, p. 623, citation for Pfc. Francis X. McGraw, 2d Bn., 26th Inf.

72. 26th Inf. Regt. S-3 Jnl entries, 1245, 1444, 1522; MacDonald, *The Siegfried Line Campaign*, pp. 489–90.

73. 26th Inf. Regt. S-3 Jnl entry, 1923 hrs, 28 Nov 44.

74. Sidney C. Miller, letter to author, 8 Dec 89.

75. 26th Inf. Regt. S-3 Jnl entries, 1445, 1536, 1540, 1810, and 2000 hrs, 29 Nov 44.

76. Ibid., entry, 1732 hrs, 29 Nov 44.

77. Sidney C. Miller, letter to author, 8 Dec 89.

78. Ibid.

79. 26th Inf. Regt. S-3 Jnl entry, 0030 hrs, 30 Nov 44.

80. Ibid., entry, 0402 hrs, 30 Dec 44.

81. Ibid., entry, 0530 hrs, 30 Dec 44; 1st Inf. Div. RO, Nov 44.

82. 26th Inf. Regt. S-3 Jnl entry, 1030 hrs, 30 Nov 44.

83. Combat Interview with Capt. Thomas W. Anderson, 1st Bn., 26th Inf., 24 May 45.

84. MacDonald, *The Siegfried Line Campaign,* pp. 492–93.

85. 18th Inf. Regt., "History for the Month of November 1944," copy in files of 1st Inf. Div. Museum.

86. Marlin Brockette, letters to author, 23 May 91 and 10 Jun 91.

87. Don A. Warner, taped comments to author, 15 Aug 89.

CHAPTER 9

1. Schmidt, MS B-810.

2. 8th Inf. Regt. UR 160, 16 Nov 44; Lt. Francis H. Fife, Combat Interview with Capt. James H. McNutt, 29th FA Bn. Liaison Officer attached to the 2d Bn., 8th Inf., and Capt. John C. Swearinger, S-3, 2d Bn., 8th Inf., n.d.

3. *Medal of Honor Recipients,* pp. 662–63, citation for 1st Lt. Bernard J. Ray, 2d Bn., 8th Inf.; McNutt CI.

4. 8th Inf. Regt. UR 161, 17 Nov 44.

5. Capt. Robert D. Moore, "The Operations of Company C, 8th Infantry (4th Infantry Division) in the Attack of the Hürtgen Forest, Germany, 19–21 November 1944" (Infantry Officer's Advanced Course, Fort Benning, GA, 1950); 4th Inf. Div. SITREP 55, 18 Nov 44; 8th Inf. Regt. UR 163, 19 Nov 44.

6. *Medal of Honor Recipients,* p. 610, citation for Maj. George L. Mabry, Jr., 8th Inf. Regt. Mabry was later commanding general, Panama Canal Zone. He retired from the army as a major general and died in Columbia, S.C., in 1990.

7. Mrs. Shirley Lanham McCreary, letter to author, 17 Mar 90; Dr. William S. Boice, *History of the Twenty-Second United States Infantry in World War II* (n.p., 1959), p. 26, copy in author's possession, used with permission of Dr. William S. Boice.

8. Barbara Becker, "Dr. Hemingstein and the General," *Washington Star Sunday Magazine,* 10 February 1963.

9. Robert S. Rush, "The 22d Infantry in the Hürtgen Forest" (n.p., n.d.); HQ, 22d Inf. Regt. Marrative Report of Operations, Nov 44.

10. Capt. Kenneth W. Hechler, Combat Interview with 1st Lt. Donald Warner, 1st Lt. Richard Bernasco, and others, 21 Dec 44 (hereafter cited as Warner CI).

11. 22d Inf. Regt. S-3 Jnl entry, 0710 hrs, 17 Nov 44.

12. Capt. Kenneth W. Hechler, Combat Interview with Maj. George M. Goforth and Capt. Clifford M. Henly, n.d. (hereafter cited as Goforth CI); 22d Inf. Regt. S-3 Jnl entry, 0835 hrs, 17 Nov 44.

13. 22d Inf. Regt. S-3 Jnl entries, 1035 and 1528 hrs, 17 Nov 44; Goforth CI; Warner CI.

14. Goforth CI; Warner CI.

15. 22d Inf. Regt. S-3 Jnl entry, 2400 hrs, 17 Nov 44.

16. Warner CI.

17. Ibid.; 22d Inf. Regt. S-3 PR 123, 18 Nov 44.

18. 22d Inf. Regt. S-3 Jnl entries, 0950, 1055, 1145, and 1205 hrs, 18 Nov 44; Boice, *History,* pp. 60–61.

19. 22d Inf. Regt. S-3 PR 124, 19 Nov 44; 22d Inf. Regt. S-3 Jnl entry, 0700 hrs, 19 Nov 44.

20. Schmidt, MS B-810.

21. 22d Inf. Regt. S-3 PR 125, 20 Nov 44.

22. 22d Inf. Regt. S-3 Jnl entry, 1140 hrs, 20 Nov 44.

23. Boice, *History,* pp. 68–69; 22d Inf. Regt. S-3 Jnl entries, 0850, 0900, 0915, 0925, 0958, 1020, 1340, 1420 hrs, 20 Nov 44.

24. 22d Inf. Regt. S-3 Jnl entry, 1538 hrs, 20 Nov 44.

25. Carlos Baker, *Ernest Hemingway: A Life Story* (New York: Scribner's, 1969), p. 436; Boice, *History,* pp. 68–69; 22d Inf. Regt. S-3 Jnl entry, 1704 hrs, 20 Nov 44.

26. 22d Inf. Regt. S-3 Jnl entry, 1825 hrs, 20 Nov 44.

27. Ibid., entry, 2400 hrs, 20 Nov 44.

28. Diary of Clifford Henley, prepared in 1973 by Tommy Harrison, New York (author's file copy provided by Donald A. Warner), p. 21.

29. MacDonald, *The Siegfried Line Campaign,* pp. 464–65; HQ 22d Inf. Regt., Narrative Report, Nov 44.

30. 22d Inf. Regt. S-3 Jnl entries, 1002–1159, 1325, 1337, and 1500–1505 hrs, 22 Nov 44.

31. CI with Lt. George Bridgeman, 3d Bn., 22d Inf. (hereafter cited as Bridgeman CI).

32. Ibid.

33. Johnson, *History of the Twelfth Infantry,* pp. 217, 220–21.

34. 12th Inf. Regt. RO, Nov 44; "4th Infantry Division Battle of Hürtgen Forest," p. 12; MacDonald, *The Siegfried Line Campaign,* pp. 438–39; First Army RO, p. 79. The 8th Infantry was unable to continue operations on 1 Dec and moved to Luxembourg soon afterward. The 12th Infantry spent 22–29 Nov securing the right flank of the 22d Inf. and improving its own positions along the Rennweg. After sustaining 1,493 battle and over 1,000 nonbattle casualties, the regiment moved to Luxembourg on 7 Dec. Neither regiment gained its final objective.

35. S. A. Stouffer, E. A. Suchman, L. C. DeVinney, S. A. Starr, and R. M. Williams, Jr., *The American Soldier: Combat and Its Aftermath,* vol. 2, *Studies in Social Psychology in World War II* (Princeton, NJ: Princeton University Press, 1949), p. 273.

36. Roland G. Ruppenthal, *Logistical Support of the Armies,* vol. 2, *September 1944–May 1945: The United States Army in World War II* (Washington, DC: GPO, 1959), pp. 337–41.

37. Stouffer et al., *The American Soldier,* p. 274.

38. Ruppenthal, *Logistical Support,* p. 341.

39. Warner CI.

40. Pogue and Topete, Combat Interview with M.Sgt. Willard Bryan, Nov 44.

41. Pogue and Topete, Combat Interview with S.Sgt. C. R. Brown, 12 Nov 44 (hereafter cited as Brown CI).

42. Frye CI.

43. Donald A. Warner, taped comments to author, Aug 89, author's files.

44. Edward B. Phillips, undated letter to author, received Nov 89.

45. Robert Moore, letter to author, 21 Nov 89.
46. Marlin Brockette, letter to author, 23 May 91.
47. Warner, taped comments, Aug 89.
48. Stouffer et al., *The American Soldier*, p. 283.
49. Eames, "Recollections," pp. 168–69.
50. Ibid.
51. Ibid.
52. Henley diary, p. 22, entry for 25 Nov 44.
53. Boice, *History*, pp. 64–65.
54. Frye CI.
55. William A. Hamberg, letter to author, 10 Feb 90.
56. Hamberg, letter to author, 13 Nov 89.
57. Weigley, *Eisenhower's Lieutenants*, pp. 548–50.

CHAPTER 10

1. HQ V Corps, *V Corps Operations*, pp. 308, 310; 8th Inf. Div. FO 16, 20 Nov 44; MacDonald, *The Siegfried Line Campaign*, pp. 440–41.
2. MacDonald, *The Siegfried Line Campaign*, p. 493.
3. V Corps RO, p. 308. Elements of the 13th and 28th Infantry Regiments held the Kall River line during the period of the 8th Division's involvement in the Hürtgen Forest. The activities of the regiments can be briefly summarized as follows. Both regiments remained in position during 21 and 22 November, and a company from the 2d Ranger Battalion entered the line between the 28th Infantry and the 121st Infantry. On 23 November, the 1st Battalion, 13th Infantry, then attached to the 28th Infantry, attacked with Company I, 28th Infantry, to clear bypassed German positions in the Tiefen Creek, north of Vossenack. The Americans took 100 prisoners but fell back under heavy German fire. Both regiments remained heavily engaged in the area for several more weeks.
4. Capt. John S. Howe, Combat Interview with Col. John R. Jeter, 30 Nov 44; 8th Inf. Div. FOs 15 (14 Nov 44) and 16 (20 Nov 44).
5. Jeter CI.
6. Pogue and Topete, Combat Interview with Maj. Wesley Hogan, 3d Bn., 121st Inf., Dec 44; Brown CI.
7. Paul M. Boesch, *Forest in Hell* (Houston: Privately printed, 1985), pp. 150–52; see also a series of 1:25,000-scale map overlays filed with the 8th Inf. Div. CIs.
8. Boesch, *Forest in Hell*, p. 156.
9. Ibid., pp. 156–58; 1:25,000-scale map overlays filed with the 8th Inf. Div. CIs.
10. V Corps RO, p. 316; Jeter CI.
11. Hogan CI; 8th Inf. Div. RO, Nov 44, Annex 3, "Summary of Enemy Action"; Brown CI.
12. *Medal of Honor Recipients*, pp. 632–33, citation for S.Sgt. John W. Minick, 3d Bn., 121st Inf.; Hogan CI; Brown CI.
13. Boesch, *Forest in Hell*, p. 158.
14. 8th Inf. Div. G-3 PR 135, 22 Nov 44; V Corps RO, p. 318; Hogan CI; Brown CI.

15. Topete, Combat Interview with S.Sgt. Anthony Rizzo, Co. G, 121st Inf., Dec 44 (hereafter cited as Rizzo CI); V Corps RO, pp. 317–18.

16. 121 Inf. Regt. RO, Nov 44.

17. Boesch, *Forest in Hell*, pp. 170–72.

18. Maj. William C. Sylvan, diary entry, 23 Nov 44; 121st Inf. Regt. S-3 Jnl entries, 1115, 1116, and 1530 hrs, 23 Nov 44. Records are unclear regarding the relief of the battalion commander; Jeter appears to have acted late on 23 Nov or early on 24 Nov.

19. Pogue, Combat Interview with Lt. Col. Henry B. Kunzig and Capt. William S. Freeman, Jr., 13 Dec 44.

20. Rizzo CI.

21. 121st Inf. Regt. S-3 Jnl entry, 1222 hrs, 24 Nov 44; 8th Inf. Div. RO, Nov 44.

22. Boesch, *Forest in Hell*, pp. 178–79.

23. Ibid.

24. Committee 7, "Armor in the Hürtgen Forest," pp. 109–10; Brown CI; 121st Inf. Regt. S-3 Jnl entry, 0915 hrs, 24 Nov 44.

25. Brown CI; 121st Inf. Regt. S-3 Jnl entry, 1820 hrs, 24 Nov 44.

26. Committee 7, "Armor in the Hürtgen Forest," pp. 109–10; 121st Inf. Regt. S-3 Jnl entry, 0420 hrs, 25 Nov 44; 8th Inf. Div. RO, Nov 44.

27. MacDonald, *The Siegfried Line Campaign,* p. 445; 8th Inf. Div. RO, Nov 44.

28. Pogue and Topete, Combat Interview with Col. Glen H. Anderson, CCR, 5th Armd. Div., 27 Dec 44; Committee 7, "Armor in the Hürtgen Forest," p. 132; 8th Inf. Div. FO 17, 24 Nov 44.

29. Pogue and Topete, Combat Interview with Capt. Frank M. Pool, 10th Tk. Bn., and 1st Lt. Richard S. Lewis, 47th Armd. Inf. Bn., 29 Dec 44 (hereafter cited as Pool CI).

30. 5th Armored Division Association, *Paths of Armor: The Fifth Armored Division in World War II* (Nashville, TN: Battery Press, 1985), pp. 157–59.

31. Pool CI; 5th Armored Division Association, *Paths of Armor*, pp. 157–59.

32. Committee 7, "Armor in the Hürtgen Forest," p. 136; V Corps RO, p. 318.

33. 121st Inf. Regt. S-3 Jnl entries, 1108 and 1442 hrs, 25 Nov 44; 8th Inf. Div. G-3 PR 138, 25 Nov 44.

34. 8th Inf. Div. RO, Nov 44; 121st Inf. Regt. S-3 Jnl entry, 1507 hrs, 26 Nov 44.

35. 121st Inf. Regt. S-3 Jnl entries, 1545 and 1550 hrs, 26 Nov 44; 8th Inf. Div. RO, Nov 44.

36. 8th Inf. Div. FO 18, 26 Nov 44; 121st Inf. Regt. S-3 Jnl entry, 1750 hrs, notes return of patrol; other information from entries for the period 1500–1650 hrs; see also 8th Inf. Div. G-3 PR 139, 26 Nov 44.

37. Chandler, *The Papers of Dwight Eisenhower,* pp. 2320–21.

38. V Corps RO, p. 319; 121st Inf. Regt. RO Nov 44; 121st Inf. Regt. S-3 Jnl entry, 0820 hrs, 27 Nov 44; 8th Inf. Div. G-3 PR 140, 27 Nov 44.

39. 121st Inf. Regt. RO, Nov 44.

40. Boesch, *Forest in Hell*, pp. 222–27.

41. Pogue and Topete, Combat Interview with Col. P. D. Ginder, 14 Dec 44.

42. Boesch, *Forest in Hell*, pp. 226–27.

43. Hubert Gees, letter to author, 15 Jun 89.

44. Paul Boesch, letter to author, 5 Mar 89.

45. Pogue and Topete, Combat Interview with Col. Thomas J. Cross, 15 Dec 44.

46. Paul Stevenson, letter to author, 24 Jan 90.

47. 8th Inf. Div. RO, Nov 44.

CHAPTER 11

1. 22d Inf. Regt. S-3 Jnl entries, 1715, 2130 hrs, 25 Nov 44.

2. Boice, *History*, p. 73; *Medal of Honor Recipients*, pp. 557–58, citation for Pfc. Marcario Garcia, 22d Inf. Regt.

3. 22d Inf. Regt. Jnl entries for the period 1105–1440 hrs, 27 Nov 44.

4. Boice, *History*, pp. 73–74.

5. Ibid., p. 74; 22d Inf. Regt. S-3 Jnl entry, 1800 hrs, 27 Nov 44.

6. 22d Inf. Regt. S-3 Jnl entries, 1535 hrs, 27 Nov 44, and 1800 hrs, 28 Nov 44.

7. Goforth CI.

8. Bridgeman CI.

9. 22d Inf. Regt. S-3 Jnl entry, 0710 hrs, 28 Nov 44.

10. Ibid., entry, 1205 hrs, 28 Nov 44.

11. Ibid., entries, 1115, 1128, and 1557 hrs, 29 Nov 44. The message as transcribed in the journal is, "Gen. Barton wants the town [Grosshau] taken today." See also Boice, *History*, p. 77.

12. Boice, *History*, pp. 77–79; Committee 7, "Armor in the Hürtgen Forest," p. 96; 22d Inf. Regt. S-3 Jnl entry, 1635 hrs, 29 Nov 44.

13. Boice, *History*, pp. 78–79.

14. Combat Interview with Lt. Lee B. Lloyd and Lt. George D. Wilson, Co. F, 22d Inf.

15. 22d Inf. Regt. S-3 Jnl entries, 1810, 1917, 1920, and 1955 hrs, 29 Nov 44; Boice, *History*, pp. 77–79.

16. 22d Inf. Regt. S-3 Jnl entries for the period; Boice, *History*, pp. 98–102; 4th Inf. Div. FO 55, 29 Nov 44.

17. Committee 7, "Armor in the Hürtgen Forest," p. 172; 5th Armored Division Association, *Paths of Armor*, pp. 168–72.

18. Rush, "The 22d Infantry in the Hürtgen Forest"; 22d Inf. Regt. S-3 Jnl, entry for 1410 hrs, 30 Nov 44.

19. Warner CI.

20. 22d Inf. Regt. S-3 Jnl entry, 1323 hrs, 1 Dec 44.

21. Warner CI.

22. Ibid.

23. 22d Inf. Regt. S-3 Jnl entry, 1648 hrs, 1 Dec 44.

24. Ibid., entry, 1730 hrs, 1 Dec 44.

25. Ibid., entries, 2210 and 2215 hrs, 1 Dec 44.

26. Ibid., entries, 0650–0903 hrs, 2 Dec 44.

27. Boice, *History*, p. 107.

28. First Army RO, pp. 88–89; MacDonald, *The Siegfried Line Campaign*, p. 474; 4th Inf. Div. RO, Nov 44, Annex 4, "Supply and Evacuation."

29. Mrs. Shirley Lanham McCreary, letter to author, Mar 90.

30. Handwritten order, Anderson to Hamberg, 28 Nov, CCR S-3 Jnl file.

31. Committee 7, "Armor in the Hürtgen Forest," pp 137–39; V Corps RO, pp. 319–20; MacDonald, *The Siegfried Line Campaign*, p. 449.

32. Handwritten order, Anderson to Hamberg, dtd 28 Nov 44; report from the CCR S-3 to Hamberg, dtd 27 Nov, both in CCR, 5th Armd. Div. Opns. files.

33. 5th Armored Division Association, *Paths of Armor*, pp. 160–61; Committee 7, "Armor in the Hürtgen Forest," pp. 140–42.

34. William A. Hamberg, letter to author, 12 Feb 90; Pogue and Topete, Combat Interview with Lt. Col. W. A. Hamberg, Maj. W. M. Daniel, and Capt. Robert V. Close, 10th Tk. Bn., 28 Dec 44.

35. Committee 7, "Armor in the Hürtgen Forest," p. 140.

36. CCR S-3 Jnl entry, 1335 hrs, 29 Dec 44.

37. Committee 7, "Armor in the Hürtgen Forest," pp. 144–45; Hamberg CI.

38. MacDonald, *The Siegfried Line Campaign*, p. 451; First Army RO, p. 83.

39. V Corps RO, pp. 320–22; 8th Inf. Div. FO 19, 30 Nov 44.

40. Brown CI; see also 1:25,000-scale map overlay prepared to supplement CI files.

41. 5th Armored Division Association, *Paths of Armor*, pp. 163–64.

42. Hamberg CI; Committee 7, "Armor in the Hürtgen Forest," pp. 149–51.

43. Earl Lutz, undated letter to author, received Dec 89.

44. Committee 7, "Armor in the Hürtgen Forest," pp. 149–51, 33.

45. Ibid., pp. 156–62; Hamberg CI.

46. Roy M. Hanf, letter to author, 30 Nov 89.

47. Gersdorff, MS A-891; MacDonald, *The Siegfried Line Campaign*, p. 460.

48. Hamberg CI; Earl Lutz, letter to author, Dec 89.

49. Hamberg CI; Committee 7, "Armor in the Hürtgen Forest," pp. 164–65.

CHAPTER 12

1. Pogue and Topete, Combat Interview with Maj. George S. Williams, Jr., and Capt. Edward Arnold, 2d Rngr. Bn., 21 Mar 45 (hereafter cited as Williams CI).

2. Earl Lutz, letter to author, Dec 89.

3. MacDonald, *The Siegfried Line Campaign*, p. 462.

4. Williams CI.

5. Bill Petty, letter to author, 12 Mar 90; 2d Ranger Battalion, "Narrative History of the 2d Ranger Battalion," part 8, pp. 3–7 (this history is based on battalion operations files and CIs).

6. Williams CI; 2d Ranger Battalion, "Narrative History."

7. Committee 7, "Armor in the Hürtgen Forest," p. 170; MacDonald, *The Siegfried Line Campaign*, p. 463.

8. First Army RO, pp. 88–89; V Corps RO, p. 324; 83d Inf. Div. FO 37, 9 Dec 44; MacDonald, *The Siegfried Line Campaign*, pp. 581–82. The field order required units to "Determine changes in elevation of streams feeding into Roer R. . . . indicating probable flooding operations."

9. 83d Inf. Div. FO 37; MacDonald, *The Siegfried Line Campaign*, p. 587. General Köchling's LXXXI Corps had responsibility for a sector facing part of the VII U.S. Corps. A stretch of the front opposite Hof Hardt, Gey, and Kleinhau belonged to the 353d Division (LXXIV Corps). Other units in the area on

10 December were the 89th and 272d Infantry Divisions. The Americans received reports from POWs and aerial reconnaissance during the second half of November that indicated large-scale troop movements behind German lines. Enemy prisoners reported seeing elements of four SS panzer divisions west of Cologne. The Americans believed these troops were a mobile reserve for use against a successful Roer crossing. They had no idea the movements were part of the preparations for the Ardennes offensive.

10. "Combat Interviews Related to the Seizure of Gey and Strass, 2d Bn., 331st Inf.," located in 83d Inf. Div. CI files (CI 175).

11. 83d Inf. Div. RO, Dec 44; MacDonald, *The Siegfried Line Campaign*, p. 589.

12. Committee 7, "Armor in the Hürtgen Forest," p. 176; 83d Inf. Div. G-3 Jnl entries, 0850 and 0945 hrs, 11 Dec 44; 83d Inf. Div. RO, Dec 44.

13. 5th Armored Division Association, *Paths of Armor*, pp. 182–85.

14. 83d Inf. Div. G-3 Jnl entry, 0930 hrs, 12 Dec 44.

15. Ibid., entry, 1230 hrs, 13 Dec 44.

16. MacDonald, *The Siegfried Line Campaign*, p. 592.

17. 83d Inf. Div. G-3 Jnl entries, 1630, 1705, 1710, and 1823 hrs, 14 Dec 44; 83d Inf. Div. RO, Dec 44; *Medal of Honor Recipients*, p. 641, citation for Sgt. Ralph G. Neppell, 3d Bn., 329th Inf.

18. 83d Inf. Div. G-3 Jnl entry, 0521 hrs, 13 Dec 44.

19. 83d Inf. Div. RO, Dec 44; 83d Inf. Div. G-2 PR 124, 13 Dec 44; 331st Inf. Regt. SITREP, 14 Dec 44.

20. 5th Armored Division Association, *Paths of Armor*, pp. 175–79, 188–91.

21. MacDonald, *The Siegfried Line Campaign*, p. 593n.

22. HQ, Ninth Army, Staff Engineer, Military Geographic Study no. 8, typed report dtd 25 Oct 44, copy in CARL.

23. MacDonald, *The Siegfried Line Campaign*, pp. 595–96; First Army RO, pp. 95–96.

24. Chandler, *The Papers of Dwight Eisenhower*, p. 2335.

25. MacDonald, *The Siegfried Line Campaign*, pp. 598, 600; HQ V Corps, *V Corps Operations*, pp. 333–34; First Army RO, pp. 96–98.

26. 78th Division Historical Association, *Lightning: The History of the 78th Infantry Division* (Washington, D.C.: Infantry Journal Press, 1947), p. 28; V Corps RO, pp. 334–36. The 78th Infantry Division ("Lightning") saw its first World War II combat in the December attack. The War Department reactivated the division at Camp Butner, NC, in August 1942. In October 1944, the division departed New York and landed at Southampton, England. By November, it was in Ninth Army reserve and later joined V Corps.

27. V Corps RO, p. 330; 2d Inf. Div. FO 12, 10 Dec 44.

28. Sylvan diary entry for 12 Dec 44.

29. Robert R. Palmer, Bell I. Wiley, and William R. Keast, *The Procurement and Training of Ground Combat Troops*, U.S. Army in World War II (Washington, D.C.: GPO, 1948).

30. 78th Division Association, *Lightning*, pp. 29–44.

31. 78th Inf. Div. G-3 Jnl entry, 1640 hrs, 13 Dec 44.

32. 78th Division Association, *Lightning*, p. 40.

33. Maj. Niram L. Sauls, "The Operations of the 2d Battalion, 310th Infantry

(78th Infantry Division) in the Attack on Kesternich, Germany, 14–16 December 1944" (Infantry Officer's Advanced Course, Fort Benning, GA, 1950); *Lightning,* pp. 43–44, 49–58; 1st Lt. Robert E. Maxwell, Combat Interview with Capt. Douglas A. Frazier, 18 May 45 (hereafter cited as Frazier CI); Graham CI.

34. Sylvan Diary entry for 13 Dec 44.

35. 2d Inf. Div. FO 12, 10 Dec 44.

36. 9th Inf. Regt. CR #164, 14 Dec 44; V Corps RO, p. 336; William C. C. Cavanagh, *Krinkelt-Rocherath: The Battle for the Twin Villages* (Norwell, MA: Christopher Publishing Co., 1986), pp. 8–9 (hereafter cited as *Krinkelt-Rocherath*).

37. Combat Interview with Capt. William E. Brubeck, 2d Battalion, 310th Infantry, 18 May 45.

38. 78th Division Association, *Lightning,* pp. 49–52, 53–56; 78th Inf. Div. RO, Dec 44; Sauls, "2d Battalion, 310th Infantry."

39. Frazier CI; Report of staff conference dtd 14 Dec 44, filed in 78th Div. Opns. files.

40. Combat Interview with Capt. Richey V. Graham, Co. E, 309th Inf., 2 Jun 45.

41. Frazier CI.

42. Sauls, "2d Battalion, 310th Infantry."

43. War Department, Table of Organization 7–15, Infantry Battalion, 30 June 1944.

44. 78th Inf. Div. FO 1, 11 Dec 44.

45. V Corps RO, pp. 346–48; Cavanagh, *Krinkelt-Rocherath,* pp. 8–10; 9th Inf. Regt. CR #166, 16 Dec 44.

46. MacDonald, *The Siegfried Line Campaign,* p. 591n.

CHAPTER 13

1. Weigley, *Eisenhower's Lieutenants,* pp. 844–46; 12th AG LOI 14, 24 Jan 45, reproduced in 12th AG RO, pp. 115–17.

2. Charles B. MacDonald, *The Last Offensive,* U.S. Army in World War II (Washington, DC.: GPO, 1973), pp. 55–67.

3. Ibid., p. 71.

4. 5th Armored Division Association, *Paths of Armor,* pp. 220–22; Pogue and Topete, Combat Interview with Capt. William Arail, Lt. Robert Flynn, and Capt. Leo McCarthy, 1st Bn., 311th Inf., 17 Feb 45 (hereafter cited as Arail CI).

5. Combat Interview summary, 78th Inf. Div. CI 148. This is a narrative account compiled from several interviews.

6. Pogue and Topete, Combat Interview with Lt. Col. William McKinney, 19 Feb 45; First Army RO, pp. 154–55.

7. 78th Division Association, *Lightning,* pp. 81–90; MacDonald, *The Last Offensive,* p. 73. The 78th Inf. Div. CI files contain a town plan of Kesternich with a set of maps showing building numbers as used in the attack.

8. Combat Interview summary, 78th Inf. Div CI 148.

9. 78th Division Association, *Lightning,* pp. 81–90.

10. Combat Interview with Col. Chester W. Willingham, filed with CI 148.

11. McKinney CI.

12. MacDonald, *The Last Offensive*, p. 74; 78th Division Association *Lightning*, pp. 95–97.

13. McKinney CI.

14. Arail CI; 78th Division Association, *Lightning*, pp. 90–91.

15. Newton CI.

16. V Corps RO, p. 372; 78th Division Association, *Lightning*, p. 97.

17. McKinney CI; 309th Inf. Regt. S-3 Jnl entries, 0345 and 0500–0800 hrs, 5 Feb 45; 309th Inf. Regt. S-3 PR 55, 5 Feb 45.

18. 311th Inf. Regt. S-3 Jnl entry, 1345 hrs, 5 Feb 45; Arail CI.

19. Arail CI; 78th Division Association, *Lightning*, p. 78.

20. Ibid., pp. 101–103; 310th Inf. Regt. RO, 1 Dec 44–31 May 45; 310th Inf. Regt. S-3 Jnl entry, 1849 hrs, 5 Feb 45.

21. 78th Inf. Div. G-3 Jnl entry, 1500 hrs, 6 Feb 45; 78th Division Association, *Lightning*, p. 104.

22. Sylvan Diary entry for 6 Feb 45.

23. V Corps RO, pp. 376–78; Pogue and Topete, Combat Interview with Lt. Col. Harry Lutz and others, 3d Battalion, 310th Infantry, 8 Feb 45.

24. Newton CI; 311th Inf. Regt. S-3 Jnl entry, 1055 hrs, 7 Feb 45.

25. Newton CI.

26. Ibid.

27. 78th Infantry Division Association, *Lightning*, pp. 112–13.

28. McKinney CI.

29. 3d Bn., 309th Inf. SITREP, 8 Feb 45.

30. MacDonald, *The Last Offensive*, p. 81; V Corps LOI 8 Feb 45, reproduced in V Corps RO, p. 378.

31. Handwritten notes prepared for 310th Inf. Regt. S-3 Jnl. These notes do not appear in the typed copy of the journal located in the same file (RG 407).

32. HQ, First Army, letter no. 824, dtd 6 Feb 45; HQ 82d Abn. Div., Annex 1 to G-2 Situation Summary No. 17, Possible Inundations of the Roer Valley, 8 Feb 45. Both documents can be found in the 82d Abn. Div. G-3 Jnl File.

33. HQ, 505th Parachute Inf. Regt., "History of Operations of the 505th Parachute Infantry Regiment in the Belgium Campaign," Part III, pp. 5–6, copy in 505th Para. Inf. Regt. Opns. files; 505th Parachute Inf. Regt. S-3 PR 8–9 Feb 45.

34. Capt. Robert J. Bigart, "The Operations of the 1st Battalion, 309th Infantry (78th Infantry Division), in the Attack on the Schwammenauel Dam, Southeast of Schmidt, Germany, 9–10 February 1945" (Anfantry Officer's Advanced Course, Fort Benning, GA, 1950).

35. Handwritten msg dtd 9 Feb 45, 309th Inf. S-3 Jnl file.

36. 78th Inf. Div. G-3 Jnl entry, 1810 hrs, 9 Feb 45; 9th Inf. Div. G-3 Jnl entry, 1820 hrs, 9 Feb 45; Bigart, "Operations of 1st Bn., 309th Inf."

37. 78th Division Association, *Lightning*, pp. 117–21; 309th Inf. Patrol Report 128, 309th Inf. Regt. S-3 Jnl File, 11 Feb 45; 9th Inf. Div. G-3 Jnl entries, 0200, 0655, and 1210 hrs, 10 Feb 45.

38. 309th Infantry S-3 Jnl, entry for 0500 hrs, 10 Feb 45.

39. Bigart, "Operations of 1st Bn., 309th Inf."

CHAPTER 14

1. Gersdorff, MS A-891.

2. Ltc. Charles C. Sperrow, interview with Gen. J. Lawton Collins, 1972, transcript on file at OCMH.

3. Wade interview with Collins, pp. 9–10.

4. Collins, *Lightnin' Joe,* p. 278.

5. MacDonald, *The Battle of the Huertgen Forest,* p. 203.

6. Blumenson, *The Battle of the Generals,* pp. 262, 272.

7. Wade interview with Collins, p. 10.

8. Weigley, *Eisenhower's Lieutenants,* pp. 635–36.

9. Fleig, *707th Tank Battalion,* p. 97.

10. William M. Pena, letters to author, 28 Dec 92 and 21 Jan 93.

11. Fowler, "3d Battalion, 112th Infantry History," Co. L entry, 3 Nov 44.

12. 22d Infantry Regiment History, 1 January 1944–1 January 1946, CARL microfilm collection, reel 2178, item 2337.

13. Boesch, *Forest in Hell,* p. 145.

14. Gersdorff, ETHINT 53, 24 Nov 45.

15. Hubert Gees, letter to author, 15 Jun 90.

Index

Aachen 1, 2, 9–13, 18–21, 30–32, 38, 46, 52, 95, 97, 105, 203, 206, 209; September situation in, 16–17
Aachen-Düren railroad, 106
Aachen-Jülich railroad, 111, 112
air attacks on dams, 180–81
Allgood, Lt. Col. J. D., 99–100, 107
Allsbrook, Billy F., 25, 45
Alzen, 24, 184
Am Gericht, 191
Anderson, Col. G. H., 147, 162, 164–65, 168
Anderson, Capt. T. W., 121
Andrus, Brig. Gen. C., 188
Antwerp, 10, 48
Ardennes, 9–10, 31
Ardennes Offensive, 2, 5, 38, 52, 96, 106, 153, 165–66, 177, 179, 189–90, 204, 209, 211
armies, US: First Army, 2, 5–6, 9–11, 13–14, 31, 32, 46, 48–50, 92, 96–97, 99, 105, 134, 140–41, 145, 168, 180, 188, 199, 205–207, 209, 211; Third Army, 11, 31, 48; Ninth Army, 31, 48, 95, 105, 134, 172, 180, 190
army groups, US: 12th Army Group, 10, 14, 31, 40, 96, 190, 203–204, 206

Barilleaux, 1st Lt. M., 79–80
Barton, Maj. Gen. R. O., 87, 95, 124, 131–34, 154, 157, 159
Basel, Switzerland, 8
battalions, German: 12th Fusilier, 104; 15th Engineer, 113; 73d Engineer, 40, 53; 116th Panzer Recon., 69, 73; 189th Anti-tank, 164; 253d Engineer, 58; 275th Engineer, 53; 275th Fusilier, 33, 38, 96, 151; Police Battalion, 39–41, XIV Luftwaffe Fortress, 53; XVIII Luftwaffe Fortress, 96; XX Luftwaffe Fortress, 28, 33, 53
battalions and companies, US: 2d Ranger, 2, 141, 167–72, 203; 12th Engineer, 152; 22d Engineer, 164; 20th Engineer, 67, 72; 146th Engineer, 81; 294th Engineer, 200; 15th Armored Infantry, 176, 179; 46th Armored Infantry, 158, 162; 47th Armored Infantry, 147–48, 162, 164–65; 10th Tank, 139, 147–48, 161–62, 164–65, 167; 34th Tank, 179; 70th Tank, 129, 157; 81st Tank, 176; 707th Tank, 51, 54–55, 60, 62–63, 71–74, 80, 82, 90; 709th Tank, 146, 150, 183; 736th Tank, 191; 745th Tank, 102; 774th Tank, 176, 186, 197; 628th Tank Destroyer, 164; 644th Tank Destroyer, 152, 172; 893d Tank Destroyer, 73, 82, 90, 191; 2d Bn., 33d Armor, 14; 2d Bn., 36th Armored Inf., 14–15; 3d Bn., 32d Armor, 110; TF 1, 15; TF 2, 14
Beach, 1st Lt. J. B., 100
Bergheim, 179
Bergstein, 12, 51–52, 139, 147, 161, 163–65, 167–69, 171–72, 200
Berndt, Maj. A., 85
Bickerath, 183, 191
Bilstein, 179
Birgel, 177–78
Blazzard, Maj. H. C., 130–31
Blumenson, Martin, 5–6, 204, 206
Boesch, 1st Lt. P. M., 142–46, 150–52, 209
Boice, Chaplain W. S., 138
Bond, Lt. Col. V. H., 25, 36
Bonn, 31
Boos, Col. F. H., 184
Boudinot, Brig. Gen. T. E., 14–15, 93
Bovenberger dairy, 108–109
Bovenberger woods, 106–108

Boyer, Lt. Col. H. E., 147, 164, 172
Bradley, Lt. Gen. O. N., 6, 10–11, 31, 96, 98, 180–81, 193, 204, 209; on Collins, 13; as commander of 28th Division, 50; on Hodges, 14; and Roer Dams, 49; tactical assessment by, 47
Brandenberg, 51, 141, 147, 161–65, 168
Brandenberg-Bergstein Ridge, 51, 61, 82, 90, 141–42, 153, 163, 168
Brandenberger, General der Panzertruppen E., 9, 18, 42, 52, 62, 165, 210
Brigades, German: 341st Sturmgechutz, 53, 69; 518th Panzer, 53, 75
Brigades, US. See Regiments, US
British Army Units: 1 Canadian Army, 190; 21 Army Group, 5, 9–11, 31, 48, 190; Special Operations HQ, 50
Brockette, 1st Lt. M. L., 121, 137
Brown, Maj. Gen. L. D., 50
Brückner, Hauptmann P., 58
Bruns, Generalmajor W., 53, 62, 200
Bryan, M.Sgt. W., 136
bunkers. See Westwall
Burgberg (Castle Hill). See Hill 400
Burley, Lt. Col. W. L., Jr., 183–86
Burton, Lt. Col. W. H., Jr., 158

Cabaniss, Lt. Col. W. L., 179
Canham, Brig. Gen. C., 142, 149
Chance, Col. R. H., 134
Carlson, 1st Lt. E. S., 60
casualties, German, 6, 23, 39, 44–45, 48, 90, 97
casualties, US, 18, 23, 37, 45, 47, 58, 87, 89–90, 100, 102–104, 109, 111, 114, 117, 120–21, 126–27, 129–30, 133–34, 147–48, 152, 158–59, 161, 163, 167, 171–72, 177, 180, 185, 188–89, 191, 193, 202
Chatfield, Lt. Col. L. W., 24, 29–30, 37, 39–40
Christensen, Maj. R. C., 74, 77
Clayman, Lt. Col. D. C., 107–109
Cole, Col. J. T., 175
Collier's magazine, 128
Collins, Maj. Gen. J. L. 2, 11–13, 16–17, 19–20, 31, 36, 46, 107, 109–10, 114–15, 118, 123, 140, 145, 147, 156, 161, 172, 176; assessment of September situation, 18; and attacks on Hürtgen, 27, 48–49; on Col. Lanham, 133; on fighting, 203, 205–206, 209
Cologne (Köln), 18, 31, 48, 62, 93, 172
combat exhaustion and stress, 54, 138–39, 163
Condon, 1st Lt. J., 78–79
Corley, Lt. Col. J. T., 118
corps, German: I SS Panzer, 9; XII SS

Panzer, 52, 95; XLVII Panzer, 62, 96; LXVII, 181; LXXXI, 9, 16, 21, 52, 62, 95–96, 105, 177; LXXIV, 9, 21, 38, 42, 52, 53, 62, 96, 177, 181
corps, US: V Corps, 12, 16, 31, 48–49, 51–52, 90–91, 96, 99, 121, 140–41, 152, 161–63, 167–68, 172, 181, 184, 188–89, 193, 195, 206, 209–10; VII Corps, 2, 10–13, 16, 18–20, 24–25, 27, 30–32, 38, 46, 48–50, 52, 86, 90, 93, 95–96, 99, 109, 121, 123, 140, 163, 172, 180, 189, 203, 205, 206, 209; VIII Corps, 31, 172; XIX Corps, 16, 31–32, 95, 200, 206
Cota, Maj. Gen. N. D., 50–52, 61–62, 66, 70, 72, 74, 77, 83, 86, 88–89, 90–91
Cowan, W. M., 37
Crabhill, Col. E. B., 175, 177–78
Craig, Maj. Gen. L. A., 24, 26–28, 36, 39, 44, 198
Cross, Col. T. J., 149–52

D-Day, 9, 98, 128
Daley, Col. E. K., 72, 81
dams. See Dreilägerbachtel Dam; Paulushof Dam; Roer Dams; Schwammenauel Dam; Urft Dam
Dana, Maj. R. A., 74–75
Daniel, Lt. Col. D. M., 119–20
Daniel, Maj. W. M., 167
Davis, Brig. Gen. G. A., 61, 66, 72, 81–83
Dead Man's Moor. See Todtenbruch
"death valley," 200
Decker, Maj. L. L., 37, 41
Dedenborn, 195
Denney, Harold, 92
Dickinson, Lt. Col. G. G., 176
divisions, German: 3d Panzengrenadier, 96; 3d Parachute, 203; 12 Volksgrenadier (Infantry), 17–18, 20–21, 23, 28, 33, 62, 95–96, 99, 105, 110, 131, 203, 210
divisions, US: 1st Infantry, 2, 12–13, 16, 18, 27, 30–31, 50, 93, 95, 99, 107, 109–10, 114, 121, 137, 140, 152, 172, 188, 203; 2d Infantry, 150, 181, 184–85, 188–89, 203, 211; 4th Infantry, 2, 48–49, 51, 83, 86–87, 91, 93, 95–96, 121, 123, 132, 136, 140, 147, 152, 154, 158, 161, 163, 172, 203; 8th Infantry, 2, 141–42, 147, 149, 152, 161, 163, 165, 167, 172, 181, 203; 9th Infantry, 2, 12–13, 16, 20–21, 23–24, 26–27, 30–33, 35–36, 38, 45, 48–49, 51, 93, 98–99, 121, 141, 152, 172, 191, 196–98, 200, 202, 203, 206; 25th Infantry, 13; 28th Infantry, 2, 48–56, 62, 67, 77, 82, 86, 90–91, 98, 141–43, 152–53, 168, 172, 184, 203, 209, 210; 29th Infantry, 50; 78th Infan-

try, 2, 181–82, 184, 188, 190–93, 195, 198, 202–203, 211; 83d Infantry, 2, 134, 161, 172, 180, 203; 99th Infantry, 141, 181, 184, 188; 104th Infantry, 49, 93, 95, 107, 109–10, 140, 161, 189; 106th Infantry, 149; 82 Airborne, 197–98, 200, 202–203; 3d Armored, 2, 9, 12–14, 16, 18, 20, 27, 30–31, 41, 93, 100, 107, 110; 5th Armored, 2, 49, 139, 141, 157–58, 163, 167, 175, 180, 203
doctrine, US, 19–20, 26, 91. *See also* training methods, US
Drake, Maj. H. L., 129
Dreiborn Ridge, 181
Dreilägerbachtal Dam, 15
Dresden, 98
Driscoll, Lt. Col. E. F., 100, 102, 104
"dragon's teeth," 8–9
Düren, 12–13, 18, 21, 32, 38–39, 46, 95, 98, 124, 141, 163, 168, 172, 175, 180, 189
Dürwiss, 98

Eames, Pvt. W. B., 115, 137–38
Eicherscheid, 181, 191
Eifel (region), 52, 123, 190
Einruhr, 190, 195
Eisenhower, Gen. D. D., 5–6, 9–10, 91, 97, 190, 193, 204; and air attacks on dams, 180–81; and assessment of Stroh, 149; and November operations, 48; and September conference, 31
Elsenborn, Belgium, 12
Elsenborn, Camp, 24, 184
Engel, Generalmajor G., 17–18, 23, 28, 62, 95, 99
Eschweiler, 16, 48, 93, 95, 98, 105
Eupen, Belgium, 11, 15, 139

Falaise, France, 5–6
Faulkner, Capt. D., 156–57, 159
Field Manual 100-15, 12, 19, 20
Finke, Capt. J. G. W., 104
Fleig, 1st Lt. R. E., 54–55, 67, 69, 71–72, 75, 77, 84
Flood, Lt. Col. A., 63, 65, 71–74, 77
Ford Maj. J. C., Jr., 56, 88
forest fighting. *See* Hürtgen Forest; *individual units*
Fort Benning, Ga., 13
Foster, Col. R. T., 175–76
Frankfurt, 190
Frazier, Capt. D. P., 186–87
Frenzerburg castle battle, 109–14

Garcia, Pfc. M., 154–55
Gees, Hubert, 38–39, 151–52, 211
Gerleman, Maj. H. E., 207

German Army units: Army Group B, 5–6, 9, 17, 52, 95, 210; Army Group Center, 6; 5th Panzer Army, 52, 62, 96; 6th Panzer Army, 5, 181; 7th Army, 9, 17, 20, 33, 52, 62, 89, 203, 210; 15th Army, 96, 105, 177; 47th Volksgrenadier, 96, 105–106, 115, 118, 177, 203; 85th Infantry, 181, 203; 89th Infantry, 24–25, 39, 42, 53, 62, 64, 69–70, 89, 96, 181, 200, 203; 116th Panzer, 16, 62, 69, 86, 96, 105, 131, 203; 272d Volksgrenadier (Infantry), 96, 165, 181, 183, 203; 275th Infantry, 29, 33, 38–39, 42, 44, 48, 53, 58, 86, 96, 123, 131–32, 181, 203, 212; 277th Volksgrenadier, 182, 203; 344th Infantry, 131–32, 203; 347th Infantry, 23; 353d Infantry, 28–29, 33, 161, 203
German operations, 210–11
Germeter, 12, 27, 31, 33, 36–38, 40–42, 44–45, 51, 53, 56, 58–60, 80, 83, 86, 91, 121, 141–42, 146–147
Gerow, Maj. Gen. L. T., 12, 31, 49–51, 54, 61, 83, 91, 145, 147, 149, 163, 168, 193, 209
Gersdorff, Generalmajor R. C., 31, 52, 62, 89, 203, 211
Gey, 12, 48, 95, 134, 157–59, 172, 175–76, 178–79
Gibb, Col. F. W., 93, 102, 103
Gibney, Col. J. L., 24, 28, 30, 36, 88
Ginder, Col. P. D., 150
Goforth, Maj. G., 129–30, 132, 156, 158
Graham, Capt. R. V., 183
Granger, Capt., 80
Gressenich, 12, 23, 93, 99–100, 105, 107, 114, 140
Grosshau, 12, 95–96, 128, 131, 133–34, 140, 142, 152, 154–61, 179
ground approaches to Roer Dams, 206–207
Guadalcanal, 13
Gunn, Lt. Col. F., 25
Gürzenich, 175, 177–78, 180
Gut Schlenderahn, 62
Gut Schwarzenbroich, 124, 127

Hackard, Capt. C. T., 61, 75
Hamberg, Lt. Col. W. A., 139, 161–65, 169, 172
Hamburg, 98
Hamich (town), 93, 99, 105–106, 113, 140; capture of, 100, 102–104
Hamich Ridge 48, 104. *See also* Hill 232
Hanf, 1st Lt. R. M., 165
Hardage, Maj. Q. A., 41
Harkinish, Michael, 41–42

Harscheidt, 64, 69, 193
Hasenfeld, 64, 70, 200
Hastenrath, 93
Hatzfeld, Maj. T. S., 60, 79
Havinghorst, Leutnant, 113–14
Hawaiian Department, 13
Hazlett, Maj. R. T., 61, 69, 72–75
Heartbreak Crossroads, 188
Hechelscheidt, 193
Heimbach, 12, 32
Heinsberg, 98
Heistern, 106, 109, 114–15
Helm, Sgt., 164
Hemingway, Ernest, 128, 132–33
Henley, Capt. C. M., 129, 133, 138
Hill 167, 107–108
Hill 187, 107–108
Hill 203, 93, 115, 117, 121
Hill 207, 93, 115
Hill 211, 175, 179
Hill 232, 93, 103–107, 114, 140. See also
    Hamich Ridge
Hill 253, 175, 179
Hill 266, 179
Hill 272, 118
Hill 400, 51, 163, 167–72, 175
Hill 401, 150
Hill 401.3, 158, 161–62
Hill 493, 197
Hill 554, 25
Hill, Col. J. G., 91
Hirschfelder, Col. C. J., 184
Hitler, Adolf, 5–6, 9, 99
Hitzfeld, General der Infanterie O., 181
Higgins, Lt. Col. W. M., 188
Höfen (town), 24, 26, 184
Höfen-Alzen Ridge, 24
Hof Hardt, 161, 175
Hogan, Maj. R. W., 142, 146–48
Hollerath, 182
Horner, Lt. Col. C. T., Jr., 103, 106
Hostrup, Capt. B. M., 51, 63, 67, 72–73,
    84
Houston, Maj. J. A., 32, 206
Hubner, Maj. Gen. C. R., 102–103, 114–
    15, 118–20, 188, 193, 195–98
Hucheln, 109–10
Huppenbroich, 191, 195
Hürtgen (town), 12, 27–29, 31, 36, 40, 42,
    48–49, 53, 58, 66, 88, 95–96, 133, 136,
    140–42, 144–50, 152, 161–62
Hürtgen Forest, 14–16, 18–19, 24, 26, 35,
    39, 42, 48, 51, 53, 54, 56, 58, 59, 60, 62,
    91, 93, 96, 98, 104–106, 109, 114–15, 117,
    119, 128, 132, 134, 136, 137, 140, 142, 144,
    148, 149, 152, 154, 160–61, 172, 179, 189,
    193, 202–206, 209–11; becomes US

objective, 10; fighting conditions in,
    27–30, 33, 38, 44–45, 66, 85, 98, 115, 118,
    121, 130, 156; location and description
    of, 1–2, 5, 8, 12–13, 200

Imgenbroich, 187, 191
Inde River, 95, 106–107, 110
Infantry Journal, 128
Infantry School, 45
Isley, Lt. Col. C. J., 81–82

Jackson, Lt. Col. L. A., 124
Jägerhaus, 30
Jeter, Col. J. R., 141–42, 145, 149
Johnson, Lt. C. R., 79
Jordan, Lt. C. H., 21, 107, 112–13
Jülich, 18, 98, 111
Jüngersdorf, 93, 115, 119

Kall River Valley, 12, 40, 51–53, 61, 63–
    67, 74, 77, 82–85, 88–89, 90, 96, 193, 200
Kall Trail, 65–67, 71–74, 81–82, 85, 90
Kalterherberg, 24
Kämmerbusch, 117. See also Hill 203
Karlsruhe, 10
Kassel, 190
Kauffman, 1st Lt. E. F., 61, 79
Kelley, S. Sgt. J. E., 192
Kenan, Lt. Col. T., 157, 159
Kesternich, 49, 181, 183–88, 191–93, 195,
    203
Kettenis, Belgium, 14
Kettlehut, 1st Lt. H. K., 171
Keyes, Lt. Col. R. W., 192
King, Lt. Col. R. H., 14
Kleinhau, 27–28, 48, 95, 139–42, 147, 149–
    50, 153, 157, 161–64
Kluge Field Marshal G., 5–6
Kleve, 8
Köchling, General der Infanterie
    F. J. M., 62, 95, 96
Kommerscheidt, 52, 61, 64–66, 69–75,
    77–78, 81, 83–84, 181, 197
Konzen, 181, 191
Koslosky, T.Sgt. J. M., 64
Köttenich, 93
Kreuzau, 175
Krinkelt, 184
Krinkelter forest, 181
Kufferath, 179
Kunzig, Lt. Col. H. B., 145–46, 149

Ladd, Lt. Col. B. W., 185–87
Lammersdorf, 25–26, 30, 32, 183
Langerwehe, 93, 95, 97, 110–11, 115, 117–
    18, 121
Lanham, Col. C. T., 95, 128–29, 131–33,
    154–61

Laufenberg castle, 118
Laurent, Sgt. R. N., 15
Leonard, 1st Lt. T. W., 75
Lewis, 1st Lt. R. S., 148
Liege, Belgium, 10–11, 97
Likes, Lt. Col. C. E., 185–87
Lindsay, T.Sgt. J. W., 100–102
Linnich, 180
Lipscomb, Lt. Col. A. A., 191, 195, 197
Littlejohn, Pvt. R., 118
Lockett, Lt. Col. L. J., 71
Lovelady, Lt. Col. W. B., 14–15
Loveless, Col. J. B., 184
Luchem, 106, 121
Luckett, Col. J. S., Jr., 86–88, 95, 134
Lüttwitz, General der Panzertruppen H. von, 62
Lutz, Lt. Col. H., 197
Lutz, T5 E. L., 165, 168
Lyga, 1st Lt. T., 69–70

Maastricht, Holland, 10
Mabry, Maj. G. L., Jr., 127
McAuley, 1st Lt. J. A., 147–48
MacDonald, Charles B., 204
McGraw, Pfc. F. X., 118
McKee, Col. R. G., 95, 119, 124–25
MacKenzie, Col. A. J., 184
McKinney, Lt. Col. C. D., 193, 196, 198
Macon, Maj. Gen. R. C., 172, 175–78
McWaters, 1st Lt. W. L., 111–12
Mahlmann, Generalleutnant P., 28–29
Mainz, 10, 190
Malmedy, Belgium, 11
Manteuffel, General der Panzertruppen H. von, 62
map exercise at Gut Schlenderahn, 62, 69
Marr, Col. R. S., 157
Marshall, Gen. G. C., 13–14, 128, 149, 181
Martin, Maj. Gen. E., 50
Masny, Capt. O., 169–70
Mausbach, 18
Merode, 95, 110, 115, 117–21, 152, 203
Mestringer Mühle, 64, 73
Meuse River, 11, 32
Miller, 1st Lt. S. B., 119–20
Miner, Col. E. M., 182, 196
Minick, S.Sgt. J., 144
Model, Field Marshal W., 6, 8–9, 17, 62, 95, 105, 165, 210
Monschau, 9, 12–13, 17, 20, 24, 26, 30–32, 53, 181, 184, 190
Monschau Corridor, 20, 23–27, 36, 41, 49, 64, 90, 181–83, 188, 190, 193, 202, 211
Mons Pocket, 11

Montgomery, Capt. H., 71
Montgomery, Field Marshal Sir B. L., 6, 9–10, 31
Moore, Bob, 137
Moore, Capt. R. D., 125–27
Morgan, T.Sgt. G., 1
Morsbach, 181
Moselle River, 9
MSR W (Road W), 128–30, 134, 143–45
MSR Y (Road Y), 133
Muhlartshütte, 16

Neitzel, Oberst Hasso, 25
Nelson, Col. G. M., 77, 83–84
Neppell, Sgt. R. G., 178
Nesbitt, Capt. J. T., 80
New York Times, 92
Niedeggen, 12
Normandy, 2, 5–6, 11, 204
Notes on Woods Fighting (pamphlet), 45
Nothberg, 107, 109–10
Nürnberg, 98, 114

Obermaubach, 32
Olef River, 181
Oliver, Maj. Gen. L. E., 176
O'Malley, Capt. E. W., 63–64, 70
Ondrick, Col. J. G., 188, 202
Operation COBRA, 97
Operation QUEEN, 96–98, 117, 131
Ord, Maj. Gen. G. J., 50
Ormont, 9
Otten, Manfred, 81
Osterhold, Oberst W., 18, 23–24, 99

Parker, Maj. Gen. E. P., Jr., 182, 184, 188, 191, 193, 195–98
Patterson, 1st Lt. R., 64–65
Patton, Lt. Gen. G. S., Jr., 31
Paul, Capt. B., 209
Paulushof Dam, 180, 196
Paustenbach, 25. *See also* Hill 554
Pearl Harbor, 13
Pena, 1st Lt. W., 58–59, 209
Peterson, Lt. Col. C. L., 51, 61, 65–66, 71–77, 83
Petty, T.Sgt. Bill, 169–71
Phillips, 1st Lt. E. B., 137
Pier, 95
Piercey, Capt. G. T., 64, 76
Pool Capt. F. M., 147–48
Potter, 1st Lt. C., 58
Pruden, Capt. J., 79–82
Prüm, 123
Püchler, General der Infanterie K., 38
Putney, Pfc. D., 74

Quesada, Maj. Gen. E. R., 97

RAF (Royal Air Force), 97–98, 180
RJ (Road Junction) 47I, 36–37, 41
Rabenheck (Raven's Hedge Ridge), 128–30
radio proximity fuze (VT), 48
Raffelsbrand, 36, 38, 40, 53
Ray, 1st Lt. B. J., 124–25
reconnaissance in force, 11–16, 30
regiments, German: 9th Parachute, 113; 16th Panzer, 53, 69, 71, 73; 24th Panzer, 53; 27th Grenadier, 18, 110; 48th Grenadier, 18, 23, 99–100, 103; 60th Panzergrenadier, 17, 58; 89th Grenadier, 110, 112; 104th Grenadier, 105, 115; 115th Grenadier, 118; 156th Panzergrenadier, 81; 189th Artillery, 53; 253d Grenadier Training, 24; 860th Infantry, 53, 75; 942d Infantry, 28, 33, 37; 943d Infantry, 160; 980th Infantry, 164–65, 183; 983d Infantry, 39, 53; 984th Infantry, 33, 53; 985th Infantry, 53, 96, 131; 1055th Infantry, 24, 53, 69, 73, 96; 1056th Infantry, 53, 86, 96
regiments, brigades, and groups, US: 8th Infantry, 86, 93, 95, 119, 124–27, 131, 134, 175; 9th Infantry, 184, 188, 196; 12th Infantry, 83, 86–88, 90, 95, 121, 131, 134, 141–42, 160, 209; 13th Infantry, 141, 149, 150, 161–62, 172; 16th Infantry, 16, 50, 93, 98, 100–101, 104–106, 108–109, 117; 18th Infantry, 16, 93, 114–15, 117–18, 121, 137; 22d Infantry, 1, 86, 95, 128–34, 136–39, 142, 152, 154–62, 209; 23d Infantry, 184; 26th Infantry, 16, 93, 115, 117, 119, 121, 137; 28th Infantry, 141, 163; 38th Infantry, 184, 188; 39th Infantry, 16, 20, 25–27, 30, 37–42, 44, 144, 198; 47th Infantry, 16, 20–21, 23–24, 27, 36, 41, 44, 93, 98–99, 107, 109–14, 117, 121, 140; 60th Infantry, 16, 20, 24, 26–27, 29–30, 36–37, 39–42, 88, 200; 109th Infantry, 51, 56, 58–59, 66, 82–84, 86–90, 141–42, 144, 168, 209; 110th Infantry, 52, 62, 66, 74, 82–83, 89, 90–91; 112th Infantry, 51, 52, 60–61, 63–65, 69–75, 77–79, 81–82, 84–85, 89, 209; 121st Infantry, 136, 139, 141–47, 149–52, 163, 172; 309th Infantry, 181–83, 185–88, 193, 195–98, 200, 202; 310th Infantry, 181–82, 185–87, 191, 193, 196–98; 311th Infantry, 191–93, 195–98, 200; 329th Infantry, 175, 177–78, 330th Infantry, 161, 175–76, 178–79; 331st Infantry, 175, 178; 393d Infantry, 184; 395th Infantry, 181, 184; 505th Parachute, 200; 517th Parachute, 200; 4th Cavalry Group, 12, 16, 119; 102d Cavalry Group, 163; CCA, 3d Armored Division, 14, 110; CCB, 3d Armored Division, 14–15, 93; CCA, 5th Armored Division, 49, 175, 179, 190–91; CCB, 5th Armored Division, 163, 175–76, 179; CCR, 5th Armored Division, 133, 141–42, 147, 149, 152–53, 157–58, 161–65, 167, 169, 172; CCR, 7th Armored Division, 193; 1171st Engineer Combat Group, 67, 72, 81
Regnier, Brig. Gen. E. A., 175
replacement doctrine, 135–36, 140
Replacement System, 135
Rhine River, 2, 10–11, 30–31, 45, 47–48, 93, 189–90, 204–205, 211
Richardson, Lt. Col. W. B., 110
Richelskaul, 36–37, 39–40, 52, 61–62, 66, 83
Riedel, Maj., 33, 38–39
Ripperdan, S.Sgt. F., 71, 76
Ripple, Lt. Col. R. W., 51, 67, 74–77, 82–84
Robertson, Maj. Gen. W., 184, 188
Rocherath, 184
Roer River, 2, 5, 10, 12–13, 16, 19, 21, 24, 27, 30–32, 38, 45–46, 48–49, 90, 93, 95–96, 106, 110–11, 114, 121, 123–24, 141, 147, 152–53, 163, 165, 168, 171–72, 175, 179–81, 189–90, 195–96, 204, 206–207, 209, 211
Roer River Dams, 2, 5, 14, 19, 32, 38, 46, 49, 52, 91, 95, 98, 141, 163, 172, 180, 189–90, 193, 200, 203–204, 206, 209, 211
Roetgen, 15, 32, 89, 142, 147–48, 189
Roetgen State Forest, 12
Rohren, 181
Rollesbroich, 25, 181–82, 193
Rose, Brig. Gen. M., 14
Rösler, Oberst E., 24, 53
Rösslershof, 106
Roter Weh Creek, 128
Rott, 15, 55, 66, 76–77, 86
"Rubble Pile," 82
Rudder, Lt. Col. J. E., 168
Ruhr, 9, 31, 48, 52, 190, 204
Rundstedt, Field Marshal G. von, 8–9, 52
Rurberg, 32, 193, 196

Saar, 9, 204
Schack, Generalleutnant F.-A., 9, 16–17, 21, 62, 95
Schafberg, 175–76, 179
Scharnhorst Line. See Westwall
Schellman, Lt. Col. R. H., 200–202
Schevenhütte, 20–21, 23–24, 27–28, 33, 36, 38, 41, 95, 99, 105, 114–15, 118, 123–24

Schill Line. *See* Westwall
Schleiden, 32
Schlich, 110
Schmidt, Generaleutnant H., 33, 35, 38–39, 42, 44–45, 48, 58, 96, 131
Schmidt (town), 2, 31–32, 36, 38, 41, 45–46, 49, 51–52, 60–66, 69–74, 77–78, 82–84, 86, 90–91, 99, 152, 172, 181, 183, 184, 193, 196, 197–98, 200, 209–10
Schönthal, 115
Schwammenauel Dam, 32, 49, 95, 114, 180–81, 193, 195, 196, 198–202, 210, 211
Schwerin, Generalleutnant G. von, 16–17
Seeley, Col. T. A., 52, 62
Seine River, 5
Seitz, Col. J. F. R., 93, 117–20
Sheridan, Pfc. C. V., 112–13
Sibert, Lt. Col. F., 86–87
Siegfried Line. *See* Westwall
Silberscheidt, 193
Simmerath, 12, 30, 49, 181–82, 185, 198
Simmerath-Düren Road, 12, 25–27, 30, 36, 38, 58, 95, 105, 183
Simon, Lt. L., 65, 70–71, 73, 74
Simonskall, 53, 66, 85, 90
Smith, Col. G. A., Jr., 93, 115, 117, 121
Smythe, Col. G. W., 21, 23, 108–11
Sonnefield, Lt. Col. J. E., 72
Spa, Belgium, 11
Spaatz, Lt. Gen. C., 97
Spooner, S.Sgt. A., 67, 71
Stolberg Corridor, 13, 16–19, 21, 23, 25–26, 31, 41, 48, 93, 95, 99–100, 106–107, 172, 210
Steckenborn, 49, 181, 193
Stevenson, 1st Lt. P., 152
Strass, 172, 175, 176, 178–79
Straube, General der Infanterie E., 9, 42, 53, 62, 131
Strickler, Lt. Col. D. B., 51, 58, 88–89
Stroh, Maj. Gen. D. A., 141–42, 145, 147, 149
Stumpf, Lt. Col. R. H., 25, 41
Stuttgen, Dr., 85
Surratt, Capt. W., 130

Tait, Lt. Col. W., 74
tank-infantry cooperation, 5, 19, 26, 37, 39–41, 54, 60–63, 65–66, 72, 75, 80, 82, 104, 109, 111–12, 117, 119, 125, 146, 150, 156–57, 178–79, 183, 186, 191–93, 197–98, 208
TF Boyer. *See* Boyer, Lt. Col. H. E.
TF Davis. *See* Davis, Brig. Gen. G. A.
TF Hamberg. *See* Hamberg, Lt. Col. W. A.
TF Richardson, 110
Thompson, Lt. Col. O., 25, 38, 44

Todtenbruch, 27, 30, 37, 62, 204
Topping, Maj. H. L., 58–60, 82–84
training methods, US, 182, 208–209

Üdingen, 179
Untermaubach, 179
Urft Dam, 32, 114, 180–81, 184, 196, 200, 210–11
USAAF units: 8th Air Force, 97–98; IX Bomber Command, 97; XXIX Tactical Air Command, 97; IX Tactical Air Command, 97
US Army: equipment of, 208; organization of, 207; weapons of, 207–208. *See also* armies, US; army groups, US; battalions, US; corps, US; divisions, US; regiments, US

Vicht (town), 16
Vicht (creek), 12, 93
Vosges mountains, 9
Vossenack (town), 36, 38, 40–41, 44, 51–53, 56, 60–67, 71, 74, 78–82, 84–86, 88, 90–91, 96, 144, 164
Vossenack Ridge, 36, 49, 60, 82

Wahlerscheid, 181, 184, 188
Waldenberg, Generalmajor S. von, 17, 62, 81
Walhorn, Belgium, 172
Walker, Capt. J., 64–65, 69–70, 77, 84
Warner, Capt. D. A., 123, 137, 158–59
Weaver, Brig. Gen. W., 149, 162, 164, 168
Wegelein, Oberst w. (Kampfgruppe), 42, 44, 51
Wehe Creek, 21, 93, 114, 124
Weigley, R. F., 206
Weisser Weh Creek valley, 12, 27–28, 33, 36, 53, 86, 88, 95–96, 128, 130–31, 134, 142–47
Weisweiler, 48, 98, 110
Welti, Oberleutnant, 40
Wenau, 115
Wenau State Forest, 12
Werth, 93
West, Capt. G. S., Jr., 60, 80
Westwall, 8–9, 11, 13, 14, 18, 20–21, 24, 26–27, 30–31, 33, 36, 37, 52, 62, 182, 184, 189, 191, 204–206, 210–11
Wharton, Brig. Gen. J. E., 50
Wilde Sau minefield, 58, 86–87, 91, 143
Wilhelmshöhe, 107, 110–11
Williams, Capt. G. S., 168–69
Williams, Lt. Col. H., 88
Willingham, Col. C., 192
Wilson, 1st Lt. G. F., 159
Winden, 179

Wittscheidt saw mill, 40–42, 53, 58, 142, 146–48
Witzerath, 183
Woffelsbach, 193
Wolf, 1st Lt. K., 103
Wood, 1st Lt. J. H., 100

Xerox Corp., 161

York, Col. R. H., 175–76, 178

Zangen, General der Infanterie Gustav von, 96, 105, 177–78
Zweifall, 16, 27, 30